Cook for a Day,
Eat for a Week

THE MAKE-AHEAD COOKBOOK

Lydia Kessler

Adamsmedia
Avon, Massachusetts

Published by

Adams Media, a division of F+W Media, Inc.

57 Littlefield Street, Avon, MA 02322. U.S.A.

www.adamsmedia.com

Contains material adapted and abridged from *The Everything® Freezer Meals Cookbook* by Candace Anderson, copyright © 2010 by F+W Media, Inc., ISBN 10: 1-4405-0612-4, ISBN 13: 978-1-4405-0612-3; and *The Everything® Meals for a Month Cookbook* by Linda Larsen, copyright © 2005 by F+W Media, Inc., ISBN 10: 1-59337-323-6, ISBN 13: 978-1-59337-323-8.

ISBN 10: 1-4405-8375-7

ISBN 13: 978-1-4405-8375-9

eISBN 10: 1-4405-8376-5

eISBN 13: 978-1-4405-8376-6

Printed in the United States of America.

10   9   8   7   6   5   4   3   2   1

Library of Congress Cataloging-in-Publication Data

Kessler, Lydia.

The make-ahead cookbook / Lydia Kessler.

    pages cm

Includes index.

ISBN 978-1-4405-8375-9 (pb) -- ISBN 1-4405-8375-7 (pb) -- ISBN 978-1-4405-8376-6 (ebook) -- ISBN 1-4405-8376-5 (ebook)

1. Make-ahead cooking. I. Title.

TX652.K43184 2014

641.5'55--dc23

2014026431

Cover design by Frank Rivera.

Cover images © Svetlana Kolpakova/Lilyana Vynogradova/Bernd Juergens/markstout/123RF.

This book is available at quantity discounts for bulk purchases.

For information, please call 1-800-289-0963.

Contents

Introduction

Tired of coming home every day and having to get dinner in the oven? Wouldn't you rather spend that time relaxing with your family or catching up with friends? Well, with *The Make-Ahead Cookbook*, you can create delicious meals that are ready when you are!

Featuring step-by-step instructions for hundreds of tasty recipes, this book shows you how to make a week's worth of dishes in just one day, so you don't have to worry about whipping up a home-cooked meal right after work or think about grabbing a quick bite at an expensive restaurant. By taking a few hours on the weekend to prepare and freeze a variety of mouthwatering dishes at home, you can fill your freezer with entrées, side dishes, and ingredients that you can turn into satisfying dishes in a matter of minutes, making them perfect for families on the go. These flavorful meals will not only come in handy on your busiest days, but they'll also save you money and time in the kitchen. Best of all, you'll not only have a variety of plates to choose from each day, but you'll also be prepared with appetizers and desserts when company drops in unexpectedly.

Whether you're looking for something light and healthy or are craving tasty comfort food, this book is guaranteed to have a dish that not only satisfies your appetite but is also stress-free and delicious. Each recipe will guide you through the make-ahead process with cooking, freezing, and reheating instructions, so that you can plan your meals based on your family's needs and weekly activities. You'll also find plenty of tips for grocery shopping, prepping your kitchen for cooking day, and keeping track of your frozen dishes—all of which will help you get dinner on the table with virtually no effort.

From Pancake Donuts (see recipe in Chapter 2) and Pumpkin Nut Bread (see recipe in Chapter 2) to Orange Chicken (see recipe in Chapter 8) and Spicy Cheese Tortellini (see recipe in Chapter 10), *The Make-Ahead Cookbook* includes easy-to-make recipes your whole family will love. So stop slaving over the stove and start preparing meals that not only taste good but also save you time when you need it most!

Part One

How to Cook for a Day, Eat for a Week

Make-Ahead Cooking

Did you know that you can cook on one day and make meals that will feed your family for the entire week? This increasingly popular form of cooking isn't as difficult as it sounds, and it can actually be a lot of fun. Inside this book, you will learn how to use your kitchen appliances to cook and store delicious, healthy meals that you can just pull out and reheat for breakfast, lunch, or dinner in a matter of minutes.

Preparing fresh, delicious meals for your family is not only simple, but it'll save you time and money. You'll never have to rely on takeout foods or expensive drive-through restaurants with their sodium-loaded, high-fat foods to get you through the week. With the hearty meals in this book, you will satisfy everyone's taste buds and appetites even on your busiest days.

Why Cook Everything in a Day?

Make-ahead cooking is about making life easier by filling your freezer with prepared meals, side dishes, and ingredients you can mix and match into meals. It's about saving money at the grocery store, and saving time in the kitchen. Best of all, it's about reducing stress in your life and giving you more time to spend with the people you love. Imagine opening your freezer door and seeing it filled with prepared meals. You took care of the hard part over the weekend, and now all you have to do is choose a meal, defrost it, and heat it. Doesn't that sound wonderful? Even on the craziest days of the week, you will be able to come home and have dinner on the table in thirty to forty minutes, with virtually no effort. Dinnertime can always be this effortless if you learn how to cook once a week and freeze your meals.

Spend Less Time in the Kitchen

People lead busy lives, and therefore time is a precious commodity. By investing a small amount of time in once-a-week cooking, you reap great benefits. For example, it takes just as much time to make three batches of spaghetti sauce as it does to make one. By simply tripling your recipe, you save cooking time for future dinners. Since you generally have more free time on the weekends, you can spend some of it making meals that your family will love. Then, when busy weeknights roll around and you are short on time, you're able to pull a meal out of the freezer and provide them with a home-cooked meal in minutes.

Saves Money

When faced with a busy day and little time to prepare dinner, the fastest solution is to eat out. This might mean ordering pizza, swinging through a fast food drive-through, or dining in a restaurant. Regardless of how you eat out, every option available is more expensive than fixing a home-cooked meal. A middle-of-the-road approach is to purchase convenience food at the grocery store. This might be precooked and packaged food, or full meals from the deli. While this solution isn't as expensive as eating out, it is still more expensive than cooking at home. The best solution is to heat up a prepared meal from your freezer. By planning ahead, you'll save a lot of money by not eating out just because you have no other options.

How to Make Meals for the Entire Week

Once-a-week cooking is a marathon cooking session that involves deciding what you want to cook, making lists, shopping, then preparing and freezing enough meals to last for a whole week. With organization, planning skills, and some food-science knowledge, you will never need to order take-out again. You'll pull delicious, healthy meals out of your freezer and reheat them in minutes.

There are a few ways to tackle making meals for a week. You can cook triple batches of your favorite recipes and freeze them in meal-size containers; you can cook ten to thirty individual recipes and freeze them; or you can buy a large quantity of meats and ingredients, cook a big batch of starter foods, and then make lots of different casseroles and entrées from the starter batch. You'll find plenty of recipes and advice in this book that will help you figure out which method and foods are best for you and your family.

Meal Planning Made Easy

What's for dinner? Chances are you've heard those words a few times in your life because just about everyone likes to know what's for dinner. Including you! Freezer cooking makes meal planning a breeze.

The easiest way to plan your meals is to print off a weekly calendar. Next, make a list of the recipes you want to serve each day, making notes regarding vacation times, times you'll be entertaining, holidays, and days when you're invited out to dinner. If you are on a tight budget, choose recipes that contain common ingredients you will use in other recipes. Assign a meal to each day and write it on the calendar. Hang your calendar on the refrigerator so that everyone knows, at a glance, what is for dinner each night. Planning your meals in advance offers another benefit. Because many make-ahead meals need to be defrosted before cooking, you know what to remove from the freezer and put into the refrigerator so the meal will have a full twenty-four hours to defrost in the refrigerator.

Grocery Shopping and Kitchen Prep

Once you have a list of meals, it's time to tackle buying and cooking all of the ingredients. Consult your calendar again and choose a shopping day and a cooking day that works with your family's schedule. You'll spend at least three to six hours cooking, so make sure these days don't fall on the same date.

Next, check which ingredients you have on hand and make a grocery list. Nothing is worse than getting halfway through a recipe only to find you are missing a key ingredient, so an accurate grocery list can be the difference between success and failure in your make-ahead cooking. Go through each recipe and write down the items and quantities you need to buy. Check your list against what's in your pantry to ensure you are not buying items you already have. Do not forget to add quart- and gallon-size freezer bags, aluminum foil, freezer wrap, and any disposable freezer containers you want to use for freezing. You'll also want to make an inventory of pots, pans, spoons, forks, and knives on hand before you shop to ensure that they are all in good working order and you don't need to make a new purchase or change up a recipe.

Once you've stockpiled your recipe ingredients, sit down and plan out your cooking session. Look for recipe steps you can combine. Do two of the recipes call for chopped onions? Chop them at the same time. When deciding the order of cooking, first do the steps that take the longest amount of time. If you need to boil a whole chicken, start this early in the day. Save dishes containing raw ingredients for last since they are the quickest to assemble and don't need cooking time.

It might seem like a bit of a challenge, but a little planning goes a long way. Just think about all the time you're going to save and how well you are treating yourself and your family. If it's your first experience with this type of cooking, try to schedule two cooking sessions instead of just one, so you aren't exhausted by the first attempt. Since you're going to be spending the entire day cooking, make sure you enjoy the process and all the sounds of cooking: the knife blade chunking into the chopping board, foods sizzling in a pan, and even the clink of metal on metal as you flip through nested measuring spoons.

The Freezer

You may want to invest in a standalone chest freezer if you are going to make this type of cooking part of your life. The freezer that is part of your refrigerator can also be used as long as it is not overpacked with food.

When adding new make-ahead meals to your freezer, try to place them in the bottom of the freezer or against the sides. These are the coldest parts of the freezer, so the food will freeze more quickly without raising the internal temperature.

Use a freezer thermometer to make sure that your freezer is at a temperature of 0°F or lower before you stock it with food. If possible, turn your freezer to −10°F when you add your meals. When the food is frozen solid, you can turn the temperature back to 0°F.

If you have an extra standalone freezer, store it in the basement or the coolest part of your home. Then, if the power goes off, the ambient air temperature will keep the temperature inside the freezer cooler for a longer period of time. If the power does go off, keep the freezer closed. You may want to wrap it in blankets or towels to help insulate it and keep the temperature down. Most standalone freezers will stay at 0°F or less for twenty-four to thirty hours without power.

Many standalone freezers need to be defrosted every six to twelve weeks. Follow manufacturer's instructions for defrosting. While defrosting your freezer, discard meals that are more than a year old and store the remaining frozen items in an insulated ice chest. Place frozen ice packs or bags of ice cubes on top of the food. The food will be safe to refreeze as long as it is still frozen solid.

Frozen Food Basics

If you are new to once-a-week cooking, the process may seem overwhelming. Just take it one step at a time. You'll get a better grasp of the tasks at hand with each step you complete. Before you start, though, there are some things you need to know about freezing food.

All food is made up of live cells, which are small building blocks. These cells contain enzymes, water, protein, and other chemicals that react with air and water to gradually cause deterioration, known as spoiling, as the food ages. When food is frozen, cell functioning slows down dramatically; this preserves the food. Freezing cannot improve the quality of food; it simply holds it at the quality it was when frozen.

There are several factors in food that affect the freezing process. Here's a brief overview of these facts so you can get the most out of make-ahead cooking.

Bacteria and Molds

Bacteria and molds are present everywhere, even on the food we eat. Freezing does stop the growth of bacteria and mold on foods; however, when the food is thawed, these microorganisms will begin to grow again. That's why it is so important to thaw foods in the refrigerator instead of at room temperature. Bacterial activity is still suppressed in the cold air of the fridge. Cooking destroys bacteria and molds, so it's very important to properly and thoroughly reheat frozen food before eating it.

Freezer Burn

A freezer is a hostile place. Foods that are not properly packaged for it will become damaged very quickly. Freezer burn is the most common problem of the freezing process. It's simply the dehydration of food. When food is improperly wrapped, the dry environment of the freezer draws off moisture as the food freezes. This damages cells in the food and results in dry, hard patches that will not revert to the hydrated state even when thawed. Food that is affected by freezer burn is not unsafe to eat, but it will be tough and lack flavor. If only a small amount of food is affected by freezer burn, you can simply cut off that area and heat and eat the rest. If there is freezer burn over a large area of the food, however, throw it out; the taste and texture will be compromised.

Stews, soups, and other liquid foods that have been affected by freezer burn may be saved. These naturally liquid foods can absorb the damage caused by the dehydration when reheated. Just add ¼ cup water to the dish when reheating, and stir gently.

To prevent freezer burn, wrap foods tightly and be sure to use containers that are specifically developed for the freezer environment.

Enzymes and Oxidation

Enzymes that are naturally present in food cause changes in color, flavor, and texture. Enzymatic processes do not stop when food is frozen, although they do slow down. Some foods, particularly fruits and vegetables, need to be blanched or briefly cooked before freezing to disable these enzymes.

Cells are complete packages with membranes that control water and air exchange. When cells have been damaged (cut, chopped, or torn) by preparing or cooking the food, air combines with enzymes inside the cells. This process is called enzymatic oxidation, and it discolors food and changes flavors. Fats in meat can become rancid.

The color of fruits and vegetables can become dull and drab. Freezing minimizes this process, and you can help by removing as much air as possible from the food when packaging it. Also, when you are preparing fruits for the freezer, coat the cut surfaces with an acidic liquid like lemon juice or an ascorbic acid solution to slow down the oxidation process.

Get the Air Out!

Air is the enemy when you're freezing foods! Remove as much air as possible when wrapping. When you package food, press down on the container to get rid of excess air. You can use a drinking straw to draw air out before sealing the package. However, liquid items such as soups and stews need a small amount of space, called head space, in the container to allow for expansion during freezing. Leave ½" of head space in these containers so the lid doesn't pop off when the food expands as it freezes.

To Freeze or Not to Freeze?

Many foods freeze well. Meats, most vegetables, dairy products (including separated egg whites), fruits, sauces, combination dishes, breads, cakes, and casseroles will all hold their quality very well in the freezer and will reheat beautifully. Handling and preparation for storage will be the key factors that determine whether the foods will retain their quality when frozen and reheated.

Foods with a high water content (lettuce, tomatoes, radishes) do not freeze well. All cells contain water, which expands when frozen. Cells of water-rich foods may break down too much as the water within them freezes, resulting in an unacceptable taste or a soggy, mushy texture when thawed. Other foods that do not freeze well include:

- Canned refrigerator dough
- Celery
- Chopped or cut potatoes
- Custard and cream fillings
- Fried foods
- Mayonnaise
- Raw eggs
- Raw tomatoes
- Sour cream
- Whole hard-cooked eggs

It's possible to work around some of these problem foods. Purchase already-frozen items, such as frozen potatoes; add them to the recipe after it has cooled; then immediately freeze the dish. When the recipe is thawed and reheated, the potatoes will be tender and perfect. Or you can also simply leave these foods out of the recipe when you're preparing it for the freezer, then add them during the thawing and reheating process.

Creamy dairy products can be frozen if a stabilizer is added to them, like flour or cornstarch. These items may separate when thawed, but a simple stir with a wire whisk will smooth out the sauce. In the accompanying freezing chart, you'll find storage times for commonly used foods to use as a guide when you're freezing your favorite ingredients.

Freezing Chart: Maximum Food-Storage Times

According to the USDA, food frozen at 0°F will remain safe to eat indefinitely. This chart represents how long a food can stay in your freezer until its quality is affected.

Food	Freezer Storage Time
Bread	2–3 weeks
Butter	6–9 weeks
Cake	2–4 weeks
Casseroles	2–3 weeks
Cheese	6 weeks
Cookies	6–12 weeks
Crab and lobster	2–3 weeks
Fish (cooked)	4–6 weeks
Fish (fatty)	2–3 weeks
Fish (lean)	6 weeks
Fruit	12 weeks
Gravy	2–3 weeks
Ice cream	2–3 weeks
Meat, cooked	2–3 weeks
Meat, ground	3–4 weeks
Meat, uncooked (excluding ground)	Up to 12 weeks
Milk	3 weeks
Muffins	6–7 weeks
Pie, baked fruit	6–8 weeks
Pie, pumpkin or chiffon	1–2 weeks
Pie crust	12 weeks
Pizza	1–2 weeks
Poultry, cooked	4 weeks
Poultry pieces, uncooked	9 weeks
Shellfish, cooked	3 weeks
Shrimp and scallops	3–6 weeks
Soups and stews	2–3 weeks
Vegetables	8 weeks

Buying and Freezing Meat

Meat falls into a special category when it comes to once-a-week cooking. Since meat will be the most expensive part of your bulk-cooking purchases, always look for sales and add recipes that use that meat to your plan. However, there are very specific rules you need to follow when purchasing and storing large quantities. Most important, pay attention to expiration dates on meat products and never buy or freeze meat that is past those dates.

If you are purchasing large quantities of meat already frozen and plan to defrost it before using it in recipes, it must be cooked before being refrozen. Never thaw frozen meat, partially cook it or use it raw in a recipe, and refreeze it. Thaw frozen meat, then cook it completely, and it can be safely refrozen.

Do not freeze meat in its original packaging. Wrap it in freezer wrap, heavy-duty foil, or zip-lock freezer bags; label; and freeze. Divide the meat into small quantities before you package it for refreezing so it will be easier to thaw and work with. Freeze chicken parts or fish fillets separately, and then combine in a larger bag. Pork chops should be separated by freezer wrap, then combined in a larger bag or wrapped together with freezer wrap. Large quantities of ground beef should be divided into thin portions and packaged divided by parchment or freezer paper.

Make sure you record the meats you are storing in the freezer. When planning each cooking session, refer to this list to use the meat stored in your freezer before you purchase more. Most frozen meat will retain its quality for six weeks to a year. Cured meats like ham and bacon hold their quality in the freezer for only about one week. Because of the curing process, these meats tend to oxidize faster and will become rancid more quickly than uncured meats.

Food Safety

Food safety is the most important part of any food preparation. It doesn't matter if you prepare gourmet foods that everyone loves; if the food makes people sick, all your work is lost. If you have doubts about the purity or safety of the food, throw it out. These rules apply to all cooking and baking, not just once-a-week cooking.

Foods that could cause trouble if mishandled include all fresh and cured meats (cooked and uncooked), eggs, dairy products like milk and cream, seafood, cooked rice and pasta, opened or unsealed home-canned foods, and all foods that contain any of these ingredients.

Whenever you touch raw meats or uncooked eggs (even the shell!), immediately wash your hands with warm, soapy water before touching anything else. Do not open a cupboard, pick up the salt shaker, or touch anything that will be eaten uncooked. Think about keeping a popup container of hand wipes in your kitchen for convenience and to help remind you of this important food-safety factor.

Foods should be left at room temperature for only two hours. At that point, foods must be refrigerated or frozen. Bacteria present in all food grow at temperatures between 40°F and 140°F. Make sure that you keep track of how long potentially hazardous food has been out of refrigeration. For instance, work with all of your ground beef recipes—finish, cool, pack, label, and freeze them—before going on to recipes using chicken. Keep raw meats separate from all other foods. Use a separate cutting board, knife, and fork for preparing raw meats.

Even if the bacteria in food are killed in the cooking process, over time, some bacteria produce toxins that are not destroyed by heat or freezing temperatures. Those toxins will make you sick. That's why you must follow food-safety procedures to the letter, heating food quickly, cooling it promptly, and never letting food stand out at room temperature for more than two hours.

How to Freeze Your Meals

Properly freezing your meals is a major factor in whether a frozen meal tastes fantastic or whether it comes out freezer burned. Each recipe in this cookbook has a suggested method of freezing. When you are ready to package your meal for the freezer, remove as much air as possible and provide sufficient protection from the freezer. Heeding the following tips will help you guard your food from freezer burn and preserve it in the best possible quality.

Cool It!

Before placing the food in your freezer, cool it as quickly as you can. Hot foods will raise the temperature of your freezer and could compromise the safety and quality of other foods stored there. When the food has been prepared as the recipe directs, place it in a metal cooking or baking pan, in an ice-water bath, or spread the food in a shallow pan and place it in the refrigerator for

thirty to fifty minutes. Then pack the food in the freezer containers or wrap, seal, label, and freeze immediately.

Think about purchasing some large, sturdy, waterproof containers or storage bins to use as ice-water baths. You are going to need all of your mixing bowls and pots for cooking the food, and your sink will be full of sudsy water for cleaning.

Flash Freezing

Flash freezing is simply freezing foods as quickly as possible. Individual appetizers, sandwiches, rolls, cookies, and other small-size foods retain their quality, shape, and form best when flash frozen. Spread a layer of food on a cookie sheet or another flat surface and freeze individually—leave a space of ½–1" between the individual pieces of food so cold air can circulate freely—then package them all in one container once frozen solid.

Pack It!

Proper packaging and wrapping will keep your food in excellent condition while it is being frozen and reheated. Make sure that there are no loose wrappings around the food. You can double wrap each recipe after it has frozen solid to make sure that each package is properly sealed. Make sure you use heavy-duty foil or freezer wrap that is heat-resistant. Use freezer tape to seal seams when you use freezer wrap to package food.

Don't store tomato-based foods in foil; the acid in the tomatoes will eat through the foil, exposing the food to air and risking freezer burn. Use heavy-duty, heatproof freezer wrap for these foods.

The types of containers you use will determine how much food you'll be able to store in your freezer. Square and flat packages and containers make the best use of space, so you can add more packages to the freezer. Most casseroles can be frozen, removed from their dishes, and then stacked to store. Different methods might work best for your budget, refrigerator, or recipe preferences, so be sure to explore them all.

Single-Serving Sizes

Single-serving-size freezer meals are perfect for lunch at work or a quick snack. Lasagna is a great example of a dish that is easily made into single-serving sizes. Make the lasagna according to the recipes in Chapter 7 (South of the Border Lasagna) and Chapter 10 (Lasagna Florentine, Spinach Lasagna, Black Bean Lasagna), but instead of freezing it as an entire meal, let it cool and then cut into single portions for freezing. Single portions mean less waste, and they also give you the advantage of being able to control your portions.

FREEZER BAG METHOD

Use either gallon- or quart-size freezer bags to freeze meals to package your make-ahead meals. This method is often used with recipes that contain a marinade, soup, gravy, or sauce. Wait until the food has cooled before adding it to the bag since putting hot food into a freezer bag can compromise the strength of the bag. In addition, putting hot food directly in the freezer raises the temperature of your freezer and makes it work too hard. Before sealing the bag, remove as much air as possible.

CASSEROLE METHOD

This method of freezing is perfect for when you make meals in a casserole dish but don't want to tie up your dish in the freezer. The idea is to flash freeze the casserole in the shape of the pan so the pan doesn't need to stay in the freezer. Before adding food, line your casserole dish with aluminum foil, and on top of the aluminum foil layer add a layer of plastic wrap. Leave enough foil and plastic wrap hanging over the edges of the dish to completely cover and seal the dish. Add your food to the dish, wrap it tightly with the wrap and foil, and place the entire dish in the freezer. After several hours, remove the dish from the freezer, take the frozen, wrapped casserole out of the dish, and place the casserole back in the freezer. Your casserole is now frozen in the shape of the dish. When you are ready to defrost or reheat the meal, unwrap the frozen casserole by removing the foil and plastic wrap. Place the frozen casserole in the same dish used when freezing, and defrost or cook.

PLASTIC WRAP METHOD

Use this method for food items that do not fit into a freezer bag. The plastic wrap method is the best choice when freezing a loaf of bread. To use this method, completely wrap your food item with plastic wrap so no part of the food is directly exposed to the freezer. Because plastic wrap does not always stick as well as it should, use tape to secure the seams.

TUPPERWARE METHOD

Tupperware and other sturdy plastic containers come in all shapes and sizes and are a great choice for freezing a variety of foods. The drawbacks to these containers are that they take up a lot of space in your freezer, and they can stain when used for spaghetti sauce, chili, and other tomato-based foods. Make sure you leave space at the top and don't fill these plastic containers to the rim.

Because food expands as it freezes, if you don't leave space, the top could pop off, exposing your food to the freezer.

Load It!

Be sure the food is thoroughly cooled before loading your freezer. It's important that food that is already frozen does not thaw or soften because of the addition of unfrozen food. Avoid opening the freezer often during the loading process. Instead, gather up several containers and place them in the freezer at the same time. Every time you open the freezer, the temperature will rise a bit.

Think about dividing your freezer into sections based on the recipes it contains. Place chicken recipes in one area, appetizers in a separate basket or container, and slow cooker recipes in another area. You'll be able to find things more easily, and you'll also be able to see which recipe category needs replenishing when you're planning your next once-a-week cooking session.

Permanently attach a notebook or dry erase board to your freezer and update it each time you add or remove food. Make sure that you've used up all the food from your current cycle of once-a-week cooking before you plan another session.

Adding too much to your freezer at once raises the temperature of the freezer and compromises the quality and safety of your stored food. Make sure that you never add the equivalent of more than 40 percent of your freezer space at one time. Be sure to refer to the manufacturer's instruction booklet for specifics for your type and size of freezer.

Label Your Meals

Always label your food before putting it in the freezer. It may be easy to tell what you're freezing before you put it in the freezer, but everything looks the same once frozen. By putting the date on your food, you know at a glance how long it has been in the freezer. Although long-term freezing will not affect the safety of your meals, it will affect the quality and taste of your meals.

Take the time to write out an inventory list at this time, too, and add to it as you freeze new meals. A freezer inventory list is a list of everything you have in your freezer and the date it was frozen. This list allows you to quickly see which make-ahead meals you have. Because you have a date next to each item, you can keep track of meals that need to be eaten first. A simple way to make a freezer inventory list is to hang a whiteboard on the freezer and attach a marker with string. It is easy to erase meals as you take them out of the freezer.

How to Cook a Freezer Meal

Now that you have a freezer full of delicious meals, it is time to reap the benefits of your labor! For health reasons, it is extremely important you follow proper defrosting procedures. Each recipe has instructions for reheating your meals, and these are different for each recipe. Follow these instructions carefully and use an instant-read thermometer to check the temperature of the food before serving.

Some meals can go directly into the oven frozen, and others need to be defrosted first. Add thawing foods to your list of chores you do before bedtime, just as you choose your clothes for the next day and check your children's homework. With a little extra planning, it's very simple to take a casserole from the freezer and store it in the refrigerator to thaw overnight, and then bake it the next evening.

When thawing meat in the refrigerator, place the bagged or wrapped meat in a container so the juices don't drip on any other food. Never thaw frozen meat at room temperature. You can thaw meat in the microwave oven, but only if you are going to cook it right away.

When you reheat thawed food, be sure it is fully cooked before serving it. Casseroles need to reach an internal temperature of 165°F before they are served. Test the casserole in the very center, since that is the last place to reach proper temperature. Meats must also be cooked to certain internal temperatures before they are safe to eat.

Safely Defrost Your Meals

Growing up, you may have watched your mother take meat out of the freezer and set it on the counter all day to defrost. While you have lived to tell the story, it is not safe practice to defrost meals this way. The safest way to defrost meals is in the refrigerator. The drawback is you need nearly twenty-four hours in the refrigerator to defrost some foods. Another option is to use the microwave or cold water. Never use hot water to defrost your freezer meals, especially those containing raw meat, since raw meat should never go between 40–140°F for any length of time.

If you follow these guidelines for preparing, cooking, and reheating your make-ahead meals, you'll create a week's worth of safe, fresh, and delicious meals for your entire family in no time. Now, let's get started in the kitchen with these easy-to-make recipes!

Part Two

Recipes

Chapter 2

Breakfast and Brunch

Zesty Breakfast Burritos

A delicious and filling breakfast, these burritos also make for a great dinner when served with hash brown potatoes and fruit or an afterschool snack the kids can pop in the microwave.

YIELDS 24 SERVINGS

2 pounds ground beef
1 onion, diced
1 green bell pepper, diced
12 eggs
1 tablespoon butter
2 cups shredded Cheddar cheese
1 (15-ounce) jar salsa
24 flour tortillas

Freezing Day

1. In a medium skillet over medium heat, brown the ground beef, onion, and bell pepper. Drain.
2. In a large mixing bowl, whisk the eggs. Melt butter in a clean large skillet, add eggs, and scramble.
3. Assemble each burrito by putting meat mixture, egg, cheese, and a spoonful of salsa inside each flour tortilla.
4. Flash freeze and transfer to a freezer bag, or wrap individually in plastic wrap and freeze.

Reheating Instructions

Heat frozen burrito in the microwave for 2 minutes. Serve.

Fresh Eggs

Wondering if your eggs are still fresh? You can tell without cracking them open. Simply put the egg in a bowl of water. If the egg floats, it means it is full of air and has gone bad; if it sinks, it is good.

Sausage and Biscuit Breakfast Sandwiches

Keep a supply of these sandwiches in your freezer for those mornings when you don't have time for breakfast. They are quick to heat up and make for a great morning breakfast on the run.

YIELDS 8 SERVINGS

8 Pillsbury Grands! refrigerator biscuits
8 sausage patties
8 eggs
8 slices American cheese

Freezing Day

1. Cook biscuits according to package directions. Split down the middle to separate the tops from the bottoms.
2. In a medium skillet over medium heat, brown the sausage patties until fully cooked, about 8–10 minutes. Drain excess fat, then add eggs and scramble.
3. Put 1 sausage patty, ⅛ of the scrambled eggs, and 1 slice of cheese on each of the biscuits. Wrap individually in plastic wrap or in quart-size freezer bags, and freeze.

Reheating Instructions

Wrap frozen sandwich in a paper towel and microwave at 30 percent for 1 minute 15 seconds, then microwave on high for 1 minute or until desired temperature is reached.

Spicy Sausage Breakfast Casserole

This breakfast casserole can be tailor-made to suit your tastes! For instance, substitute the sausage with ground beef, and add a layer of bacon or ham. Switch the Cheddar cheese for pepper jack, and add a tomato or broccoli layer. The possibilities are endless.

YIELDS 6-8 SERVINGS

1 pound ground sausage, hot
1 small onion, chopped
½ green bell pepper, chopped
1 loaf Italian bread
1-2 cups shredded Cheddar cheese, to taste
1 (4-ounce) can chopped green chilies
6 eggs
3 cups milk
1 teaspoon yellow mustard
½ teaspoon salt
¼ teaspoon cayenne pepper, or to taste

Freezing Day

1. Prepare a 9" × 13" casserole dish for freezing. See instructions for the Casserole Method in Chapter 1, or use an aluminum pan.

2. In a medium skillet over medium heat, brown the sausage, onion, and bell pepper 8–10 minutes until the sausage is fully cooked. Drain and remove from heat.

3. Cut the bread into 1" slices and layer the bottom of the casserole dish.

4. Layer the meat on top of the bread, followed by the cheese, then the green chilies.

5. In a large mixing bowl, add the eggs, milk, mustard, salt, and cayenne pepper and mix to combine.

6. Pour the egg mixture over the casserole layers. Wrap tightly according to the Casserole Method and freeze.

Reheating Instructions

Following the Casserole Method, defrost casserole in the refrigerator overnight. Bake at 350°F for 45 minutes–1 hour until the egg is fully cooked and a knife inserted in the dish's middle comes out clean.

Breakfast Pizza

These little pizzas are so fun to make and eat. You can eat them as soon as they are baked. They will taste different every time if you use a mild sausage or one that's spicier and vary the cheese topping.

YIELDS 8 SERVINGS

2 tablespoons butter

4 English muffins, split

½ pound bulk pork sausage

½ cup finely chopped onion

8 eggs, beaten

⅓ cup whole milk

1 cup shredded Colby cheese

½ cup shredded mozzarella cheese

YIELDS 24 SERVINGS

6 tablespoons butter

12 English muffins, split

1½ pounds bulk pork sausage

1½ cups finely chopped onion

24 eggs, beaten

1 cup whole milk

3 cups shredded Colby cheese

1½ cups shredded mozzarella cheese

Freezing Day

1. Preheat the oven to 350°F. Butter the split sides of English muffins and toast in a toaster oven until light brown and crisp. Set aside. In a heavy skillet over medium heat, cook pork sausage until almost done. Drain off excess fat and add onion. Cook and stir for 3–4 minutes, until sausage is cooked and onion is crisp-tender. Remove pork and onion from the pan, leaving drippings.

2. In a large bowl, beat eggs and milk until combined. Pour into the hot skillet and cook over medium heat until just set, about 5–8 minutes. Fold sausage and onion mixture into eggs.

3. Divide egg mixture among toasted English muffins and top with cheeses. Place on a cookie sheet and bake for 10–15 minutes or until thoroughly heated and cheese is melted. Cool on a wire rack for 30 minutes, then flash freeze in a single layer on a cookie sheet. When frozen solid, wrap well and place in ziplock bags. Seal bag, label, and freeze.

Reheating Instructions

Microwave frozen pizzas one at a time on high power for 1–3 minutes or until thoroughly heated.

Turkey Apple Sausage

It's fun to make your own sausage, and this recipe is so easy. To serve without freezing, simply cook the patties until no longer pink in the center, about 8–10 minutes.

YIELDS 6–8 SERVINGS

1 Granny Smith apple
½ cup finely chopped onion
3 tablespoons olive oil, divided
1 pound ground turkey
¼ pound ground pork
2 tablespoons mustard
½ teaspoon dried sage leaves
½ teaspoon dried marjoram leaves
1 teaspoon salt
⅛ teaspoon white pepper

YIELDS 18–24 SERVINGS

3 Granny Smith apples
1½ cups finely chopped onion
3 tablespoons olive oil
3 pounds ground turkey
¾ pound ground pork
6 tablespoons mustard
1½ teaspoons dried sage leaves
1½ teaspoons dried marjoram leaves
1 tablespoon salt
⅜ teaspoon white pepper
6 tablespoons olive oil

Freezing Day

1. Peel and finely chop apple. Cook apple and onion in 1 tablespoon olive oil in a heavy skillet over medium heat until crisp-tender, about 5–10 minutes. Cool mixture, then combine with the rest of the ingredients, except remaining olive oil, in a large bowl; mix gently.

2. Form sausage mixture into 3" patties, each about ½" thick. Heat remaining olive oil in a heavy nonstick skillet. Cook patties over medium heat for 8–10 minutes, turning once, until thoroughly cooked. Cool patties in the refrigerator, then individually wrap and place in a rigid container. Label container and freeze.

Reheating Instructions

Remove patties from freezer and microwave from frozen for 3–4 minutes on medium per sausage patty. Or place frozen patties in a baking pan and bake in a preheated 400°F oven for 10–12 minutes, until thoroughly heated.

Sausage Scones

These easy scones are perfect for breakfast on the run. To serve immediately without freezing, let cool for a few minutes after baking.

YIELDS 8 SCONES

½ pound bulk pork sausage
1½ cups flour
½ cup whole-wheat flour
3 tablespoons sugar
1 tablespoon baking powder
¼ teaspoon salt
¼ cup grated Parmesan cheese
⅓ cup heavy cream
1 egg
¼ cup butter, melted

YIELDS 24 SCONES

1½ pounds bulk pork sausage
4½ cups flour
1½ cups whole-wheat flour
9 tablespoons sugar
3 tablespoons baking powder
¾ teaspoon salt
¾ cup grated Parmesan cheese
1 cup heavy cream
3 eggs
¾ cup butter, melted

Freezing Day

1. Preheat the oven to 400°F. In a heavy skillet over medium heat, cook sausage until crumbly and brown. Drain on paper towels. In a large bowl, combine the dry ingredients and mix to combine. In a small bowl, combine cream, egg, and melted butter and beat well; add all at once to the dry ingredients along with drained sausage. Stir until dough forms.

2. Pat out dough into an 8" round on an ungreased cookie sheet. Cut the circle into 8 wedge-shaped scones. Bake scones for 11–13 minutes, until very lightly browned and set. Cool on a wire rack, then flash freeze on a cookie sheet. Pack into rigid containers, separating the layers with waxed paper; label, seal, and freeze.

Reheating Instructions

Place frozen scones on a baking sheet and bake at 400°F for 10–15 minutes, until golden brown and hot. Let cool a few minutes before serving.

Egg Muffin Sandwiches

You could substitute Dinner Rolls (see recipe in Chapter 6) for the English muffins. To serve these little sandwiches without freezing, microwave each on high for about 50–60 seconds to melt the cheese.

YIELDS 8 SERVINGS

2 tablespoons butter
8 English muffins, split
6 slices bacon
8 eggs
⅓ cup evaporated milk
¼ teaspoon salt
⅛ teaspoon white pepper
½ teaspoon dried thyme leaves
16 slices American cheese, unwrapped

YIELDS 24 SERVINGS

6 tablespoons butter
24 English muffins, split
18 slices bacon
24 eggs
1 cup evaporated milk
¾ teaspoon salt
⅜ teaspoon white pepper
1½ teaspoons dried thyme leaves
48 slices American cheese, unwrapped

Freezing Day

1. Spread butter on the split sides of English muffins and toast in a toaster oven until light golden brown. Set aside. In a heavy skillet over medium heat, cook bacon until crisp; remove from skillet and drain on paper towels. Pour off all but 1 tablespoon bacon drippings from skillet.

2. In a large bowl, beat eggs with milk and seasonings. Pour into hot drippings and cook over medium-low heat, stirring frequently, until just set. Remove from heat, and then crumble bacon and stir into egg mixture.

3. Place 1 slice American cheese on 1 split half of each English muffin. Top with egg mixture, dividing evenly among muffins. Top egg mixture with remaining cheese slices and cover with remaining English muffin halves. Flash freeze sandwiches in a single layer on a cookie sheet until solid. Wrap in a microwave-safe paper towel, then pack into ziplock bags. Label bags, seal, and freeze.

Reheating Instructions

Place frozen, wrapped muffins, one at a time, in the microwave and heat on high power for 1–3 minutes, until thoroughly heated and cheese has melted.

Pancake Donuts

Try these Pancake Donuts with butter and confectioners' sugar for a sweet treat. These also make a great way to grab a quick breakfast in the mornings when you are short on time.

YIELDS 6 DONUTS

2 cups flour
4 teaspoons baking powder
¼ teaspoon salt
⅛ teaspoon cinnamon
⅛ teaspoon nutmeg
2 eggs
1 cup sugar
1 cup milk
½ cup oil

Freezing Day

1. In a medium bowl, combine flour, baking powder, salt, cinnamon, and nutmeg and whisk together.

2. In a mixing bowl, beat eggs slightly, add sugar, and beat at medium speed until the mixture is lemon colored and well blended (about 2 minutes).

3. Add milk, oil, and dry ingredients alternately to egg mixture. Beat well after each addition.

4. Preheat a griddle to medium low. Ladle batter on the hot griddle; spread slightly with back of ladle as batter is thick. Turn only once, after approximately 1–5 minutes when edges look done. Use your spatula to lift the edge of the donut and peek underneath. They should be light brown in color when ready.

5. Flash freeze and wrap in bundles of 3 or use sandwich-size freezer bags.

Reheating Instructions

Pancake Donuts can be warmed in the microwave for 30–60 seconds or the toaster.

Pecan Corn Waffles

These crunchy and tender waffles are perfect for a special weekend breakfast or brunch. They can be eaten immediately after cooking in the waffle iron.

YIELDS 8 SERVINGS

1½ cups flour
½ cup yellow cornmeal
⅓ cup sugar
¼ teaspoon salt
½ teaspoon baking powder
3 eggs
½ cup buttermilk
⅓ cup melted butter
1 cup corn
½ cup chopped pecans

YIELDS 24 SERVINGS

4½ cups flour
1½ cups yellow cornmeal
1 cup sugar
¾ teaspoon salt
1½ teaspoons baking powder
9 eggs
1½ cups buttermilk
1 cup melted butter
3 cups corn
1½ cups chopped pecans

Freezing Day

1. In a large mixing bowl, combine flour, cornmeal, sugar, salt, and baking powder and blend well. In a small bowl, combine eggs, buttermilk, and melted butter and beat well. Pour into dry ingredients and stir just until a batter forms. Fold in corn and pecans just until combined.

2. Cook in a preheated, oiled waffle iron until golden brown. Cool on a wire rack, then place in ziplock bags, seal, label, and freeze.

Reheating Instructions

Bake frozen waffles in a toaster oven or regular oven heated to 375°F until hot and crisp, about 4–8 minutes. Serve with maple syrup or fruit.

Classic French Toast

Sour cream adds wonderful flavor and makes the slices of French toast almost cakelike in the center. You can serve without freezing along with maple syrup, powdered sugar, and assorted jams and jellies.

YIELDS 4–6 SERVINGS

¼ cup butter
3 eggs
⅓ cup cream
2 tablespoons sour cream
½ cup milk
¼ cup powdered sugar
2 teaspoons vanilla
¼ teaspoon salt
8 slices whole-wheat bread

YIELDS 12–18 SERVINGS

¾ cup butter
9 eggs
1 cup cream
6 tablespoons sour cream
1½ cups milk
¾ cup powdered sugar
2 tablespoons vanilla
¾ teaspoon salt
24 slices whole-wheat bread

Freezing Day

1. Preheat the oven to 400°F. Place butter in a jellyroll pan and set aside. In a shallow bowl, combine eggs, cream, sour cream, milk, sugar, vanilla, and salt and mix well with an egg beater until blended.

2. Dip each slice of whole-wheat bread into the egg mixture and let stand for 1–2 minutes until the bread absorbs some of the egg mixture. Set bread on a platter and place the jellyroll pan in the oven. Heat the pan for 2–4 minutes or until the butter is melted. Carefully place each piece of coated bread into the hot butter. Bake for 4–6 minutes until bottom of toast is golden brown. Carefully turn slices with a spatula and bake for 4–7 minutes longer, until bottoms are golden brown. Remove from pan and let cool completely on a wire rack.

3. Flash freeze slices in a single layer on cookie sheets. When frozen solid, pack into ziplock freezer bags, label bags, seal, and freeze.

Reheating Instructions

Place frozen French toast slices in the toaster and toast until thoroughly heated and crisp, or bake in a preheated 375°F oven for 9–12 minutes or until thoroughly heated and crisp.

Bran Muffins

These little muffins have a wonderful taste and a very tender texture because of the brown sugar and maple syrup. Serve them while warm with some softened butter for a great healthy breakfast.

YIELDS 48 MUFFINS

1 (15-ounce) box raisin bran cereal
4 cups flour
1 cup whole-wheat flour
1½ cups sugar
1 cup brown sugar
2 teaspoons baking soda
½ teaspoon salt
½ cup maple syrup
4 eggs, beaten
1 cup safflower oil
4 cups buttermilk
1 cup raisins

YIELDS 144 MUFFINS

3 (15-ounce) boxes raisin bran cereal
12 cups flour
3 cups whole-wheat flour
4½ cups sugar
3 cups brown sugar
2 tablespoons baking soda
1½ teaspoons salt
1½ cups maple syrup
12 eggs, beaten
3 cups safflower oil
12 cups buttermilk
3 cups raisins

Freezing Day

1. Preheat the oven to 400°F. In a large bowl, combine cereal, flours, sugars, baking soda, and salt and mix well to blend. In a medium bowl, combine maple syrup, eggs, oil, and buttermilk and beat to blend. Add liquid ingredients to dry ingredients along with raisins and stir just until combined.

2. *To freeze baked muffins:* Line 48 muffin tins with paper liners and fill ¾ full with batter. Bake for 13–19 minutes or until muffins are golden brown and tops spring back when touched lightly with fingertip. Cool on a wire rack, then pack into rigid containers, seal, label, and freeze. *To freeze batter:* Line 48 muffin tins with paper liners and fill ¾ full with batter. Flash freeze in a single layer on a cookie sheet; when frozen solid, pack into rigid containers, separating layers with waxed paper. Seal container, label, and freeze.

Reheating Instructions

To thaw and serve baked muffins: Let stand at room temperature for 2–3 hours until thawed. When thawed, remove paper liners and reheat muffins in a microwave on high for 1 minute, if desired. *To thaw and bake batter:* Place frozen, unbaked muffins in muffin tins and bake in a preheated 400°F oven for 30–35 minutes, until muffins are golden brown and tops spring back when touched lightly with a fingertip.

Blueberry Muffins

If you're using frozen blueberries in these delicious muffins, add them to the batter while they are still frozen. You can serve these muffins after baking as soon as they have cooled slightly.

YIELDS 24 MUFFINS

3 cups flour
½ cup ground oatmeal
½ cup sugar
1 tablespoon baking powder
1 teaspoon baking soda
½ teaspoon salt
1½ cups buttermilk
⅓ cup vegetable oil
⅓ cup butter, melted
2 eggs
3 tablespoons flour
3 cups fresh or frozen blueberries
2 cups chopped pecans
¼ cup sugar
1 tablespoon cinnamon

YIELDS 72 MUFFINS

9 cups flour
1½ cups ground oatmeal
1½ cups sugar
3 tablespoons baking powder
1 tablespoon baking soda
1½ teaspoons salt
4½ cups buttermilk
1 cup vegetable oil
1 cup butter, melted
6 eggs
9 tablespoons flour
9 cups fresh or frozen blueberries
6 cups chopped pecans
¾ cup sugar
3 tablespoons cinnamon

Freezing Day

1. Preheat the oven to 400°F. Line 24 muffin cups with paper liners and set aside. In a large bowl, combine 3 cups flour, oatmeal, ½ cup sugar, baking powder, baking soda, and salt and mix well. In a medium bowl combine buttermilk, oil, melted butter, and eggs and beat until blended. Pour into dry ingredients and mix just until combined.

2. In a medium bowl, combine 3 tablespoons flour with blueberries and pecans and toss gently. Fold into batter just until combined. Spoon batter into prepared muffin cups, filling each ¾ full. In a small bowl, combine ¼ cup sugar and cinnamon and mix well. Sprinkle this mixture over the muffin batter.

3. Bake for 18–25 minutes or until muffins are golden brown and spring back when lightly touched in the center. Remove from pan immediately and cool on a wire rack. When muffins are completely cool, flash freeze in a single layer on cookie sheets. Place muffins in ziplock bags, label, seal, and freeze.

Reheating Instructions

Let muffins stand at room temperature for 1–2 hours until thawed. Or microwave each unwrapped frozen muffin for 40–50 seconds on high, let stand, and repeat if necessary.

Cherry Oat Muffins

Make sure to carefully pick over the dried cherries to make sure the pits have all been removed. These little muffins have a wonderful flavor and texture, and they freeze beautifully.

YIELDS 24 MUFFINS

1 cup oatmeal
1 cup oat bran
⅔ cup brown sugar
1 cup flour
1 teaspoon baking powder
½ teaspoon baking soda
⅛ teaspoon salt
1 cup buttermilk
½ cup safflower oil
2 eggs
1½ cups chopped dried cherries

YIELDS 72 MUFFINS

3 cups oatmeal
3 cups oat bran
2 cups brown sugar
3 cups flour
1 tablespoon baking powder
1½ teaspoons baking soda
⅜ teaspoon salt
3 cups buttermilk
1½ cups safflower oil
6 eggs
4½ cups chopped dried cherries

Freezing Day

1. Preheat the oven to 375°F. Line 24 muffin cups with paper liners and set aside. In a large bowl, combine oatmeal, oat bran, brown sugar, flour, baking powder, baking soda, and salt and mix well. In a medium bowl, combine buttermilk, oil, and eggs and beat well. Add liquid ingredients to dry ingredients along with chopped cherries and mix just until blended.

2. Fill prepared muffin cups ¾ full and bake for 17–21 minutes or until golden brown and tops spring back when lightly touched with a finger. Cool on a wire rack, then flash freeze in a single layer on a cookie sheet. When frozen, pack into rigid containers, layers separated by waxed paper.

Reheating Instructions

Let muffins stand at room temperature for 1–2 hours until thawed. Or place frozen muffins, one at a time, in a microwave and heat on 30 percent power for 2–4 minutes, until thawed and warm.

Healthy Apple Muffins

Make several batches of muffins to freeze, and you have a ready supply of healthy afterschool snacks or a low-calorie dessert for your lunch.

YIELDS 12 MUFFINS

2½ cups whole-wheat flour

2 cups honey

1 tablespoon pumpkin pie spice

1 teaspoon baking soda

½ teaspoon salt

2 eggs

1 cup puréed pumpkin

½ cup applesauce

2 cups apples, peeled and diced

Freezing Day

1. Preheat the oven to 350°F. In a large mixing bowl, combine all the ingredients except the apples. Mix well. Fold in apples.
2. Pour into paper-lined muffin tins. Bake for 35 minutes. Cool, flash freeze, and transfer to a freezer bag.

Reheating Instructions

Defrost muffins at room temperature for about 1 hour. Serve at room temperature, or heated in the microwave for 20–30 seconds.

Folding In

When you "fold in" an ingredient, you use a spatula or large spoon in a vertical up-and-down motion to gently blend the ingredients from the bottom to the top. The process introduces air into the mixture.

Pumpkin Nut Bread

To make fresh pumpkin purée, cut your pumpkin into large chunks, cover with water, and bring to a boil. Cook the pumpkin until tender. Once it has cooled, use a food processor to purée it.

YIELDS 2 LOAVES

1 cup vegetable oil

3 cups sugar

2 cups pumpkin purée

1½ teaspoons salt

1 teaspoon cinnamon

1 teaspoon nutmeg

½ teaspoon cloves or ginger

½ teaspoon black walnut flavoring

1 teaspoon burnt sugar flavoring

3½ cups flour

2 teaspoons baking soda

⅔ cup water

1 cup chopped nuts

4 eggs

Freezing Day

1. Preheat the oven to 350°F. In a large mixing bowl, combine all the ingredients.
2. Spray a 9" × 5" baking pan with cooking oil and pour batter into the pan.
3. Bake for 1 hour or until a knife inserted comes out clean.

Reheating Instructions

To defrost bread, wrap the loaf in plastic wrap and defrost at room temperature for 2–3 hours and serve.

Cranberry Oatmeal Quick Bread

If using frozen cranberries to make this delicious quick bread, chop while frozen, then return to the freezer until you're ready to add them to the batter. These little breads taste best if allowed to sit overnight before eating.

YIELDS 2 LOAVES

1 cup oatmeal
1¼ cups hot water
¾ cup butter
1½ cups brown sugar
½ cup sour cream
2 tablespoons orange peel
1 egg
1 teaspoon vanilla
2½ cups flour
2 teaspoons baking powder
½ teaspoon baking soda
¼ teaspoon salt
1 teaspoon cinnamon
1 cup chopped cranberries
½ cup finely chopped walnuts

YIELDS 6 LOAVES

3 cups oatmeal
3¾ cups hot water
2¼ cups butter
4½ cups brown sugar
1½ cups sour cream
5 tablespoons orange peel
3 eggs
1 tablespoon vanilla
7½ cups flour
2 tablespoons baking powder
1½ teaspoons baking soda
¾ teaspoon salt
1 tablespoon cinnamon
3 cups chopped cranberries
1½ cups finely chopped walnuts

Freezing Day

1. Preheat the oven to 350°F. Grease and flour 8" × 4" loaf pans and set aside. In a medium bowl, combine oatmeal and hot water, mix, and let stand for 5 minutes. Meanwhile, cream butter and brown sugar until fluffy. Add sour cream, orange peel, egg, vanilla, and oatmeal mixture and blend. Add flour, baking powder, baking soda, salt, and cinnamon and stir just until combined; then fold in cranberries and walnuts.

2. Spoon batter into prepared pans and bake for 55–65 minutes or until golden brown and set. Cool 10 minutes; then remove from pans and cool on wire rack. Wrap well in freezer wrap, seal, label, and freeze.

Reheating Instructions

Loosen wrappings and let bread stand at room temperature for 1–3 hours, until thawed.

Chocolate Banana Nut Bread

Heat up a slice of bread and spread on a little butter for a delicious treat. Try substituting the chocolate chips with chopped strawberries or apples.

YIELDS 1 LOAF

1¾ cups flour
2 teaspoons baking powder
¼ teaspoon baking soda
½ teaspoon salt
½ cup butter, softened
⅔ cup sugar
2 eggs, beaten
1½ cups bananas, mashed
½ cup chocolate chips
¼ cup walnuts, chopped

Freezing Day

1. Preheat the oven to 350°F. In a small mixing bowl, mix flour, baking powder, baking soda, and salt.

2. In a large mixing bowl, mix the butter, sugar, and eggs.

3. Alternate adding the flour mixture and bananas to the large mixing bowl, a little at a time. Mix just enough to combine—do not overmix. Fold in chocolate chips and walnuts.

4. Pour into a greased loaf pan and bake for 1 hour–1 hour 10 minutes. A knife inserted into the center should come out clean.

Reheating Instructions

To defrost the bread, wrap the loaf in plastic wrap and defrost at room temperature for 2–3 hours and serve.

Apple Quick Bread

This is great bread for breakfast on the run. You can add a glaze if you like: Combine 1 cup confectioners' sugar, ½ teaspoon vanilla, and 2–3 tablespoons milk and mix well; then drizzle over loaves.

YIELDS 2 LOAVES

4 medium apples
1 cup butter, softened
2 cups sugar
1 teaspoon cinnamon
4 eggs
3½ cups flour
1 teaspoon baking soda
½ teaspoon baking powder
¼ teaspoon salt
1 cup buttermilk
1 teaspoon vanilla
1 cup chopped pecans

YIELDS 6 LOAVES

12 medium apples
3 cups butter, softened
6 cups sugar
1 tablespoon cinnamon
12 eggs
10½ cups flour
1 tablespoon baking soda
1½ teaspoons baking powder
¾ teaspoon salt
3 cups buttermilk
1 tablespoon vanilla
3 cups chopped pecans

Freezing Day

1. Preheat the oven to 325°F. Generously grease and flour 2 (9" × 5") loaf pans and set aside. Peel and core apples and chop finely, by hand or in a food processor.

2. In a large bowl, combine chopped apples, butter, sugar, cinnamon, and eggs. Stir for 2–3 minutes, until blended. Add remaining ingredients and mix well to blend. Pour batter into prepared baking pans. Bake for 60–75 minutes, until dark golden brown.

3. Cool bread in pans for 5 minutes, then turn out of pans and cool on a wire rack. Wrap loaves in freezer-safe plastic wrap, label, and freeze.

Reheating Instructions

Loosen wrapping and thaw loaves 2–3 hours at room temperature.

Cinnamon Raisin Monkey Bread

This bread is easy for kids to make as well as fun to eat—just pull off pieces! Try adding diced apples or pears to the bread instead of raisins.

YIELDS 14 SERVINGS

¾ cup white sugar

3 tablespoons cinnamon

3 tubes refrigerator buttermilk biscuits

½ cup pecans, chopped and divided

½ cup raisins

½ cup unsalted butter

1 cup brown sugar

1 teaspoon vanilla extract

Freezing Day

1. Preheat the oven to 350°F. Mix sugar and cinnamon together in a plastic bag.

2. Cut biscuit dough into quarters, and put in the bag with the cinnamon sugar. Shake to coat the pieces.

3. Grease the bottom and sides of a bundt pan. Place ¼ cup pecans in the bottom of the pan. Put a layer of biscuit pieces on top of the pecans. Continue to add biscuit pieces to the pan. Intersperse the raisins and remaining pecans among the biscuit pieces.

4. In a small saucepan over medium-low heat, melt butter. Add brown sugar and vanilla. Heat until brown sugar is dissolved in the butter. Pour the melted butter and sugar over the top of the biscuits.

5. Bake for 35–40 minutes. Remove from the oven and turn out on a plate. Let cool, wrap tightly, and freeze.

Reheating Instructions

Defrost bread at room temperature for 2–3 hours. Bread can be served at room temperature or heated in the oven at 350°F for 10–15 minutes.

Coffee Cake

Coffee cake seldom contains coffee, but it was originally made to eat with your coffee as a snack or dessert. This light and fluffy Coffee Cake, with its delicious topping, will certainly complement your morning coffee or afternoon tea.

YIELDS 6 SERVINGS

½ cup vegetable oil
¾ cup sugar
1 egg
½ cup milk
1½ cups flour
1½ teaspoons baking powder
¼ teaspoon salt
1 teaspoon vanilla extract
2 tablespoons butter
¼ cup brown sugar
1 teaspoon flour
1 teaspoon cinnamon
½ cup chopped pecans

Freezing Day

1. Preheat the oven to 350°F. In a medium bowl, mix oil and sugar. Add egg and milk and mix.

2. In a separate bowl, sift together 1½ cups flour, baking powder, and salt. Add flour mixture to egg mixture a little at a time and mix well.

3. In a separate bowl, prepare topping by mixing the vanilla extract, butter, brown sugar, 1 teaspoon flour, cinnamon, and nuts.

4. Pour coffee cake batter into a greased 9" × 9" pan. Add topping.

5. Bake for 35 minutes or until edges are browned and a knife inserted in the center comes out clean. Cool, wrap with plastic wrap, and freeze.

Reheating Instructions

Defrost Coffee Cake at room temperature for 1–2 hours and serve at room temperature.

Divinity Salad

This delicious salad makes a refreshing break-fast on a hot day, or a wonderful addition to a summer cookout. You can also freeze it in an 8" round pan for 3–4 hours; then simply cut into wedges to serve.

YIELDS 8 SERVINGS

1 (10-ounce) can crushed pineapple
3 tablespoons reserved pineapple juice
1 (8-ounce) package cream cheese, softened
1 cup mayonnaise
¼ cup buttermilk
½ cup honey
1 cup finely chopped apricots
1 cup heavy cream
3 tablespoons powdered sugar
½ cup finely chopped toasted pecans

YIELDS 24 SERVINGS

3 (10-ounce) cans crushed pineapple
9 tablespoons reserved pineapple juice
3 (8-ounce) packages cream cheese, softened
3 cups mayonnaise
¾ cup buttermilk
1½ cups honey
3 cups finely chopped apricots
3 cups heavy cream
9 tablespoons powdered sugar
1½ cups finely chopped toasted pecans

Freezing Day

1. Thoroughly drain pineapple, reserving juice; set aside. In a large bowl, beat cream cheese until light and fluffy. Gradually add mayonnaise and beat until very fluffy. Add buttermilk, pineapple juice, and honey and mix well until blended.

2. Add drained pineapple and chopped apricots to cream cheese mixture. In a small bowl, combine cream and powdered sugar and beat until stiff peaks form. Fold into cream cheese mixture along with pecans.

3. Spoon salad into paper-lined muffin cups and flash freeze in a single layer until solid. Store in ziplock bags; label, seal bags, and freeze.

Reheating Instructions

Let salad stand at room temperature for 15–20 minutes.

Appetizers and Snacks

Pita Bread Crackers

The red pepper flakes give these Pita Bread Crackers a bit of heat, and you can add more or fewer pepper flakes according to your taste. Try these crackers with Hummus (see recipe in Chapter 4).

> **YIELDS 32 CHIPS**
> 4 round pieces of pita bread
> Olive oil to taste
> ¼ cup Parmesan cheese, freshly grated
> ½ teaspoon dried Italian seasoning
> ¼–½ teaspoon red pepper flakes, to taste
> ¼ teaspoon garlic salt

Freezing Day

1. Preheat the oven to 350°F. Separate the two sides of pita bread from each other, and tear each side into 4 crackers.
2. With the rough side up, brush each piece with olive oil and sprinkle with Parmesan cheese, Italian seasoning, red pepper flakes, and garlic salt.
3. Bake chips on a baking sheet for about 8 minutes, or until the crackers are browned. Cool completely. Flash freeze and transfer to a freezer bag.

Reheating Instructions

Defrost pita crackers at room temperature for about 1 hour. Eat at room temperature, or bake at 350°F for 5–10 minutes to heat through.

Spiced Pecans

The chili powder in these pecans gives them a spicy little kick! Wrap them in cellophane, or put them into a small Mason jar, tie with a ribbon, and give as a gift.

> **YIELDS 1 POUND PECANS**
> 1 egg white
> 1 teaspoon cold water
> 1 pound pecan halves
> 1 cup sugar
> ½ teaspoon salt
> ½ teaspoon chili powder
> 1 teaspoon cinnamon
> ¼ teaspoon nutmeg

Freezing Day

1. Preheat the oven to 300°F. In a mixing bowl, beat egg white and water until it is frothy. Add pecans and stir to coat.
2. In a separate bowl, mix sugar, salt, chili powder, cinnamon, and nutmeg. Add pecans and mix well.
3. Line a baking sheet with foil and put the pecans on the foil. Bake for 20–30 minutes. Stir pecans every 8–10 minutes.
4. Cool pecans and freeze in a freezer bag or plastic container.

Reheating Instructions

Defrost at room temperature for 1–2 hours and use as desired.

Spiced Pecan Salad

The Spiced Pecans are a great snack by themselves, but they are also a flavorful addition to most salads. For a real taste treat, sprinkle the pecans over a salad of fresh spring greens, dried cranberries, baby spinach, crumbled goat cheese or blue cheese, pine nuts, and balsamic or raspberry vinaigrette.

Spicy Snack Mix

To serve immediately, let snack mix cool for 30–35 minutes after baking, and serve.

YIELDS 8–10 SERVINGS

2 cups salted mixed nuts

2 cups small pretzels

2 cups potato sticks

½ cup butter, melted

3 tablespoons Worcestershire sauce

2 teaspoons dried Italian seasoning

½ teaspoon crushed red pepper flakes

⅛ teaspoon white pepper

YIELDS 24–30 SERVINGS

6 cups salted mixed nuts

6 cups small pretzels

6 cups potato sticks

1½ cups butter, melted

9 tablespoons Worcestershire sauce

6 teaspoons dried Italian seasoning

1½ teaspoons crushed red pepper flakes

⅜ teaspoon white pepper

Freezing Day

1. Preheat the oven to 300°F. Pour nuts, pretzels, and potato sticks onto 2 cookie sheets with sides. In a small saucepan, combine melted butter with remaining ingredients. Drizzle over the nut mixture. Toss to coat. Bake for 20–25 minutes, or until mixture is glazed and fragrant, stirring once during baking.

2. Cool snack mix and pack into ziplock bags. Label bags and freeze.

Reheating Instructions

Thaw at room temperature for 1–3 hours. Spread on a baking sheet and reheat in a 300°F oven for 5–8 minutes, until crisp.

Garlic Parmesan Rolls with Marinara Sauce

Try coating these savory treats with cheeses or herbs. After dipping the rolls in butter, sprinkle them with rosemary or basil.

YIELDS 8–12 SERVINGS

½ cup butter

3 tablespoons minced garlic

2 cans (13.8-ounce) refrigerated pizza crust

¼–½ cup Parmesan cheese, to taste

1 jar chunky marinara sauce for dipping (used on reheating day)

Freezing Day

1. Preheat the oven to 400°F. In a small saucepan over medium heat, melt 1 tablespoon butter and sauté garlic for 1–2 minutes. Add remaining butter and mix. Remove from heat.

2. Remove the pizza dough from the cans and roll it out a bit. Cut the dough into strips, and tie the strips into knots.

3. Place knots on a greased baking sheet and bake for 15–20 minutes until knots begin to turn a light golden brown.

4. While still hot, dip each knot into the garlic butter, sprinkle with Parmesan cheese, and cool. Flash freeze on a baking sheet. Transfer to a freezer bag.

Reheating Instructions

1. Defrost knots at room temperature for 1 hour. Put on a greased baking sheet and bake at 400°F until knots are golden brown, 3–5 minutes.

2. Heat marinara sauce in the microwave for 30–60 seconds and serve with garlic knots for dipping.

Freezing Parmesan Cheese

Canned Parmesan cheese just cannot hold a candle to the taste of real fresh-ground cheese. Unfortunately, fresh block Parmesan has a shelf life of only a few weeks in the refrigerator and therefore does not store well. Grated Parmesan cheese, however, does freeze well. Finely grate and seal in an airtight container (preferably in small, single-use amounts) and freeze.

Cheese and Bacon Potato Skins

If you like your potato skins extra crunchy, scoop out the potatoes and then rub both the inside and outside with canola oil. Broil the skins on both sides until browned. Potato skins taste delicious topped with chopped chives and dipped in ranch dressing or sour cream.

YIELDS 8 SERVINGS

8 large potatoes
1 stick salted butter or margarine
½ pound bacon
½–1 cup shredded Cheddar cheese

Freezing Day

1. Preheat the oven to 400°F. Bake potatoes for 1 hour. Let cool completely.

2. Cut potatoes lengthwise into quarters. Carve out the inside of each of the potato quarters and discard.

3. In a small saucepan, melt the butter. Once melted, brush on the inside and outside of each potato quarter.

4. In a medium skillet over medium heat, cook the bacon, turning frequently, 10–15 minutes until crispy. Crumble into small pieces.

5. Top each potato quarter with grated Cheddar cheese and bacon. Flash freeze then transfer to freezer bag.

Reheating Instructions

Place frozen potato skins on a baking sheet and bake at 450°F for 15–25 minutes.

How to Freeze Bacon

Having cooked bacon on hand makes cooking much easier. To freeze cooked bacon, cook as usual, removing the bacon a minute or so earlier than normal. Drain and cool the bacon and freeze slices separated by wax paper. Thawed bacon can be reheated in the microwave for 20–40 seconds on high or in a hot pan for 1–2 minutes.

Buffalo Chicken Wings

Raw vegetables, especially celery, and blue cheese or ranch dressing are the perfect complement to these spicy wings. Guests will also enjoy dipping their wings directly into the dressing.

YIELDS 8–12 SERVINGS

1½ cups butter
1 (12-ounce) bottle hot sauce
2 tablespoons white vinegar
12 whole chicken wings

Freezing Day

1. In a small saucepan over medium heat, melt the butter. Remove from heat.
2. Mix in hot sauce and vinegar. Remove from heat and let cool.
3. When you buy your wings, they are large and need to be cut into smaller pieces by making two cuts. The first cut is made at the joint between the two meaty portions. After the first cut, the larger piece contains two sections, one being the tip of the wing. Make your second cut and discard the tip of the wing.
4. Place 1" water in the bottom of a 6-quart saucepan. Put a steamer basket inside the pan and cover. Bring the water to a boil. Put wings in the steamer basket and steam over medium heat for 10 minutes. Pat dry and cool.
5. Put cooled wings in a gallon-size freezer bag and pour the prepared sauce over the wings. Seal the bag and freeze.

Reheating Instructions

1. Defrost chicken wings in the refrigerator for 24 hours.
2. Place wings and sauce in a 9" × 13" baking dish.
3. Bake at 425°F for 40 minutes until wings are fully cooked.

Sesame-Encrusted Teriyaki Chicken Bites

This recipe will teach you how to serve a platter of teriyaki chicken bites your guests will rave about. Pair each chicken bite on a toothpick with a chunk of fresh pineapple.

YIELDS 8 SERVINGS

2 pounds boneless, skinless chicken breasts
1 (10-ounce) bottle teriyaki sauce
3 tablespoons soy sauce
6 tablespoons honey
1 (3-ounce) container sesame seeds

Freezing Day

1. Cut chicken into bite-size cubes and marinate in teriyaki sauce for 1–3 hours in a medium bowl in the refrigerator.
2. Gently pat chicken dry with paper towels.
3. In a separate bowl, mix soy sauce with honey.
4. Put sesame seeds on a small plate.
5. Dip each chicken bite into the soy sauce and honey mixture, fully coating the bite.
6. Then dip one side of the coated chicken in the sesame seeds.
7. Flash freeze on a baking sheet lined with wax paper, sesame seed–side up. Transfer to a freezer bag.

Reheating Instructions

Bake the frozen chicken on a lightly greased baking sheet at 400°F for 15–20 minutes, or until chicken is fully cooked. Do not overcook.

Teriyaki Sauce

Bottled teriyaki sauce is readily available at the grocery store, but you can also make a similar sauce. To make your own style of teriyaki sauce, mix the following in a food processor: ¼ cup soy sauce, ¼ cup water, 2 tablespoons honey, 1 clove minced garlic, ¼ teaspoon allspice, and ⅛ teaspoon ground ginger.

Bruschetta Turnovers

These turnovers are a variation of traditional Italian bruschetta. Traditional bruschetta was made by rubbing toasted bread with olive oil and garlic.

YIELDS 4 OR 5 SERVINGS

1 (17-ounce) box frozen puff pastry
3 cloves garlic, minced
1 small tomato, chopped
4–6 fresh basil leaves, chopped
¼–½ cup shredded mozzarella cheese
2 tablespoons olive oil (used on reheating day)
4 tablespoons Parmesan cheese (used on reheating day)

Freezing Day

1. Defrost puff pastry on the counter for about 30 minutes. Spread puff-pastry sheet on a floured surface and roll it out a few times to flatten folds in the pastry.

2. Use a 3"-diameter circle and cut out 9 circles.

3. On half of each pastry circle put garlic, tomato, basil, and mozzarella cheese.

4. Fold over half of each circle (making a half-moon shape) and seal edges by pressing down.

5. Place on a baking sheet and flash freeze. Transfer to a freezer bag.

Reheating Instructions

1. Place frozen pastries on a baking sheet and bake at 400°F for 10 minutes.

2. Brush each turnover with olive oil and sprinkle with Parmesan cheese.

3. Return to the oven for 10–15 additional minutes until pastry turns a golden brown.

Cheesy Artichoke and Spinach Spirals

When cutting the spirals, use a serrated knife. You will get a clean cut and it will help prevent the bread from tearing.

YIELDS 4 SERVINGS

1 (11-ounce) can refrigerated French bread loaf

1 (10-ounce) package frozen spinach

1 (14-ounce) jar artichoke hearts

1 (5-ounce) can sliced water chestnuts

2 tablespoons minced onion

1 (8-ounce) package cream cheese

2 cups shredded Monterey jack cheese

¼ teaspoon red pepper flakes

Freezing Day

1. Preheat the oven to 375°F. Unroll the dough from the can and roll it out with a rolling pin to a 12" × 13" rectangle.

2. Defrost the spinach and squeeze out the extra water. Drain the artichoke hearts and chop into pieces.

3. In a large mixing bowl, mix chopped artichoke hearts with the spinach.

4. Add the remaining ingredients to the bowl and mix thoroughly.

5. Spread the mixture on the dough, and roll up into a tight roll using wet fingers to seal the seam. Pinch and seal the ends closed.

6. Bake for 25–30 minutes or until it is golden brown.

7. Cool, wrap with plastic wrap, and freeze.

Reheating Instructions

Defrost in the refrigerator overnight. Bake at 350°F for 15 minutes or until heated. Cut into 6–8 slices.

Best Ways to Defrost and Squeeze-Dry Spinach

Try these tips for defrosting and squeezing water out of spinach. One method is to defrost spinach in a microwave. Fold a towel around the defrosted spinach and, holding the towel over the sink, twist one end of the towel in one direction and the other end in the opposite direction squeezing out the water. A second way to accomplish this is to use a mesh strainer under running water to defrost the spinach, then press spinach against the mesh to squeeze out water.

Italian Pastry Roll-Ups

Try your own variation of these roll-ups! Add vegetables (sweet red peppers, sliced mushrooms, or onions, for example) or meat (like crumbled ground beef or sausage).

YIELDS 12 SERVINGS
1 (17-ounce) box frozen puff pastry
1 cup ricotta cheese
1 cup jarred spaghetti sauce
1 cup mozzarella cheese, shredded

Freezing Day

1. Defrost pastry on the counter for 30 minutes.
2. Evenly spread ricotta cheese on sheets, followed by sauce, and top with mozzarella cheese.
3. Starting on the long side, roll up the pastry like a jellyroll. Wet the tips of your fingers with water and seal the edge of the pastry so it stays rolled.
4. Using a serrated knife, cut each roll into 6–8 slices.
5. Lay the slices on a baking sheet lined with wax paper and flash freeze. Transfer to a freezer bag.

Reheating Instructions

Place the frozen slices on a baking sheet and bake at 400°F for 15–20 minutes.

Basil and Mozzarella Stuffed Tomatoes

Basil can be expensive to buy out of season, but it is easily grown at home. This herb needs about 7 hours of sunlight a day, and can be grown indoors or outdoors after the last frost.

YIELDS 6–8 SERVINGS
10 ounces cherry tomatoes (about 18)
½ cup mozzarella cheese
1 tablespoon olive oil
1–3 tablespoons fresh basil, chopped
   (according to taste)
¼ teaspoon salt
1 small clove garlic, minced

Freezing Day

1. With a paring knife, remove the tops and insides of tomatoes.
2. In a large mixing bowl, combine the cheese, olive oil, basil, salt, and garlic. Mix well.
3. Spoon the stuffing into each tomato.
4. Flash freeze on a baking sheet and transfer to a freezer bag.

Reheating Instructions

Defrost in the refrigerator overnight and serve cold.

Asiago Baked Olives

Asiago is a delicious and versatile cheese that originated in Northern Italy. If you don't have access to Asiago cheese, you can substitute either Romano or Parmesan cheese.

YIELDS 10 SERVINGS

2 cups grated Asiago cheese

1¼ cups flour

½ cup butter, plus 2 tablespoons if needed

1 teaspoon Worcestershire sauce

⅛ teaspoon cayenne pepper

40 green olives

Freezing Day

1. In a large mixing bowl, combine the cheese, flour, butter, Worcestershire sauce, and cayenne pepper to make a dough. Add more flour or butter to the dough as needed.

2. Roll dough into balls a little larger than the size of your olives. Push an olive into each ball so it is covered completely with the dough.

3. Place olives on a baking sheet lined with wax paper and flash freeze. Transfer to a freezer bag.

Reheating Instructions

Place frozen olives on baking sheet and cook for 20–25 minutes at 400°F.

Appetizers Relieve Stress?

It is always a good idea to have a handful of frozen appetizers in your freezer. You'll be prepared when unexpected company drops by, and if you are asked to bring a dish to a party, you can do so with ease. Having something on hand saves you the stress of grocery shopping and the worry over what to make. Anything that can relieve stress in your life is definitely a good thing!

Sesame Shrimp Toast

Traditionally, shrimp toast is most often deep-fried, but it can also be baked. To deep-fry, brush the shrimp toast lightly with egg. Put into oil shrimp-side down, then turn. Fry until golden brown. It is not recommended you freeze the toast once it has been deep-fried.

YIELDS 6 SERVINGS

6 slices white bread

8 ounces cooked shrimp, peeled

2 tablespoons water chestnuts, finely chopped

1 egg white

½ teaspoon garlic, minced

½ teaspoon sesame oil

½ teaspoon fresh ginger, minced

2 tablespoons scallions, minced

1 tablespoon sesame seeds

Freezing Day

1. Remove crusts from bread, cut diagonally into 4 pieces, and toast lightly.

2. In a food processor, combine shrimp, water chestnuts, egg white, garlic, sesame oil, and ginger. Pulse 5–10 times, but do not purée. Stir in scallions.

3. Spread shrimp mixture on the toasted bread slices, and sprinkle with sesame seeds.

4. Flash freeze and transfer to a Tupperware container.

Reheating Instructions

Bake frozen shrimp toast at 400°F for 10–15 minutes.

Dim Sum

Shrimp toast is a Chinese dish often included in dim sum. Dim sum (which means "heart warmers") consists of a variety of both sweet and savory snacks that are shared with pots of tea. In restaurants, the freshly cooked dim sum selections are brought to the tables, stacked on rolling carts and often served in steaming bamboo baskets.

Dijon Kielbasa Bites

Puff pastry is a layered pastry made by a time-consuming and repetitive process of folding layers of dough and butter, and then letting the pastry rest in a temperature-controlled environment. Frozen puff pastry is readily available and is a huge timesaver.

YIELDS 4–6 SERVINGS

1 (17-ounce) package frozen puff pastry
1 pound kielbasa
1 (8-ounce) jar Dijon mustard

Freezing Day

1. Defrost puff pastry on the counter for about 30 minutes.
2. Cut kielbasa into bite-size pieces and brown in a medium skillet over medium heat for 10–15 minutes.
3. Once defrosted, roll out puff pastry on a floured surface to smooth out the folds in the pastry.
4. Cut pastry into 3" circles.
5. In the center of each circle, put ¼ teaspoon Dijon mustard (or more to taste) and a piece of kielbasa on top of the Dijon.
6. Pull up the edges of the circles so it looks like a Hershey's Kiss. Use water on your fingers to seal the top together.
7. Flash freeze and transfer to a freezer bag.

Reheating Instructions

Place frozen Dijon Kielbasa Bites on a greased baking sheet and bake at 400°F for 15–20 minutes or until golden brown.

Mini Chicken Turnovers

These little pastries are the perfect finger food for your next party. They also make great game-day snacks.

YIELDS 30 TURNOVERS

Filling

2 tablespoons onion, minced

4 tablespoons mushrooms, diced

2 tablespoons butter

¼ teaspoon garlic, minced

1½ cups cooked chicken

3 ounces cream cheese

¼ teaspoon salt

¼ teaspoon pepper

3 tablespoons white wine

Pastry

1½ cups flour

¾ teaspoon salt

½ cup shortening

3 tablespoons water, as needed

Freezing Day

1. Make the filling: In a large skillet over medium heat, sauté onions and mushrooms in butter for 5–6 minutes. Add the garlic and sauté 1–2 more minutes.

2. Add chicken, cream cheese, salt, pepper, and wine. Heat over medium-low heat 5–7 minutes until cream cheese melts. Remove from heat and set aside.

3. Make the pastry: Sift the flour and salt together in a medium bowl. Cut in the shortening until it is crumbly.

4. Add water, a tablespoon at a time, until the dough holds together. Make dough into a ball and roll out on a floured surface to ⅛" thick. Cut into 30 circles.

5. Line a baking sheet with wax paper. Put a spoonful of chicken mixture on one half of each pastry circle, and fold it over. Moisten the edge of the turnover to help seal the dough. Press around the outside with a fork. Put on a baking sheet and flash freeze.

6. Transfer to a freezer bag once flash frozen.

Reheating Instructions

Place frozen turnovers on a baking sheet and bake at 400°F for 15–20 minutes or until turnovers are golden brown.

Puff-Pastry Chicken Turnovers

If you prefer a simpler route, purchase frozen puff pastry. You need 2 (17-ounce) boxes. Defrost the pastry on the counter for about 30 minutes, and roll it out on a floured surface. Cut out 3" circles and fill with the chicken mixture. Fold, seal the edges with a fork, and flash freeze. To bake, defrost and bake at 400°F for 5 minutes or until pastry is golden brown.

Ham and Pineapple Bites

These appetizers are sweet and spicy. The red pepper flakes give the bites a spicy kick, while the honey gives them a sweet flavor.

YIELDS 12 SERVINGS

25 cubes cooked ham
¼ cup honey
Red pepper flakes to taste
25 pineapple chunks

Freezing Day

1. Coat one side of each cube of ham with honey. Sprinkle a small amount of red pepper flakes on top of the honey, and top that with a pineapple chunk. Hold it together with a toothpick.
2. Flash freeze and transfer to a freezer bag.

Reheating Instructions

Defrost Ham and Pineapple Bites overnight in the refrigerator and serve cold.

Spicy Beef Kabobs with Cucumber Dipping Sauce

Fresh ginger should be kept in the refrigerator, but it will last longer if you freeze it. When using frozen ginger, there is no need to defrost. Simply grate however much ginger you need, and return the rest to the freezer.

YIELDS 6–8 SERVINGS

¼ cup lime juice
2 cloves garlic, minced
1 cup soy sauce
2 teaspoons fresh ginger, grated
1 teaspoon crushed red pepper flakes
2 pounds lean steak, cut into cubes
2 red bell peppers (used on reheating day)
2 green bell peppers (used on reheating day)
2 yellow bell peppers (used on reheating day)
Cucumber Dipping Sauce (see recipe in Chapter 4) (used on reheating day)

Freezing Day

1. In a small bowl, combine lime juice, garlic, soy sauce, ginger, and red pepper flakes.
2. Put marinade in a freezer bag, add cubed steak, and freeze.

Reheating Instructions

1. Defrost meat and marinade in the refrigerator overnight.
2. Cut red, green, and yellow peppers into 1½" pieces.
3. Place meat and vegetables on skewers and grill over medium-high heat 8–12 minutes, or until desired doneness.
4. Serve with Cucumber Dipping Sauce.

Egg Rolls

To serve immediately, fry in peanut oil at 375°F for 2–3 minutes, until golden brown. To make a dipping sauce, mix 3 tablespoons soy sauce with 1 teaspoon sugar, 1 tablespoon mustard, and 1 tablespoon vinegar.

YIELDS 24 SERVINGS

½ pound ground pork
½ pound ground shrimp
1 carrot, shredded
2 cloves garlic, minced
1 bunch green onions, finely chopped
1 cup shredded napa cabbage
2 tablespoons soy sauce
1 tablespoon oyster sauce
2 tablespoons cornstarch
1 tablespoon water
1 package egg roll wrappers
3 cups peanut oil

YIELDS 72 SERVINGS

1½ pounds ground pork
1½ pounds ground shrimp
3 carrots, shredded
6 cloves garlic, minced
3 bunches green onions, finely chopped
3 cups shredded napa cabbage
6 tablespoons soy sauce
3 tablespoons oyster sauce
6 tablespoons cornstarch
3 tablespoons water
3 packages egg roll wrappers
3 cups peanut oil

Freezing Day

1. In a large skillet over medium heat, brown ground pork until almost done. Add ground shrimp, carrot, and garlic; cook and stir for 4–6 minutes or until pork is cooked. Remove from heat, drain well, and add green onions, cabbage, soy sauce, and oyster sauce.

2. Combine cornstarch and water in a small bowl and blend well.

3. To form Egg Rolls, place one wrapper, point-side down, on the work surface. Place 1 tablespoon of the filling 1" from the corner. Brush all edges of the Egg Roll wrapper with the cornstarch mixture. Fold the point over the filling, then fold in the sides and roll up the Egg Roll, using the cornstarch mixture to seal as necessary.

4. At this point, Egg Rolls may be flash frozen, or you can flash freeze them after frying. Once frozen, pack, label, and freeze in rigid containers.

Reheating Instructions

To reheat unfried Egg Rolls, fry the frozen rolls in peanut oil heated to 375°F for 2–3 minutes, turning once, or until deep golden brown. To reheat fried Egg Rolls, place frozen Egg Rolls on a baking sheet; bake at 375°F for 8–10 minutes or until crisp and hot.

Stuffed Mushrooms

Lemon juice prevents the mushrooms from darkening during freezing and adds a fresh flavor. To serve immediately, bake filled mushrooms at 375°F for 8–10 minutes or until hot and cheese is melted.

YIELDS 30 SERVINGS

30 large mushrooms
2 tablespoons lemon juice
2 tablespoons olive oil
1 onion, finely chopped
1 tablespoon olive oil
1 Granny Smith apple, peeled and finely chopped
½ cup chopped walnuts
1 cup cubed Havarti cheese
½ teaspoon salt
⅛ teaspoon pepper

YIELDS 90 SERVINGS

90 large mushrooms
6 tablespoons lemon juice
6 tablespoons olive oil
3 onions, finely chopped
3 tablespoons olive oil
3 Granny Smith apples, peeled and finely chopped
1½ cups chopped walnuts
3 cups cubed Havarti cheese
1½ teaspoons salt
⅜ teaspoon pepper

Freezing Day

1. Preheat the oven to 375°F. Remove stems from mushrooms; chop stems and set aside. Combine lemon juice and olive oil in a small bowl and dip mushroom caps into this mixture. Place mushroom caps upside down on a baking sheet and bake for 6–8 minutes, or until slightly softened. Remove from the oven and cool.

2. In a heavy skillet over medium heat, sauté onion and chopped mushroom stems in olive oil until tender. Add chopped apple and walnuts; mix well. Remove from heat and cool for 20 minutes. Stir in cheese, salt, and pepper.

3. Stuff mushrooms with the filling mixture, smoothing the top of the filling. Flash freeze mushrooms on baking sheets. When frozen, pack mushrooms in rigid containers, with waxed paper separating layers. Label mushrooms and freeze.

Reheating Instructions

Bake frozen mushrooms at 375°F for 15–18 minutes or until mushrooms are hot and beginning to brown and the cheese is melted.

Italian Pork Skewers

These skewers are tender and full of flavor. To serve immediately, marinate for 2-3 hours, then cook over a grill or broil until done.

YIELDS 6–8 SERVINGS

2 pounds pork tenderloin
¼ cup balsamic vinegar
¼ cup olive oil
¼ cup finely minced onion
1 teaspoon dried Italian seasoning
½ teaspoon salt
⅛ teaspoon pepper

YIELDS 18–24 SERVINGS

6 pounds pork tenderloin
¾ cup balsamic vinegar
¾ cup olive oil
¾ cup finely minced onion
1 tablespoon dried Italian seasoning
1½ teaspoons salt
⅜ teaspoon pepper

Freezing Day

1. Trim excess fat from the tenderloin. Cut pork, on a slant, into ¼"-thick slices, each about 4" long. In a large bowl, combine the remaining ingredients and mix well with a wire whisk. Add tenderloin slices and mix gently to coat. Cover and refrigerate for 2–3 hours. Meanwhile, soak 8" wooden skewers in cold water.

2. Remove pork from the marinade and thread onto the soaked skewers. Flash freeze on a baking sheet in a single layer. When frozen solid, pack skewers in rigid containers, with layers separated by waxed paper. Label skewers and freeze.

Reheating Instructions

Thaw overnight in the refrigerator. Cook skewers 4–6" from medium coals on a grill, or broil 4–6" from the heat source, for about 4–6 minutes or until cooked (160°F on an instant-read thermometer), turning once.

Chicken Verde Quesadillas

Prepare a large batch of Chicken Verde and use it to make Chicken Verde Wraps (see recipe in Chapter 11).

Freezing Day

1. In a large skillet over medium-high heat, sauté the chicken 4–5 minutes in vegetable oil until white in color. Add the onion and sauté 8–10 minutes until most of the juices have disappeared. Drain any remaining juices.

2. Add the tomatillo and cook over low heat until the mixture thickens, 20–30 minutes. Season the mixture with salt and pepper.

3. Place spoonfuls of Chicken Verde on one half of a flour tortilla, and sprinkle with cheese. Fold the tortilla in half covering the filling. In a large skillet, cook quesadillas in olive oil over medium heat for 2 minutes on each side. Let cool and flash freeze.

4. Once frozen, transfer to a freezer bag.

Reheating Instructions

Defrost each frozen quesadilla in a microwave for 1 minute. In a skillet over medium heat, put 1 teaspoon vegetable oil. Add a quesadilla to the skillet and cook on each side for 2 minutes or until quesadilla is browned.

Chapter 4

Marinades, Sauces, Dips, and Seasonings

Pork Marinade

This is a great marinade to have on hand to marinate a pork roast. You can also inject this marinade into your pork.

YIELDS 1½ CUPS

1 cup apple juice
2 tablespoons Worcestershire sauce
2 tablespoons apple cider vinegar
1 tablespoon oil
1 tablespoon lemon juice
1½ teaspoons hot sauce
2 tablespoons dark brown sugar
½ teaspoon cumin
¾ teaspoon salt

Freezing Day

1. In a medium saucepan over medium heat, combine apple juice, Worcestershire sauce, apple cider vinegar, oil, lemon juice, and hot sauce. Simmer for 10 minutes.
2. Add dark brown sugar, cumin, and salt. Whisk until dry ingredients are completely dissolved. Remove from heat, cool, and freeze.

Reheating Instructions

Defrost in the refrigerator overnight and use as desired.

Chicken Marinade

Marinating your chicken lets it soak up delicious flavors until you are ready to cook. Slice up the chicken and wrap it in a burrito with enchilada sauce, or put on top of a green salad.

YIELDS 1 CUP

2 teaspoons soy sauce
¼ cup chicken broth
½ cup lime juice
¼ cup olive oil
1 teaspoon salt
2 teaspoons brown sugar
1 teaspoon onion powder
½ teaspoon liquid smoke
1 teaspoon chili powder
½ teaspoon black pepper

Freezing Day

Combine all the ingredients in a food processor and mix. Freeze in a freezer bag.

Reheating Instructions

Defrost marinade in the refrigerator overnight and use as desired.

Teriyaki Marinade

Cayenne is a hot spice used to flavor dishes. Adjust the cayenne to suit your tastes, and be sure to add extra cayenne slowly—the heat can sneak up on you!

YIELDS ½ CUP

½ cup teriyaki sauce
2 tablespoons orange juice concentrate
1 clove garlic, minced
¼ teaspoon ground ginger
⅛ teaspoon cayenne pepper

Freezing Day

In a food processor, combine all the ingredients and mix. Freeze in a freezer bag or plastic container.

Reheating Instructions

Defrost marinade in the refrigerator overnight and use as desired.

Sesame Ginger Dipping Sauce/Marinade

Dip homemade Pot Stickers (see recipe in Chapter 7) in this sauce, or use it as a marinade for chicken, fish, or beef. It also tastes delicious mixed with vegetables and stir-fried.

YIELDS 1 CUP

⅓ cup sesame oil
⅓ cup soy sauce
2½ tablespoons grated fresh ginger
2 cloves garlic, minced
2½ tablespoons brown sugar
1 teaspoon red pepper flakes

Freezing Day

Combine all the ingredients in a food processor and mix. Freeze in a freezer bag.

Reheating Instructions

Defrost the marinade in the refrigerator overnight and use as desired.

Sesame Ginger Grilled Chicken

Prepare the marinade as instructed and divide the result in half. Freeze half the marinade with boneless chicken breasts, and the other half in its own freezer bag to be used for basting. Grill chicken over medium heat for 12–15 minutes or until no longer pink. Brush chicken with extra marinade throughout cooking.

Sweet-and-Sour Sauce

This versatile sauce will carry you through many meals. Try it with Meatballs (see recipe in Chapter 7), shredded pork, chicken, or as a dipping sauce.

YIELDS 3¾ CUPS

1 (15-ounce) can pineapple chunks with juice
½ cup white vinegar
¼ cup ketchup
¾ cup brown sugar
1 tablespoon Worcestershire sauce
Dash hot sauce
3 tablespoons cornstarch (optional)
¼ cup cold water (optional)

Freezing Day

1. Pour the pineapple juice into a measuring cup. Add enough water to make 1 cup. Save the pineapples to serve with dinner, or for use in another recipe.

2. Combine all the ingredients in a medium saucepan and bring to a boil. Simmer 5 minutes. Freeze in a freezer bag or in Tupperware.

3. If you prefer your Sweet-and-Sour Sauce thick, mix 3 tablespoons cornstarch with ¼ cup cold water. Mix until the cornstarch is completely dissolved. Pour the cornstarch mixture into the saucepan and stir continually until the sauce thickens.

Reheating Instructions

Defrost sauce in the refrigerator overnight and serve at room temperature.

Stir-Fry Sauce

This sauce is easy to whip up, tastes fantastic on both beef and chicken, and is a great option to keep on hand in the freezer to prepare for a quick dinner.

YIELDS 1¼ CUPS

¼ cup soy sauce
¼ cup honey
¾ cup olive oil
2 tablespoons balsamic vinegar
2 cloves garlic, minced
1 tablespoon onion, minced
¼ teaspoon fresh ginger

Freezing Day

In a food processor, mix all the ingredients. Freeze in a freezer bag.

Reheating Instructions

Defrost sauce in the refrigerator overnight and use as desired.

Thicken Your Stir-Fry Sauce

If you want your Stir-Fry Sauce to also act as a thickening agent, whisk in 1 teaspoon cornstarch for every 6 tablespoons of liquid in your Stir-Fry Sauce. Make sure your liquids are not hot, or the cornstarch will form clumps.

Alfredo Sauce

Alfredo Sauce is very versatile. You can serve it with grilled chicken and fettuccine noodles, as a topping for vegetables, or with seafood.

YIELDS 5 CUPS

⅓ cup butter

1 small clove garlic, minced

2 cups heavy cream

1½ cups fresh Parmesan cheese, grated

¼ cup fresh parsley, chopped

1 (8-ounce) can sliced mushrooms

⅛ teaspoon black pepper, or more to taste

Freezing Day

1. In a medium saucepan over medium-low heat, melt butter. Add garlic and heavy cream.

2. Little by little add the Parmesan cheese. Let it fully melt before adding more. Stir constantly.

3. Stir in parsley, mushrooms, and pepper to taste.

4. Freeze in a freezer bag.

Reheating Instructions

Defrost sauce in the refrigerator overnight and heat in a medium saucepan over medium heat for 8–12 minutes, or until desired temperature is reached. If sauce is too thick, it can be thinned out by adding milk or more butter.

Homemade Pizza Sauce

This recipe contains enough sauce to make 4 pizzas, so freeze the sauce accordingly and you'll always have just the right amount for pizza night!

YIELDS SCANT 3 CUPS

1 (15-ounce) can tomato sauce

1 (6-ounce) can tomato paste

2 teaspoons basil

2 teaspoons oregano

1½ teaspoons garlic powder

1 teaspoon paprika

½ teaspoon onion powder

½ teaspoon sugar

Freezing Day

Add all the ingredients to a food processor and mix well. Divide into 1-cup portions and freeze in a freezer bag.

Reheating Instructions

Defrost overnight in the refrigerator and use as desired.

Basil and Pine Nut Pesto

Pesto, a sauce that originated in Italy, is traditionally made using a mortar and pestle. It is most commonly served over pasta, but it can be used in a wide variety of ways such as over baked potatoes, on top of a steak, or even with steamed vegetables.

YIELDS 3½ CUPS

½ cup pine nuts

2 cups fresh basil

4 cloves garlic, peeled

¾ cup fresh Parmesan cheese, grated

1 tablespoon salt

1½ cups olive oil

Freezing Day

1. In a food processor, mix the pine nuts, basil, garlic, cheese, and salt. Gradually add olive oil until pesto reaches desired consistency. You may enjoy a thinner consistency for tossing with pasta, or a thicker consistency for spreading on Pita Bread Crackers (see recipe in Chapter 3).

2. Transfer to a freezer bag and freeze.

Reheating Instructions

Defrost pesto in the refrigerator overnight and use as desired.

Substitution for Pine Nuts

Pine nuts are an essential ingredient in classic Italian pesto recipes, but they can be a bit pricey. To save money when making your pesto, try using a combination of pine nuts and walnuts, or skip the pine nuts completely and use walnuts. Make sure the skin has been removed from the walnut before using.

Gravy for Any Occasion

This basic gravy recipe can be used with any type of broth, and as a complement to a variety of dishes. To make this gravy, you can use broth (or meat juices) from the dish you are cooking, canned broth, or even make broth from bouillon cubes.

YIELDS 1½ CUPS
3 tablespoons cornstarch
½ cup cold water
2 cups broth
¼ cup milk
3 tablespoons butter or margarine
Salt and pepper to taste

Freezing Day

1. In a small dish, combine cornstarch with cold water. Mix well.
2. Add broth to a saucepan. Slowly stir in the cornstarch and water mixture.
3. Cook over medium heat, stirring constantly until gravy thickens and begins to boil.
4. Add milk, butter, and salt and pepper to taste, then remove from heat.
5. Let gravy cool, and freeze in a freezer bag.

Reheating Instructions

Defrost in the refrigerator overnight and heat gravy.

Add Variety to Your Gravy

You can add to this basic recipe to match any meal you are cooking. Make gravy to go with a beef dish by using beef broth as your base and adding mushrooms, onions, and extra pepper. For giblet gravy, use the pan drippings from the turkey to make your broth, and add cooked and cut-up giblets to the gravy.

Dill Sauce

Dill seeds have a stronger flavor than dill weed and add a crunch to your dip. You can also use ¼ cup fresh dill in place of the dried dill weed.

YIELDS ½ CUP
½ cup plain yogurt
1 teaspoon dried dill weed
½ teaspoon sugar
1 teaspoon lemon zest
2 teaspoons lemon juice
Salt to taste

Freezing Day

Combine all the ingredients in a small bowl and freeze in a freezer bag.

Reheating Instructions

Defrost sauce in the refrigerator overnight and serve chilled.

Dill, Three Ways

Dill is typically available three ways: dried dill, fresh dill, and dill seeds. Dried dill has the mildest flavor but holds up better when cooking for longer times. Fresh dill has a stronger flavor and will keep a reasonable amount of time in the refrigerator. Dill seed is much spicier in nature and stronger in flavor than even fresh dill.

Traditional Marinara Sauce

This sauce can be paired with a variety of dishes such as Meatballs (see recipe in Chapter 7) or with Eggplant Parmigiana (see recipe in Chapter 10). Dress up the sauce by adding sautéed bell peppers, zucchini, and mushrooms.

YIELDS 4–6 CUPS
½ cup chopped onion
2 tablespoons olive oil
2 cloves garlic, minced
2 (14.5-ounce) cans diced tomatoes
1 (6-ounce) can tomato paste
1½ teaspoons basil
1½ teaspoons oregano
1 whole bay leaf

Freezing Day

1. In a large skillet over medium heat, sauté onion in olive oil for 8–10 minutes. Add garlic and sauté an additional 1–2 minutes. Add the diced tomatoes with liquid, tomato paste, and spices. Bring to a boil, reduce heat, and simmer 1–2 hours. If you like a thinner sauce, add water.
2. Remove bay leaf. Freeze in Tupperware or a freezer bag.

Reheating Instructions

Defrost sauce in the refrigerator overnight and use as desired.

Sweet Barbecue Sauce

This is a sauce that kids love. Put a batch of chicken legs in a freezer bag, pour the barbeque sauce over them, and freeze. When you are ready to cook, defrost the chicken and throw the legs on the grill.

YIELDS 3 CUPS
2 cups ketchup
1 cup brown sugar
2 teaspoons liquid smoke
1 teaspoon garlic powder
½ teaspoon Worcestershire sauce

Freezing Day

Combine all the ingredients in a medium bowl and mix well. Freeze in a freezer bag.

Reheating Instructions

Defrost sauce in the refrigerator overnight and use as desired.

Cucumber Dipping Sauce

This sauce is wonderful served with *Spicy Beef Kabobs (see recipe in Chapter 3)* or a variety of cut-up vegetables such as red and green bell peppers, carrots, and celery.

YIELDS 2½ CUPS

1 medium cucumber

2 cups plain yogurt

1 tablespoon fresh dill

2 teaspoons lemon juice

Salt and pepper to taste

1 clove garlic, minced (used on reheating day)

2 tablespoons red onion, finely chopped (used on reheating day)

Freezing Day

1. Peel, seed, and chop the cucumber.
2. In a medium mixing bowl, mix cucumber, yogurt, dill, lemon juice, salt, and pepper.
3. Freeze in a freezer bag or Tupperware.

Reheating Instructions

Defrost dip in the refrigerator overnight. Stir in garlic and red onion, and serve chilled.

Cool as a Cucumber

Cucumbers are the quintessential summer vegetable. They are low in calories, mild in taste, and are made up of over 90 percent water. Cucumbers are a common component in recipes for everything from salad to sandwiches. This refreshing vegetable is even featured in recipes for drinks and smoothies.

Spicy Black Bean Dip

This dip tastes great served with tortilla chips, toasted bread, or bagel chips. It also makes a great filling for tacos and burritos!

YIELDS 1 CUP

1 (15-ounce) can black beans, drained (reserve liquid)

¼ cup fresh cilantro, chopped

1 teaspoon chili powder

1 teaspoon cilantro

1 teaspoon salt

1 (4-ounce) can green chilies, drained

Freezing Day

1. Combine all the ingredients in a food processor and process until smooth. Use the reserved liquid from the black beans to bring the dip to the desired consistency.
2. Freeze dip in a freezer bag.

Reheating Instructions

Defrost dip in the refrigerator overnight and serve either hot or cold.

Cilantro Ice Cubes

A fun way to freeze herbs such as cilantro is to make herb cubes! Place chopped herbs in the bottom of a plastic ice-cube tray. Fill the remaining space in the ice-cube tray with water and freeze. Once frozen, transfer the herb cubes to a freezer bag. Now when a recipe calls for cilantro, you can pop in a cube.

Pico de Gallo

The secret to making delicious Pico de Gallo is fresh ingredients. Using high-quality ingredients, from beautiful ripe tomatoes to garden-fresh cilantro, is a surefire way to make this Pico de Gallo a wonderful accompaniment to your food.

YIELDS 1½ CUPS

2 large ripe tomatoes, diced

1 red onion, diced

3 tablespoons fresh cilantro, chopped

1 jalapeño pepper, diced

½ clove minced garlic

Juice of 1 or 2 limes, or to taste

Salt to taste

Freezing Day

In a large bowl, mix tomatoes, onions, cilantro, jalapeños, and garlic. Add lime juice and salt to taste. Freeze in a freezer bag or Tupperware.

Reheating Instructions

Defrost in the refrigerator overnight and serve.

Salsa Verde

This Salsa Verde is made primarily from tomatillos. Try making your own recipe of salsa verde using fresh herbs by combining fresh thyme, a little sage, parsley, cilantro, garlic, shallot, basil, salt, pepper, and olive oil in a blender. Taste as you go to come up with the perfect recipe!

YIELDS 6–8 SERVINGS

1 pound fresh tomatillos

½ cup water

1 shallot, peeled

1 clove garlic

2 poblano chilies

½ cup fresh cilantro

3 tablespoons fresh oregano

½ teaspoon cumin

3 tablespoons lime juice

Olive oil as needed

Salt to taste

Freezing Day

1. Remove husks from tomatillos and put in a medium saucepan with ½ cup water. Bring to a boil. Reduce heat and simmer about 10 minutes until the tomatillos are soft.
2. Add all the ingredients, including the tomatillos and water, to a food processor and purée. Add olive oil to reach the desired consistency and salt to taste.
3. Freeze in a freezer bag.

Reheating Instructions

Defrost sauce in refrigerator overnight and use as desired.

Hot Peppers

There is quite a variety of peppers to choose from, each containing different levels of heat. The poblano pepper used in this recipe is a mild pepper. To go a bit hotter try a jalapeño or red Fresno pepper. Try a serrano pepper to go even hotter. The most daring will try one of the very hottest, the habanero.

Queso Dip

This cheesy dip is delicious served with tortilla chips or as a topping on tacos or burritos. Spice up the dip with chopped jalapeños or green chili peppers.

Freezing Day

1. In a medium skillet over medium heat, brown ground beef with chopped onion for about 8–10 minutes until beef is fully cooked. Drain.
2. In a large saucepan, melt Velveeta.
3. Add salsa and ground beef mixture to melted cheese. Mix thoroughly.
4. Let the mixture cool and freeze in a freezer bag.

Reheating Instructions

Defrost in the refrigerator overnight. Heat defrosted Queso Dip in a medium saucepan over medium heat for 5–10 minutes, or until desired temperature is reached.

No More Tears

Do you find yourself avoiding cutting onions because they burn your eyes? To avoid the tears and burning that comes with chopping an onion, try these tricks: Place the onion briefly in the freezer before cutting, or cut the onion under cold running water.

Hummus

If you like your Hummus spicy, add cayenne pepper and sliced jalapeño peppers. Serve the Hummus with Pita Bread Crackers (see recipe in Chapter 3).

Freezing Day

1. Combine the garbanzo beans, lemon juice, sesame oil, sesame seeds, onion, and garlic in a food processor. Mix until blended.
2. Add the reserved garbanzo bean liquid a tablespoon at a time until the hummus reaches a creamy consistency.
3. Freeze in a freezer bag or Tupperware.

Reheating Instructions

Defrost in the refrigerator overnight and serve at room temperature.

Taco Seasoning Mix

This seasoning mix can be used with ground beef, turkey, or pork to make a variety of Mexican dishes such as Spicy Taco Roll-Ups (see recipe in Chapter 11).

YIELDS 2½ TABLESPOONS
1 tablespoon chili powder
2 teaspoons dried minced onion
1 teaspoon cumin
1 teaspoon garlic powder
1 teaspoon paprika
Dash cayenne, or more according to taste

Freezing Day

Mix all the ingredients in a small bowl and freeze in a freezer bag. To make with meat before freezing, add to browned meat with 1 cup water. Bring to a boil, reduce heat, and simmer 10–15 minutes. Freeze in a freezer bag.

Reheating Instructions

Use spices according to recipe.

Ground Beef Seasoning Mix

Add this seasoning to make delicious hamburgers, add it to your meatloaf, or even mix it in your meatballs. This recipe is enough to season 2 pounds of ground beef.

YIELDS 4 TEASPOONS
½ teaspoon salt
½ teaspoon black pepper
½ teaspoon brown sugar
1½ teaspoons paprika
¼ teaspoon garlic powder
¼ teaspoon onion powder
¼ teaspoon cumin
⅛ teaspoon cayenne pepper

Freezing Day

Mix all the ingredients in a small bowl and store in an airtight container. Either freeze on its own or add to food before freezing (as called for in the recipe).

Reheating Instructions

Use according to chosen recipe.

Barbecue Rub

Keep a container of this rub in your freezer so it'll be ready to go for your next cookout. Rub oil over the meat followed by this rub before putting it in the freezer. When you are ready to cook, you'll have a deliciously seasoned meat.

YIELDS 6 TABLESPOONS

3 tablespoons paprika
1 tablespoon salt
2 teaspoons onion powder
2 teaspoons garlic powder
2 teaspoons pepper
Dash cayenne, or to taste

Freezing Day

Combine all the ingredients in a small bowl and freeze in a freezer bag or plastic container.

Reheating Instructions

Use straight from the freezer.

Chapter 5

Soups, Stews, and Chilies

Minestrone

Minestrone is a hearty Italian soup loaded with vegetables and beans. You may substitute any of the vegetables in this recipe with ones you have on hand. Pasta has been omitted since fully cooked pasta gets mushy when frozen.

YIELDS 6–8 SERVINGS

2 tablespoons tomato paste

2 (14-ounce) cans beef broth

1 (10-ounce) package frozen chopped spinach, thawed

1 onion, chopped

2 carrots, cut into bite-size pieces

1 red bell pepper, cut into bite-size pieces

1 zucchini, sliced

4 teaspoons dried parsley

2 cloves garlic, minced

1 teaspoon dried basil

½ cup grated Parmesan cheese

2 (15-ounce) cans kidney beans with juice

1 (28-ounce) can chopped tomatoes with juice

Freezing Day

1. In a mixing bowl mix tomato paste and beef broth. Set aside.
2. Put the remaining ingredients into a slow cooker. Pour beef broth mixture over the top.
3. Cook on low for 8–10 hours. Cool and freeze in a freezer bag or in individual portions in Tupperware containers.

Reheating Instructions

Defrost soup in the microwave or the refrigerator overnight. Warm on the stovetop in a large saucepan for 20–25 minutes over medium heat or microwave individual portions 2–3 minutes in the microwave, and serve.

Gazpacho

This refreshing summer soup is served chilled. Spice it up by adding sliced jalapeño peppers and cayenne pepper to suit your tastes.

YIELDS 2–4 SERVINGS

4 cups tomato juice
2 seedless cucumbers, peeled and chopped
½ green bell pepper, chopped
2 green onions, chopped
¼ teaspoon Worcestershire sauce
1 clove garlic
1 tablespoon fresh basil
2 tablespoons wine vinegar
1 tablespoon plus 1 teaspoon olive oil

Freezing Day

Place all the ingredients into a blender or food processor and mix until smooth. Freeze in a freezer bag.

Reheating Instructions

Defrost Gazpacho in the refrigerator overnight. Serve chilled and topped with diced onions, green peppers, and tomatoes.

Split Pea and Ham Soup

Divide and freeze this soup into single-serving portions to create a delicious homemade option you can pair with a sandwich or salad for lunch or a light dinner.

YIELDS 8 SERVINGS

4 strips bacon
1 cup sweet onion, chopped
1 clove garlic, minced
1 cup carrots, shredded
1 pound dried split peas
2 cups cooked, lean ham
1 ham bone (optional)
10 cups water
Salt and pepper to taste

Freezing Day

1. In a medium skillet over medium heat, cook bacon until crisp. Drain all but 1 tablespoon bacon grease, add onions, and sauté for 5–6 minutes. Add garlic and sauté 1 more minute.
2. To the slow cooker add the bacon, onions, garlic, carrots, dried split peas, ham, and ham bone. Add water and season with salt and pepper.
3. Cover and cook on high 4–5 hours.
4. Remove ham bone and let soup cool. Freeze in a freezer bag or plastic container.

Reheating Instructions

Defrost soup in the refrigerator overnight and heat in a medium saucepan over medium heat for 15–20 minutes, or until desired temperature is reached.

Vegetable Bean Soup

Keep a batch of this delicious soup on hand for those cold evenings when you want something warm and comforting to eat. It also makes the perfect meal to bring to a sick friend.

- 4 cups vegetable broth
- 1 (14-ounce) can diced tomatoes
- 3 cloves garlic, diced
- 3 large carrots, peeled and sliced
- 2 stalks celery, sliced
- ½ head cabbage, shredded
- 1 medium yellow onion, chopped
- 3 medium leeks, whites only, sliced
- 6–8 small red potatoes, cubed
- Pinch rosemary
- 1 (16-ounce) can white beans, drained
- Salt and pepper to taste

Freezing Day

1. Combine vegetable broth, tomatoes, garlic, carrots, celery, cabbage, onion, leeks, potatoes, and rosemary in a Crock-Pot. Cook on low for 8 hours. Add beans, salt, and pepper and cook for 30 minutes more.
2. Freeze using freezer bags.

Reheating Instructions

Defrost soup in the refrigerator overnight and heat in a stockpot over medium heat for 15–20 minutes or until the desired temperature is reached.

Butternut Squash Soup

When serving the soup, ladle into bowls and then drizzle additional cream over the surface of the soup. Drag a toothpick through the cream to create a marbled effect.

YIELDS 6 SERVINGS

1 medium apple
4 cups butternut squash, cooked and puréed
3 cups chicken broth
2 tablespoons mild onion, grated
¼ teaspoon dried ginger
1 tablespoon dark brown sugar, packed
1 teaspoon fresh sage, minced
½ cup heavy cream (used on reheating day)

Freezing Day

1. Peel, core, and finely chop the apple. To the slow cooker, add the apple, squash, chicken broth, onion, ginger, and brown sugar. Cook on low for 6 hours. Add sage during the last 30 minutes of cooking time.
2. Put soup in a blender and purée. Freeze in a freezer bag.

Reheating Instructions

Defrost soup in the refrigerator overnight. Heat the soup in a medium saucepan over medium heat for 15–20 minutes or until the desired temperature is reached. Pour cream in just before serving.

How to Cook and Purée Butternut Squash

Cut the top and bottom of the squash off and peel the skin. Cut down the center lengthwise and remove and discard the seeds and membranes. Cut the squash into chunks and put into a pot of water. Boil for 7–10 minutes until squash is soft. Drain the water, put squash into a blender, and purée.

Taco Soup

Serve this soup with a variety of toppings, just like a taco! Cheddar cheese, sour cream, jalapeño peppers, and tortilla chips all taste delicious paired with this soup.

YIELDS 8 SERVINGS

1½ pounds ground beef
1 (15-ounce) can whole-kernel corn, with liquid
1 (15-ounce) can cream corn
1 (15-ounce) can hominy, with liquid
1 (15-ounce) can kidney beans, with liquid
1 (15-ounce) can pinto beans, with liquid
2 (14.5-ounce) cans diced tomatoes, with liquid
1 (1.25-ounce) package taco mix
1 (1-ounce) package dry ranch dressing mix

Freezing Day

1. Brown ground beef in a medium skillet over medium heat. Drain.
2. Add beef and remaining ingredients to the slow cooker and mix well.
3. Cover and cook on low for 6–7 hours. Cool and freeze in a freezer bag.

Reheating Instructions

Defrost in the refrigerator overnight, heat in a medium saucepan over medium heat for 15–20 minutes or until the desired temperature is reached, and serve.

Portion-Control Your Soup

Line your favorite microwavable soup mug with a quart-size freezer bag. Pour the soup into the lined mug and flash freeze. Once the soup is frozen, lift the bag of soup from the mug, and return the soup to the freezer. Now you have a perfectly shaped portion of soup that can go from the freezer straight to your mug. To heat, you can defrost, microwave, and serve the soup in the same cup!

Hamburger Soup

This thick, hearty beef and vegetable soup is great to have on hand. Serve it with crusty French bread for a delicious meal.

YIELDS 8 SERVINGS

1 pound ground beef, lean
1 cup carrots, chopped
1 cup onion, chopped
1 (16-ounce) package frozen corn
4 cups beef broth
1 (28-ounce) can Italian-seasoned tomatoes with juice
1 (14-ounce) can tomato sauce
¼ cup ketchup
1½ teaspoons Italian seasoning
Salt and pepper to taste

Freezing Day

1. Brown the ground beef in a medium skillet over medium heat and drain.
2. Add beef to a large stockpot with all the remaining ingredients.
3. Simmer, uncovered, for 1½ hours. Stir often.
4. Cool and freeze in a freezer bag.

Reheating Instructions

Defrost soup in the refrigerator overnight and heat in a stockpot over medium heat for 15–20 minutes or until the desired temperature is reached.

Sweet Italian Sausage and Tortellini Soup

This soup is the perfect dinner to enjoy on a cold winter night in front of a roaring fire. Try topping your soup with freshly grated Parmesan cheese.

YIELDS 6 SERVINGS

1 pound sweet Italian sausage
1 onion, chopped
1 clove garlic, chopped
2 (9-ounce) bags three-cheese stuffed tortellini
1 bag frozen Italian vegetables
2 (14-ounce) cans chicken broth
1 (14.5-ounce) can diced tomatoes
1 cup water
1 teaspoon oregano
1 teaspoon basil

Freezing Day

1. Cut sausage into small, bite-size pieces. In a large stockpot, brown sausage and onion over medium heat for about 10 minutes. Add garlic and cook an additional minute. Drain.
2. Add remaining ingredients and bring to a boil. Reduce heat and simmer for 5 minutes. Remove from heat and cool.
3. Freeze in a freezer bag.

Reheating Instructions

Defrost soup in the refrigerator for 24 hours. Bring to a boil in a stockpot and simmer for 5–10 minutes.

Seafood Chowder

To serve this easy chowder without freezing, cook pasta and add it along with the evaporated milk; simmer until hot.

YIELDS 8 SERVINGS

1 tablespoon olive oil
1 onion, chopped
1 green pepper, chopped
1 carrot, chopped
2 cloves garlic, minced
½ teaspoon dried thyme leaves
½ teaspoon salt
⅛ teaspoon white pepper
¼ cup flour
1 cup dry white wine
3 cups fish broth
½ pound frozen uncooked medium shrimp
1 (6-ounce) can crabmeat
1 pound red snapper fillets, cubed
1 cup uncooked shell pasta
1 (13-ounce) can evaporated milk (used on reheating day)

YIELDS 24 SERVINGS

3 tablespoons olive oil
3 onions, chopped
3 green peppers, chopped
3 carrots, chopped
6 cloves garlic, minced
1½ teaspoons dried thyme leaves
1½ teaspoons salt
⅜ teaspoon white pepper
¾ cup flour
3 cups dry white wine
9 cups fish broth
1½ pounds frozen uncooked medium shrimp
3 (6-ounce) cans crabmeat
3 pounds red snapper fillets, cubed
3 cups uncooked shell pasta
3 (13-ounce) cans evaporated milk (used on reheating day)

Freezing Day

1. In a large stockpot, add olive oil, onion, green pepper, carrot, and garlic. Cook and stir over medium heat until almost tender. Add thyme, salt, pepper, and flour to the pot; cook and stir for 3 minutes, until bubbly. Add wine and broth; cover and simmer for 15 minutes, stirring twice.

2. Uncover the pot and add the seafood. Bring to a simmer and cook for 5–10 minutes, until the fillets flake when tested with a fork and the shrimp curls and turns pink. Chill soup in an ice-water bath or the refrigerator. Pour into a rigid container, attach a bag with the pasta, label, and freeze. Reserve evaporated milk in the pantry.

Reheating Instructions

Thaw soup overnight in the refrigerator. Cook pasta according to package directions until al dente; drain and reserve. Pour soup into a large stockpot and bring to a simmer. Add evaporated milk and pasta; simmer for 4–5 minutes, until heated through.

Creamy Leek Soup

Goes great with the Open-Faced Italian Sandwiches (see recipe in Chapter 11), or served with a side of toasted, sliced Italian bread topped with melted mozzarella or Swiss cheese.

YIELDS 6 SERVINGS

3 tablespoons butter

4 leeks, thinly sliced

2 large potatoes, peeled and cubed

2 (14-ounce) cans chicken broth

½ teaspoon salt

¼ teaspoon pepper

2 cups half-and-half

¼ cup sherry

Freezing Day

1. In a medium skillet over medium heat, melt butter and sauté leeks until tender.

2. In a large saucepan, add potatoes, chicken broth, salt, and pepper. Bring to a boil and immediately reduce heat. Simmer until potatoes are tender. Remove from heat and cool.

3. Pour into a blender and mix until smooth. Pour back into the saucepan and add the leeks with butter and half-and-half. Simmer for 20 minutes. Remove from heat and stir in sherry. Cool and freeze in a freezer bag or plastic container.

Reheating Instructions

Defrost soup in the refrigerator for 24 hours. Warm in a saucepan over medium-low heat for 25–30 minutes or until the desired temperature is reached.

Cheesy Bacon and Potato Soup

This thick and hearty soup makes a delicious dinner when served with a loaf of crunchy French bread and a salad.

YIELDS 10–12 SERVINGS

6 slices bacon

5 medium potatoes, cooked

6 tablespoons butter

⅔ cup flour

6 cups milk

1 cup sour cream

2 cups Cheddar cheese

Salt and pepper, to taste (used on reheating day)

3–5 tablespoons chopped green onions, to taste (used as a topping on reheating day)

3–5 tablespoons crumbled cooked bacon, to taste (used as a topping on reheating day)

Freezing Day

1. Cook the bacon in a medium skillet over medium heat until cooked through and cut into small pieces. Cut cooked potatoes into cubes.

2. In a large stockpot, melt butter over medium-low heat. Add flour and whisk until combined.

3. Slowly pour in milk. Continue to stir 5–10 minutes until milk thickens slightly.

4. Add potatoes, bacon, sour cream, and Cheddar cheese. Heat until cheese is melted, about 5 minutes. Remove from heat and cool.

5. Divide into serving portions and freeze in a freezer bag.

Reheating Instructions

1. Defrost soup in the refrigerator for 24 hours. Heat in a stockpot over medium heat until the desired temperature is reached. Add salt and pepper to taste.

2. Top each serving with chopped green onions and crumbled bacon.

Cool Soup

Soup must be cool before it can be put into the freezer. To quickly cool your soup, fill your kitchen sink with cold water and ice cubes. Place your soup pot into the cold water and stir the soup. The surrounding ice water will help it to cool quickly.

Chicken Tortilla Soup

To serve, put corn tortilla chips in the bottom of each bowl and ladle the soup over them. Top with a dollop of sour cream and fresh cilantro leaves. Season with Tabasco to taste.

YIELDS 8 SERVINGS

6 boneless, skinless chicken thighs
½ teaspoon olive oil
¼ teaspoon ground cumin
1 (32-ounce) carton chicken broth
1 (15-ounce) can whole corn, drained
1 (15-ounce) can black beans
1 (15-ounce) can kidney beans, drained
1 cup onion, chopped
1 clove garlic, minced
½ teaspoon chili powder
3 teaspoons lime juice
1 (10-ounce) can Ro-Tel diced tomatoes with liquid
1 teaspoon salt
1 (8-inch) corn tortilla, cut into thin strips (used on reheating day)
1 cup chopped fresh cilantro (used on reheating day)

Freezing Day

1. In a large pot over medium heat, cook the chicken in oil until lightly browned, about 3–5 minutes per side.
2. Add all the remaining ingredients except cilantro and corn tortilla strips.
3. Cover, reduce heat to low, and simmer for 60 minutes. Cool and freeze in a freezer bag.

Reheating Instructions

Defrost soup in the refrigerator for 24 hours, and warm in a stockpot on the stovetop over medium heat for 15–20 minutes, or until the desired temperature is reached.

Vegetarian Chili

You can use any kind of canned bean in this easy and delicious recipe. To serve immediately, add corn with beans and simmer for 15–20 minutes until blended.

Freezing Day

1. In a large stockpot over medium heat, cook onion, garlic, and carrots in olive oil until crisp-tender. Drain rinsed beans well and add to the stockpot with the remaining ingredients except the corn. Bring to a boil; then reduce heat and simmer for 5 minutes.

2. Cool in an ice-water bath or the refrigerator; then pour into a rigid container. Label, seal container, and freeze. Reserve canned corn in pantry.

Reheating Instructions

Let chili thaw overnight in the refrigerator. Remove bay leaf. Pour into a large saucepan and bring to a simmer. Add undrained corn and simmer for 15–20 minutes or until thoroughly heated, stirring occasionally.

Cold Carrot Soup

This is the perfect choice to serve at a light luncheon on a hot summer day as well as an ideal complement to cool cucumber sandwiches.

Freezing Day

1. In a large saucepan over medium heat, melt butter and sauté shallots for 5–8 minutes.
2. Meanwhile peel and chop carrots and potato.
3. Once shallots are tender, add chicken broth, carrots, potatoes, lemon juice, and spices. Add enough water so potatoes and carrots are covered. Bring to a boil, then reduce heat to medium-low and simmer until carrots and potatoes are tender, about 30–40 minutes.
4. Pour into a blender and mix until smooth. Let cool.
5. Add half-and-half and freeze.

Reheating Instructions

Defrost soup in the refrigerator for 24 hours and serve chilled.

Buy Whole Spices Whenever Possible

Spices such as nutmeg, cinnamon, and allspice will last years longer when bought whole than when bought ground because the essential oils are still contained within the spice. They will also have a much stronger flavor. Purchase a spice grinder or file grater, and store your whole spices in a small freezer bag in the freezer.

Corn Chowder

Serve this Corn Chowder with Cheddar Garlic Biscuits (see recipe in Chapter 6). To add variety to the chowder, add cooked ham or cooked chicken.

Freezing Day

1. Cook bacon in a medium skillet over medium heat until crisp; cool and crumble. In about 3 tablespoons of bacon drippings, sauté onion and carrot until onion is translucent, about 5–10 minutes. Add garlic and sauté 1–2 minutes.
2. In a large pot, add chicken broth and sherry. Bring to a boil, add white corn, cover, reduce heat, and maintain a low boil for 15 minutes. Add sautéed vegetables to the corn stock.
3. Add the remaining ingredients except bacon, and season with ground black pepper to taste. Simmer for 15 minutes.
4. Add bacon and simmer 15 more minutes.
5. Cool and freeze in a freezer bag or a plastic container.

Reheating Instructions

Defrost Corn Chowder in the refrigerator overnight and heat in a saucepan over medium heat for 15–20 minutes or until it reaches the desired temperature.

Homemade Chicken Broth When You're Ready

Anytime you roast a whole chicken, the leftover carcass is great for making chicken broth. Simply freeze the carcass until you are ready. To make broth, put the carcass in water with celery, onion, carrots, ½ teaspoon dried thyme, ½ teaspoon dried rosemary, 1 bay leaf, and 8 whole peppercorns. Bring it to a boil, skim the foam, lower the heat, and cook for 2 hours covered. Strain and you have broth.

Spanish-Style Lentil Stew

Spanish chorizo comes both dry-cured and fresh. Fresh chorizo needs to be fully cooked, but dry chorizo can be eaten as is.

YIELDS 8 SERVINGS

3 cloves garlic

1 medium onion

1 large tomato

1 pound Spanish chorizo sausage, preferably well cured

2–3 tablespoons olive oil

1 tablespoon cumin, or to taste

1–2 teaspoons Tabasco, to taste

1 cup red wine

1 large potato, cut into small cubes

4 large carrots, peeled and chopped

1½ pounds dried lentils

1 ham bone

¼ pound lard

¼ pound prosciutto, cut into pieces

2 (14-ounce) cans chicken broth

1 cup cream (optional)

Freezing Day

1. Purée the garlic, onion, and tomato in a food processor or blender and set aside.

2. Peel the chorizo, chop into very small pieces, and place in boiling water. When the red grease from the chorizo has gone to the surface after about 3–4 minutes, strain and set aside.

3. Put a large pot over medium heat and add the olive oil.

4. Add the onion, tomato, and garlic purée to the pot along with the cumin and Tabasco and cook for about 5 minutes.

5. Add the red wine, potatoes, and carrots and cook for another 5 minutes.

6. Add the lentils, ham bone, lard, prosciutto, and the chorizo and mix. Cover with the chicken broth and water if needed.

7. Cook over low-medium heat, stirring occasionally, for about 1–1½ hours until the lentils are tender and the stew has a creamy texture. If desired, add the cup of cream when nearly finished.

8. Let cool, separate into desired portions, and freeze in a freezer bag.

Reheating Instructions

Defrost stew in the refrigerator for 24 hours. Heat in a large saucepan over medium heat for 15–20 minutes or until the desired temperature is reached.

Black Bean Soup

After you ladle soup in each bowl, top it with a dollop of sour cream and fresh cilantro. Soup is delicious served with Sweet Cornbread (see recipe in Chapter 6).

YIELDS 4 SERVINGS

1 sweet onion, chopped

2 tablespoons olive oil

2 cloves garlic, minced

¼ cup sherry

1 teaspoon cumin

1 teaspoon oregano

¼ teaspoon thyme

¼ teaspoon cayenne pepper

2 (15.2-ounce) cans black beans

2 (14-ounce) cans chicken broth

Freezing Day

1. In a large stockpot over medium-high heat, sauté the onion in olive oil for 5–10 minutes. Add garlic and sauté 1 additional minute. Add the sherry, cumin, oregano, thyme, and cayenne pepper. Mix well and remove from heat.

2. Drain and rinse the black beans. Put half the beans in a blender and purée. Add the whole beans and puréed beans to the stockpot.

3. Pour the broth into the stockpot. Mix well.

4. Put soup into a freezer bag or plastic container and freeze.

Reheating Instructions

Defrost soup in the refrigerator for 12–24 hours. Put into a stockpot and heat over medium for 15–20 minutes or until soup reaches the desired temperature.

Homestyle Beef Stew

Your home will be filled with delicious aromas as this stew simmers all day in the slow cooker. Serve this stew over mashed potatoes for a hearty dinner.

YIELDS 6–8 SERVINGS

2½ pounds beef stew meat, cubed
4 tablespoons flour
3 tablespoons olive oil
4 carrots
2 onions
2 beef bouillon cubes
4 cups water
½ cup red wine
2 tablespoons Worcestershire sauce
1 bay leaf

Freezing Day

1. Dredge meat in the flour. In a large skillet over medium-high heat, add the olive oil and beef and brown the beef on all sides, 7–10 minutes. Put beef in a slow cooker.

2. Cut carrots into 1" pieces, and peel and quarter the onions. Add to the slow cooker.

3. Dissolve bouillon cubes in 4 cups boiling water. Add to slow cooker.

4. Add the remaining ingredients, cover, and cook in the slow cooker on low for 7–8 hours or until beef is fork-tender.

5. Cool, portion, and freeze.

Reheating Instructions

Defrost in the refrigerator overnight. Heat stew in a large saucepan over medium heat for 20–25 minutes or until fully heated.

Portion Control

Beef stew is a delicious meal to have on a cold wintery day, and with portion-control freezing you can make it into a delicious lunch. Once the stew has cooled, divide it into lunch-size portions and freeze in individual Tupperware containers. Defrost overnight in the refrigerator and you now have an easy meal you can heat in the microwave in minutes.

Goulash

Goulash has evolved over the years, but authentic Hungarian Goulash was cooked in a large cast-iron kettle over an open fire. The hearty soup was used to feed the herdsmen working the fields.

YIELDS 8–10 SERVINGS
2 cups uncooked macaroni
1 pound ground beef
1 pound ground sausage
1 onion, chopped
2 cloves garlic, minced
2 (29-ounce) cans tomato sauce
2 (15-ounce) cans corn, drained
2 tablespoons dried Italian seasoning
Parmesan cheese (used on reheating day)

Freezing Day

1. In a large saucepot, cook macaroni 8–9 minutes until it is just underdone. Drain and return to the saucepot.

2. In a large skillet over medium-high heat, brown the ground beef, ground sausage, and onion for 15 minutes, or until the meat is thoroughly cooked. Add garlic and cook an additional 1–2 minutes. Drain off fat.

3. Add the remaining ingredients to the saucepot, remove from stove, and cool. Cool and freeze in a freezer bag.

Reheating Instructions

Defrost Goulash in the refrigerator for 24 hours. In a large skillet, bring Goulash to a boil, turn heat down, and simmer for 20 minutes. Serve with Parmesan cheese sprinkled over the top.

Blue-Ribbon Chili

This award-winning chili tastes fantastic served over rice. Have toppings such as grated Parmesan cheese, shredded Cheddar cheese, sliced jalapeño peppers, sour cream, and oyster crackers available for even more flavor.

YIELDS 20 SERVINGS

5 pounds 80/20 or 75/25 ground beef

1 large sweet onion, diced

3 tablespoons jalapeños, diced

3 cloves garlic, minced

4 tablespoons cumin

3 tablespoons cocoa

5 tablespoons chili powder

2 tablespoons salt

2 cups beef broth

3 tablespoons oregano

8 tablespoons minced, dried onion

½–1 teaspoon cayenne pepper, according to taste

2 (6-ounce) cans tomato paste

4 (14.5-ounce) cans diced tomatoes with green chilies

⅛ cup ketchup

2 tablespoons dark brown sugar

Freezing Day

1. In a large skillet over medium heat, brown ground beef with the diced onion, jalapeño peppers, and garlic. Drain.

2. Transfer meat to a large stockpot, and add all the other ingredients. Mix well.

3. Simmer on low for 60–90 minutes. Add water as necessary to achieve desired thickness.

4. Remove from heat, cool, and freeze using freezer bags or plastic containers.

Reheating Instructions

Defrost chili in the refrigerator for 24 hours (less time for small portions). Warm chili in a large saucepan over medium-low heat for 20–30 minutes, or until it reaches the desired temperature.

Thoughts on Chili

Cooking chili is all about getting the right balance between the heat of the chili and the savory of the meat and spices. Purists will maintain that real chili does not have beans and that it should make you sweat, even if it's just a little bit! Chili is a great food to experiment with to develop your personal recipe.

White Chili

This spicy chili, made with chicken and can-
nellini beans, is a twist on traditional chili. If
you prefer, you may substitute Great Northern
beans for the cannellini beans.

YIELDS 4 SERVINGS

1 pound boneless chicken thighs

1 tablespoon olive oil

1 onion, chopped

2 cups chicken broth

1 teaspoon cumin

1½ teaspoons chili powder

3 jalapeño peppers, chopped

1 (15-ounce) can cannellini beans, rinsed and drained

1 tablespoon lime juice

Sour cream (used as a topping on reheating day)

Monterey jack cheese (used as a topping on reheating day)

Fresh cilantro (used as a topping on reheating day)

Freezing Day

1. Cut chicken into bite-size cubes; in a medium skillet over medium-high heat, stir-fry the chicken in the oil with the onion for 4–5 minutes.

2. Add chicken and onion to a large saucepan along with the chicken broth, cumin, chili powder, and chopped jalapeños. Bring to a boil, reduce heat, and simmer for 15 minutes. Add beans and lime juice and cook an additional 5 minutes.

3. Cool chili and freeze in a Tupperware container or freezer bag.

Reheating Instructions

Defrost in the refrigerator for 24 hours. Warm chili in a large saucepan over medium heat for 20–30 minutes until the desired temperature is reached. Serve with desired toppings.

Frozen Herb Butter

Flavor butter with fresh parsley, basil, or dill. Put 2 tablespoons of one herb in the food processor to purée. Add ½ cup softened butter and blend. Add more butter according to taste. Spoon the butter into ice-cube trays and freeze. Once frozen, put cubes into a freezer bag. Use the herb butter to season vegetables, on bread, or in recipes.

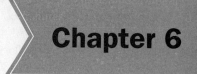

Side Dishes

Dinner Rolls

To quickly warm, place these rolls in a paper bag and heat in a microwave for 20–30 seconds (until warm, but not hot); serve with honey butter.

YIELDS 12 SERVINGS

2 (.25-ounce) packages yeast
2 cups warm water
Pinch sugar
½ cup butter
3 eggs
½ cup sugar
1 teaspoon salt
6 cups flour

Freezing Day

1. In a large bowl, mix the yeast, warm water, and pinch of sugar. Let mixture sit for about 10 minutes until it starts to froth on top.

2. Add butter and eggs to yeast and mix. Add sugar, salt, and 3 cups flour and mix. Continue to add flour until the dough is easy to handle.

3. Knead the dough on a lightly floured surface until it becomes elastic.

4. Put the dough in a lightly greased bowl, cover it with a towel, and set the bowl in a warm place for about 1 hour until the dough has doubled in size.

5. Shape into rolls and put in a greased baking pan. Cover the rolls with a towel and let rise for 30 minutes.

6. Preheat the oven to 400°F. Bake rolls for 15–20 minutes.

7. Let rolls cool, then flash freeze on a baking sheet. Once frozen, transfer to a freezer bag.

Reheating Instructions

Let rolls defrost at room for 1 hour, and serve. If you want to warm the rolls, heat in a 350°F oven for 5–10 minutes.

Honey Butter

This butter is delicious on almost any roll. Mix ½ pound butter (softened), ⅓ cup honey, ¼ teaspoon cinnamon, ¼ teaspoon vanilla extract, and a dash of salt. Use a melon baller to form scoops of butter, and flash freeze on a baking sheet covered with wax paper. Once frozen, transfer to a freezer bag.

Sweet Cornbread

This bread tastes great with butter and is a delicious accompaniment to Blue-Ribbon Chili (see recipe in Chapter 5) and Sweet Italian Sausage and Tortellini Soup (see recipe in Chapter 5).

YIELDS 4-6 SERVINGS

1 cup yellow cornmeal
1 cup flour
¼ cup sugar
½ teaspoon salt
2½ teaspoons baking powder
1 cup heavy cream
¼ cup applesauce
¼ cup honey
2 eggs

Freezing Day

1. Preheat the oven to 400°F. In a large bowl, sift together the cornmeal, flour, sugar, salt, and baking powder.
2. In a separate bowl, mix the heavy cream, applesauce, honey, and eggs.
3. Combine the wet and dry ingredients, and stir just enough to mix them.
4. Pour batter into a greased 9" × 9" pan. Bake for 20–25 minutes until a knife inserted in the center comes out clean. Cool, wrap well with plastic wrap, and freeze.

Reheating Instructions

Defrost cornbread at room temperature for 1–2 hours and serve. To warm the bread, place in an oven at 350°F for 10 minutes.

Cornbread Muffins

This recipe can also be used to make cornbread muffins! Line each cup of your muffin tin with muffin (cupcake) papers and use a ladle to pour in the batter. Bake the muffins at 400°F for 15–20 minutes, or until a toothpick inserted comes out clean.

Flavored White Rice

This rice is lightly flavored with onion and garlic. It is delicious enough to stand on its own as a side dish, yet mild enough to go with a sauce or gravy.

YIELDS 4–6 SERVINGS

1 small onion, chopped
1 tablespoon olive oil
1 clove garlic, minced
1 cup white rice
2 cups water

Freezing Day

1. In a large saucepan over medium heat, sauté onion in the olive oil for 5–10 minutes until onions are soft and translucent. Add the garlic and sauté 1–2 minutes until garlic is golden brown.
2. Add rice and cook for 3–5 minutes, stirring constantly.
3. Add 2 cups water and bring to a boil.
4. Reduce heat to low, cover tightly, and cook for 20 minutes. Let stand an additional 5 minutes off the heat with the lid still on tight.
5. Freeze in a freezer bag.

Reheating Instructions

Defrost in the refrigerator overnight. Heat rice in the microwave for 1–5 minutes (depending upon portion size), and serve.

Portion Control

You can freeze rice by the serving. Fill a large ice-cream scoop with rice, and place it onto a wax-covered baking sheet. Flash freeze the scoop of rice, then transfer to a freezer bag. When you are ready to reheat the rice, simply choose the number of scoops you will need and heat them!

Cornbread Stuffing

This stuffing is a real crowd pleaser! You can make this side dish into a main dish by adding cubed, cooked chicken into the stuffing.

YIELDS 6 SERVINGS

1 (6-ounce) package cornbread mix (this recipe tastes better if you do not use a sweet cornbread mix)

½ cup butter or margarine

½ cup onion, chopped

½ cup celery, chopped

1 (10.75-ounce) can cream of chicken soup

1 (10.75-ounce) can chicken and rice soup

1 cup chicken broth

1–2 teaspoons sage, to taste

Salt and pepper to taste

Freezing Day

1. Bake cornbread according to package directions and cool. Crumble into pieces.

2. In a large skillet over medium heat, melt butter. Add chopped onion and celery and sauté 5–10 minutes until vegetables are tender.

3. Remove skillet from heat and add the soups, broth, and crumbled cornbread. Add sage, salt, and pepper to taste. Mix well and freeze in a freezer bag.

Reheating Instructions

1. Defrost mixture in the refrigerator overnight and pour into a greased casserole dish.

2. Bake at 350°F for 45 minutes or until firm.

German Potato Salad

A roux is a mixture of flour and fat that is used to thicken sauces. The ratio is 1:1; one part fat to one part flour. Be careful not to cook your roux too long; you need to start over if it burns or has black specks in it.

YIELDS 20 SERVINGS

1 (8–10-pound) bag new red potatoes
1½ cups sweet pickle juice (like the juice from a jar of bread-and-butter pickles)
5½ cups cold water
1½ cups apple cider vinegar
1 cup sugar
¼ teaspoon salt
1½ pounds bacon, chopped
1 large onion, chopped
Olive oil (if needed)
Flour (enough to form roux)

Freezing Day

1. Boil potatoes until a fork easily inserts into one. Drain and cool immediately in cold water, changing water as needed until it stays cool. Drain and peel potatoes. Cut into bite-size pieces. Set aside.
2. In a mixing bowl, combine the sweet pickle juice, water, apple cider vinegar, sugar, and salt. Set aside.
3. In a medium skillet over medium heat, cook bacon until almost crisp, then add onion. Cook onion until translucent, 8–10 minutes.
4. You should have at least 4–5 tablespoons of grease in the skillet. If you don't, add olive oil until that amount is achieved.
5. Whisk in an equal amount of flour as grease in the pan. It should have a slightly glossy look. Cook roux over medium heat for 4–5 minutes, stirring constantly.
6. Slowly add the pickle juice mixture until a thin sauce is formed. Pour over potatoes and stir to combine. Freeze.

Reheating Instructions

Defrost potato salad in the refrigerator for 24 hours. It may be served warm or cold.

Spicy Refried Beans

Divide the beans into portions to make vegetarian bean burritos, or put them on your tacos with meat. Use them as a layer in South of the Border Lasagna (see recipe in Chapter 7), a topping for nachos, or a dip for chips.

YIELDS 8–10 SERVINGS

6 (15.5-ounce) cans refried beans
2 (10-ounce) cans enchilada sauce
1 (4.5-ounce) can green chilies

Freezing Day

Mix all the ingredients in a large bowl, separate into desired portions, and freeze in a freezer bag or plastic container.

Reheating Instructions

Defrost in the refrigerator overnight, heat in a large skillet over medium heat, and use as desired.

Coleslaw

To serve this zesty dish without freezing, let cabbage mixture marinate in the refrigerator for 1–2 hours. Serve as a side or with Fish Tacos (see recipe in Chapter 9).

YIELDS 4–6 SERVINGS

½ head cabbage, shredded
1 red bell pepper, chopped
1 red onion, finely chopped
1 cup sugar
½ teaspoon salt
½ teaspoon celery salt
¼ cup apple cider vinegar
½ cup water

YIELDS 12–18 SERVINGS

1½ heads cabbage, shredded
3 red bell peppers, chopped
3 red onions, finely chopped
3 cups sugar
1½ teaspoons salt
1½ teaspoons celery salt
¾ cup apple cider vinegar
1½ cups water

Freezing Day

1. Toss cabbage, pepper, and onion in a large bowl and set aside.
2. In a medium saucepan, combine sugar, salt, celery salt, vinegar, and water and bring to a boil. Boil vigorously for 3 minutes, then cool completely in the refrigerator.
3. Pour liquid over vegetables and place in a rigid container. Label and freeze.

Reheating Instructions

Thaw Coleslaw overnight in the refrigerator. Serve slaw when it's completely thawed.

Drunken Sweet Potatoes

Bourbon adds a delicious vanilla and caramel flavor to the dish. If you want to avoid adding alcohol to the sweet potatoes, substitute 1½–2 teaspoons vanilla extract for the bourbon.

YIELDS 6–8 SERVINGS

5 medium sweet potatoes (orange variety)
½ cup butter or margarine
2 tablespoons brown sugar
½ cup light cream
2 tablespoons bourbon
½ cup flour (for topping)
½ cup brown sugar (for topping)
¼ cup butter or margarine (for topping)
1 cup chopped pecans (for topping)

Freezing Day

1. Peel potatoes and cut into chunks. Boil in water until a fork inserts easily into the potatoes. Drain and whip potatoes in a large mixing bowl.
2. Prepare a casserole dish for freezing or use an aluminum pan.
3. To the potatoes add ½ cup butter, 2 tablespoons brown sugar, light cream, and bourbon. Mix well and add to the casserole dish.
4. In a separate bowl prepare the topping: Mix the flour and brown sugar. Cut in the butter until crumbly. Mix in chopped pecans.
5. Add topping to the casserole dish, wrap tightly, and freeze.

Reheating Instructions

For a defrosted casserole, bake at 350°F for 25 minutes. For a frozen casserole, add 45–60 minutes to defrosted casserole baking time.

Cheesy Double-Baked Potatoes

Double-baked potatoes make a wonderful side dish, as well as an easy afternoon snack. Try topping reheated potatoes with chopped scallions or bacon for added flavor.

8 medium baking potatoes
1 cup shredded Cheddar cheese
¼ cup milk
¼ cup butter
1 cup sour cream
Salt and pepper to taste

Freezing Day

1. Preheat the oven to 350°F. Lay potatoes directly on the oven rack and bake for 1 hour. Do not wrap potatoes in foil when baking.

2. Let cool 10 minutes, and then slice in half lengthwise. Scoop out the potatoes from each half, leaving about ¼" of potato next to the skin. Put the scooped-out potato filling in a large mixing bowl.

3. In the mixing bowl add the remaining ingredients to the potatoes and mash.

4. Spoon mashed potatoes back into the skins and flash freeze. Transfer to a freezer bag.

Reheating Instructions

Put frozen potatoes on a baking sheet. Heat potatoes in the oven at 350°F until potatoes are heated through, approximately 45–60 minutes. Potatoes can also be heated in the microwave for approximately 3 minutes per potato. Cooking times will vary depending on potato sizes.

Beautiful Double-Baked Potatoes

When filling double-baked potatoes, use a wide-tipped pastry bag to create swirls and patterns on the top of the potato for an artistic touch. For a creamier potato filling, overcook the potato the first time in order to render it much softer and easier to mix.

Cheddar Garlic Biscuits

These biscuits are easy to make and are a delicious addition to many meals. Serve them with Vegetable Bean Soup (see recipe in Chapter 5) or Grilled Citrus Chicken (see recipe in Chapter 8).

YIELDS 12 BISCUITS

2 cups all-purpose baking mix such as Bisquick
⅔ cup buttermilk
1 cup Cheddar cheese
¾ teaspoon garlic powder, divided
¼ cup butter
¼ teaspoon parsley flakes

Freezing Day

1. Preheat the oven to 400°F. In a large bowl, mix the baking mix, buttermilk, Cheddar cheese, and ¼ teaspoon garlic powder. Mix well.
2. Using a teaspoon, drop the batter onto a lightly greased baking sheet to form 12 biscuits.
3. Bake for 18–20 minutes until tops begin to brown.
4. In a medium saucepan, melt the butter and mix with the remaining ½ teaspoon garlic powder and parsley flakes. Brush butter mixture over the top of biscuits and let cool.
5. Flash freeze, then transfer to a freezer bag.

Reheating Instructions

Defrost biscuits at room temperature for 1–2 hours. Biscuits can either be served at room temperature or heated in a 350°F oven for 6–10 minutes, or until they reach the desired temperature.

Spicy Corn Casserole

This corn casserole is an easy side dish. Serve it with Blue Cheese Burgers, Sweet Ginger Sloppy Joes, or Avocado Chicken Burgers (see recipes in Chapter 11).

YIELDS 6–8 SERVINGS

3½ cups frozen corn
8 ounces cream cheese, softened
1 stick butter, softened
¼ cup milk
1 (4-ounce) can green chili peppers, drained
½ pound cooked bacon, crumbled

Freezing Day

In a large bowl, mix all the ingredients. Freeze in a freezer bag.

Reheating Instructions

Defrost corn casserole in the refrigerator overnight and heat at 350°F for 25–30 minutes or until fully heated.

Mashed Potatoes

Try adding 1 bulb of roasted garlic to Mashed Potatoes. Serve Mashed Potatoes with Home-style Beef Stew (see recipe in Chapter 5) or Steak and Tomatoes (see recipe in Chapter 7).

YIELDS 15 SERVINGS

5 pounds (about 15) potatoes, peeled
2½ cups half-and-half
½ cup butter, softened
1 egg

Freezing Day

1. Cut potatoes into large chunks, put in a large pot, cover with water, and bring to a boil. Cook over medium heat for 15–20 minutes until potatoes are tender. Drain.
2. Mash potatoes. Add half-and-half, butter, and egg to the potatoes and mix well.
3. Freeze in a freezer bag, casserole dish, or Tupperware container.

Reheating Instructions

Defrost potatoes in the refrigerator for 24 hours and heat at 350°F until potatoes are heated through, 30–45 minutes. Micro-waving is not recommended for heating.

Portion Control

Rather than freezing 5 pounds of Mashed Potatoes, divide them into smaller portions. To make single-serving portions, freeze potatoes in muffin tins. Once potatoes have frozen, remove them from the muffin tins and put them into a freezer bag. Heat frozen potatoes in the oven according to the reheating instructions.

Mashed Potato Bombs

These bombs are great to serve at parties. Make them a bit bigger when serving them as a side dish—the kids will love them! This is a great solution for your leftover Mashed Potatoes, or you can make a batch just for fun.

YIELDS 15 SERVINGS

1 batch Mashed Potatoes (see previous recipe)
½ cup flour
3 eggs, beaten
½ cup bread crumbs
1 quart peanut oil for frying (used on reheating day)

Freezing Day

1. Prepare Mashed Potatoes and let them cool in the refrigerator.
2. Form them into balls the size of a golf ball.
3. Apply breading by rolling them first in flour, then in beaten egg, then in bread crumbs.
4. Flash freeze, then transfer to freezer bag.

Reheating Instructions

Defrost for 30 minutes, then deep-fry the bombs at 325°F until they turn gold in color, approximately 3 minutes.

Hush Puppies

This traditionally Southern dish is best known for being served with fried catfish, but it tastes wonderful served with any type of seafood. Hush Puppies also taste great with fried chicken and are always a hit with the kids.

YIELDS 20 SERVINGS

1 cup yellow cornmeal
1 cup flour
3 teaspoons baking soda
½ teaspoon salt
1½ teaspoons sugar
1 small onion, grated
1 (15-ounce) can creamed corn
2 eggs
1 quart peanut oil for frying

Freezing Day

1. In a mixing bowl combine the cornmeal, flour, baking soda, salt, and sugar. In a separate mixing bowl combine the onion, corn, and eggs. Combine both mixtures. If the batter is too runny, add more cornmeal until it can hold its shape.

2. Heat 2" oil to 365°F. Drop batter into the oil by the spoonful and cook on both sides until browned. Remove from oil and place on paper towels to drain. Cool.

3. Flash freeze and transfer to a freezer bag.

Reheating Instructions

Place frozen Hush Puppies on a baking sheet and cook at 425°F for 14–16 minutes. Turn once after 7 minutes.

What's in a Name?

There are a lot of stories about how Hush Puppies got their name. One interesting story tells of Confederate soldiers sitting around a campfire at night cooking their dinner. They tossed their dogs Hush Puppies to stop them from barking when Yankee soldiers were approaching.

Spaghetti

To serve immediately, cook sauce over low heat for 30–40 minutes, stirring frequently, until thick. Cook pasta according to package directions, drain, and serve sauce over pasta.

YIELDS 4 SERVINGS

1 pound ground beef

1 onion, chopped

3 cloves garlic, minced

1 carrot, grated

1 teaspoon dried basil leaves

¼ teaspoon salt

1 (26-ounce) jar pasta sauce

½ cup grated Parmesan cheese

1 (8-ounce) package spaghetti pasta (used on reheating day)

YIELDS 12 SERVINGS

3 pounds ground beef

3 onions, chopped

9 cloves garlic, minced

3 carrots, grated

1 tablespoon dried basil leaves

¾ teaspoon salt

3 (26-ounce) jars pasta sauce

1½ cups grated Parmesan cheese

3 (8-ounce) packages spaghetti pasta (used on reheating day)

Freezing Day

Brown ground beef with onion and garlic in a heavy skillet over medium heat. Drain well, and then add carrot, basil, salt, and pasta sauce. Simmer for 10–15 minutes; then cool sauce in fridge, pour into a 1-gallon ziplock bag, attach a 1-pint ziplock bag filled with the cheese, label, and freeze. Reserve pasta in pantry.

Reheating Instructions

Thaw overnight in the refrigerator. Pour sauce into a heavy saucepan and add ¼ cup water. Heat, stirring frequently, until sauce comes to a boil. Cook pasta according to package directions, drain, and serve with hot sauce and grated cheese.

Chicken Risotto

To serve immediately, continue cooking rice mixture, adding 1 cup water and condensed chicken broth, until rice is tender and chicken is cooked through. Add remaining ingredients and cook until hot.

YIELDS 4 SERVINGS

3 boneless, skinless chicken breasts
2 tablespoons olive oil
1 onion, chopped
½ cup chopped leeks
2 cups long-grain white rice
1 cup white wine
1 cup chicken broth
½ cup grated Parmesan cheese
1 (10-ounce) can condensed chicken broth (used on reheating day)
3 tablespoons heavy cream (used on reheating day)
3 tablespoons butter (used on reheating day)

YIELDS 12 SERVINGS

9 boneless, skinless chicken breasts
6 tablespoons olive oil
3 onions, chopped
1½ cups chopped leeks
6 cups long-grain white rice
3 cups white wine
3 cups chicken broth
1½ cups grated Parmesan cheese
3 (10-ounce) cans condensed chicken broth (used on reheating day)
9 tablespoons heavy cream (used on reheating day)
9 tablespoons butter (used on reheating day)

Freezing Day

1. Cut chicken breasts into 1" pieces. Heat olive oil in a large stockpot. Add chicken, onion, and leeks; cook and stir for 5–7 minutes until onion is crisp-tender and chicken turns white.

2. Add uncooked rice and stir well until rice is coated. Cook for 2–3 minutes over medium heat, until rice begins to look translucent. Add white wine and cook, stirring frequently, until liquid is absorbed. Turn heat down to low; add plain chicken broth and cook, stirring frequently, until liquid is absorbed.

3. Remove pan from heat and place mixture in rigid containers. Chill in the refrigerator or an ice-water bath; then wrap, pack, and freeze. Attach a ziplock bag with the grated cheese. Reserve condensed chicken broth in the pantry, and cream and butter in the fridge.

Reheating Instructions

Thaw overnight in the refrigerator. Place in a large saucepan over low heat, stirring occasionally, until hot. Combine reserved condensed chicken broth with 1 cup water and add to the rice mixture. Cook and stir over medium heat until the liquid is absorbed, the rice is tender, and the chicken is cooked through. Add cheese, cream, and butter, and stir until cheese and butter are melted.

Chicken Fried Rice

Jasmine or basmati rice is a good choice for this dish because they both tend to be less sticky than other white rice.

> **YIELDS 4-6 SERVINGS**
> 2 cups rice
> 4 cups chicken broth
> 1 shallot, chopped
> ¼ teaspoon ginger
> 3 tablespoons vegetable oil
> 2 eggs, beaten
> 1 cup chicken, cooked
> ½ cup frozen peas
> ¼–½ cup oyster sauce, to taste
> ⅓ cup soy sauce, or to taste
> Sesame oil, to taste (used on reheating day)

Freezing Day

1. In a large saucepan, bring rice and chicken broth to a boil over medium heat. Turn the heat down to low and cover the pan. Cook for 20 minutes. Put rice in the refrigerator until it is cold.

2. In a large skillet (or wok), sauté shallot with ginger in vegetable oil for 6–8 minutes. Add eggs and stir until scrambled, about 5 minutes. Remove from heat. Stir in rice, chicken, peas, oyster sauce, and soy sauce. Cool.

3. Freeze in a freezer bag.

Reheating Instructions

Defrost in the refrigerator overnight and heat in a large skillet over medium heat for 15–20 minutes until it reaches the desired temperature. Toss with sesame oil.

Baby Carrot Herb Medley

In a hurry? Steam baby carrots in the microwave with ½ cup water and a tablespoon of butter. Cover and cook 4–5 minutes or until desired tenderness is reached.

YIELDS 4 SERVINGS

1 tablespoon lemon juice
25 baby carrots
2 tablespoons butter
1 tablespoon chopped fresh sage
1 teaspoon chopped fresh dill
¼ teaspoon salt
¼ teaspoon pepper

Freezing Day

1. Place ½" water and 1 tablespoon lemon juice in the bottom of a saucepan. Put carrots in a steamer basket and hang over the water. The basket should not touch the water. Cover the saucepan and heat to boiling. Reduce heat and steam carrots for 7 minutes until they are tender-crisp. The carrots should just begin to get tender, but still retain a crisp texture.

2. In a medium skillet, melt butter over medium heat. Add sage, dill, salt, and pepper. Add carrots and mix well. Allow to cool, and freeze in a freezer bag or plastic container.

Reheating Instructions

Defrost carrots in the refrigerator overnight. Sauté uncovered in a medium skillet over medium heat 2–3 minutes, stirring gently until hot.

Rosemary Herb Butter

Here is an all-purpose herb butter suitable for topping almost any vegetable. Ingredients: ¼ cup softened butter, ½ teaspoon dried and crumbled rosemary, ¼ teaspoon dried and crushed marjoram, and ½ teaspoon dried parsley flakes. Cream or whip butter until fluffy. Stir in rosemary, marjoram, and parsley until evenly mixed. Yields ¼ cup.

Gourmet Potatoes

Prosciutto is a dry-cured ham that is sliced very thin. Try stirring Greek yogurt into your potatoes with the milk!

YIELDS 12 SERVINGS

4 pounds Idaho potatoes
1 cube chicken bouillon
2 tablespoons butter
2 cups chopped wild mushrooms
2 tablespoons dried shallots
Milk, as needed for desired texture
5 slices prosciutto, finely chopped
2 cups freshly grated Gouda cheese
2 tablespoons dried chives
Pepper to taste

Freezing Day

1. Peel potatoes and place in boiling water with chicken bouillon.
2. In a large skillet, melt the butter over medium heat and lightly sauté the mushrooms, approximately 5 minutes. Add shallots and cook 1 more minute.
3. When potatoes are done (a fork inserts easily into them), drain and put back in the pan and mash. Add milk to potatoes until they are creamy.
4. Mix in the prosciutto, cheese, chives, and cooked mushroom mixture; mix well. Add pepper to taste.
5. Freeze in a freezer bag or Tupperware.

Reheating Instructions

1. Defrost potatoes in the refrigerator for 24 hours and put in a greased casserole dish. Stir well.
2. Bake, covered, at 350°F for 30 minutes.

Roasted Peppers and Tomatoes

Green, yellow, and red peppers are all the same pepper, but they are harvested at different stages of ripening. Red peppers are sweeter and fruitier in taste and have a higher nutritional value.

YIELDS 4 SERVINGS

2 red, yellow, or green bell peppers
2 Roma tomatoes
1 garlic clove
Olive oil to taste (used on reheating day)
Salt to taste (used on reheating day)

Freezing Day

1. Cut each pepper in half lengthwise. Remove stems and seeds.

2. Place peppers skin-side up on a plate and cook on high in the microwave for 3 minutes. Transfer the peppers to a foil-lined cookie sheet (skin-side up).

3. Cut tomatoes in half lengthwise. Squeeze out most of the seeds. Place tomatoes on the cookie sheet.

4. Turn the oven on broil. Place the cookie sheet on the top shelf of the oven. Watching carefully, broil approximately 8–10 minutes, until the skins turn partially black and loose.

5. Remove from the oven and place peppers and tomatoes in a bowl; cover with foil.

6. When they are cool to the touch, peel skin off. Slice or chop peppers and tomatoes. Slice garlic clove and add to the peppers. Freeze the peppers, tomatoes, and garlic in a freezer bag or plastic container.

Reheating Instructions

1. Defrost vegetables in the refrigerator overnight and put on a baking sheet.

2. Drizzle olive oil over peppers and tomatoes and sprinkle salt to taste. Heat at 425°F for 5 minutes or until vegetables reach the desired temperature. As an alternative heating method, you can heat in the microwave for 2–3 minutes on high.

The Benefits of Red Bell Peppers

Red bell peppers are very nutrient-rich and are an excellent source of vitamins A, B_6, and C. Red bell peppers also provide a good source of fiber and the antioxidant vitamin E. This diet-friendly vegetable has no fat, cholesterol, or sodium, and very few carbohydrates.

Tomatoes and Okra

Freshly cut okra releases a sticky substance that works well in thickening soups and stews. To freeze fresh okra, first blanch for 2 minutes, cool in ice water, drain, and package for the freezer.

YIELDS 6–8 SERVINGS

1½ pounds fresh okra

4 or 5 Roma tomatoes

3 tablespoons butter

1 onion, chopped

½ teaspoon salt

¼–½ teaspoon red pepper flakes, to taste

1 cup tomato sauce

3 tablespoons chopped parsley (used on reheating day)

Freezing Day

1. Cut off stems of okra and slice into ½" pieces. Cut tomatoes into pieces and set aside.
2. In a medium skillet over medium heat, melt butter. Sauté okra and onion for about 3 minutes. Add tomatoes and sauté an additional 2–3 minutes.
3. Stir in salt, red pepper flakes, and tomato sauce.
4. Remove from heat and cool. Pour into a freezer bag and freeze.

Reheating Instructions

1. Defrost okra and tomatoes in the refrigerator overnight. Pour into a lightly greased baking dish and top with parsley.
2. Bake at 350°F for 30 minutes.

An Alternative to Canned Tomatoes

You can freeze fresh tomatoes with either the skin on or off. Thawed tomatoes will become mushy, so they should be used in recipes calling for cooked tomatoes. Clean tomatoes, cut away the stem scar, and place on cookie sheets in the freezer. To freeze skinless, dip in boiling water for 60 seconds, peel when cool, and freeze on a cookie sheet. Bag when frozen solid.

Chapter 7

Beef and Pork

Basic Ground Beef Mixture

Keep this on hand, in 1-pound portions, for easy meals. Mix with Gravy for Any Occasion (see recipe in Chapter 4) and serve over open-faced biscuits. Make a meaty dip by combining with Queso Dip (see recipe in Chapter 4), or add Traditional Marinara Sauce (see recipe in Chapter 4) and make a quick spaghetti dinner.

YIELDS 30–32 SERVINGS

8 pounds ground beef

½ cup onion, chopped

4 batches Ground Beef Seasoning Mix (see recipe in Chapter 4)

Freezing Day

1. In a medium skillet over medium heat, brown ground beef with onion. Drain pan if necessary.
2. Add 4 batches of Ground Beef Seasoning Mix and simmer for 5–10 minutes.
3. Divide mixture into 8 equal portions and freeze in freezer bags.

Reheating Instructions

Defrost meat in the refrigerator overnight and use as desired.

Freezer Burgers

Instead of browning the ground beef, mix the raw beef with the seasoning mix and form into hamburger patties. Flash freeze the patties on a baking sheet, and then transfer them to freezer bags. Separate layers of burgers with wax paper to keep them from sticking together.

Meatballs

Who doesn't love a good meatball? These can be paired with Traditional Marinara Sauce (see recipe in Chapter 4) for spaghetti and meatballs, or Alfredo Sauce (see recipe in Chapter 4), or made into meatball sandwiches topped with mozzarella cheese.

YIELDS 6 SERVINGS

2 pounds ground beef

1 cup bread or cracker crumbs

½ cup grated Parmesan

1 sprig chopped parsley

1 teaspoon garlic salt

2 beaten eggs

Red wine, as needed for meatballs to hold together

Diced mushrooms (optional)

Freezing Day

1. Preheat the oven to 350°F. Combine all the ingredients in a large bowl. Form into balls, place them on a cookie sheet, and bake for 30 minutes–1 hour, depending upon the size of the meatball, until they are no longer pink in the middle.
2. Flash freeze on a baking sheet and transfer into a freezer bag.

Reheating Instructions

Add frozen Meatballs to desired sauce and cook over medium temperature for 20–25 minutes or until heated to the desired temperature. Meatballs can also be defrosted in the refrigerator overnight and used as desired.

Mushroom Beef Stroganoff

Serve the Mushroom Beef Stroganoff over egg noodles or rice. Don't forget to serve bread so you can soak up every last bit of the delicious sauce.

YIELDS 4 SERVINGS

½ cup flour
½ teaspoon salt
¼ teaspoon pepper
1 pound top round steak or equivalent, cut into cubes
2 tablespoons cooking oil
1 (10.75-ounce) can cream of mushroom soup
1 cup water
2 (8-ounce) cans sliced mushrooms
¼ cup white wine
1 cup sour cream (used on reheating day)

Freezing Day

1. In a 1-gallon plastic bag, put flour, salt, and pepper. Add beef and shake to coat completely.

2. Heat oil in large skillet over medium heat. Add beef and brown on all sides, about 7–10 minutes.

3. In a separate bowl, mix soup and water. Slowly add soup and water to the skillet, scraping the bottom as you mix with beef.

4. Add mushrooms and wine.

5. Cook over medium-low heat for 1 hour, stirring frequently. Scrape the bottom of the skillet when you stir.

6. Cool and freeze in a freezer bag.

Reheating Instructions

Defrost stroganoff overnight in the refrigerator; stir in sour cream and heat in a medium saucepan over medium-low heat for 30–45 minutes or until it is thoroughly heated.

Make It Last

One of the benefits to owning a freezer is the ability to stock up on meat when it goes on sale. To help your meat taste as fresh as possible for as long as possible, rewrap it when you come home from the grocery store. Rather than put it directly in the freezer, repackage it in freezer bags or freezer wrap.

Ricotta and Beef Stuffed Shells

An alternative preparation of this dish is to prepare and freeze it as an entire casserole rather than flash freezing the shells and assembling the casserole on serving day.

YIELDS 6 SERVINGS

1 pound ground beef

1 small onion, chopped

1 clove garlic, minced

3 slices white bread

1 cup mozzarella cheese

½ cup ricotta cheese

1 egg

½ cup milk

1 teaspoon Italian seasoning

1 (12-ounce) box jumbo pasta shells, uncooked

2 (24-ounce) jars spaghetti sauce (used on reheating day)

1 cup mozzarella cheese (used on reheating day)

Freezing Day

1. In a heavy skillet over medium heat, brown ground beef and onion for 7–10 minutes or until meat is thoroughly cooked. Add garlic and cook 1 more minute. Drain if needed.

2. Put ground beef mixture in a large mixing bowl.

3. Add bread, torn into small pieces, mozzarella cheese, ricotta, egg, milk, and Italian seasoning to the mixing bowl. Mix well.

4. Carefully stuff each shell with the meat mixture.

5. Flash freeze shells and transfer to a freezer bag.

Reheating Instructions

1. Put frozen shells in a 9" × 12" baking dish.

2. Pour up to 2 jars of sauce over the top of shells, depending upon your taste. Spread 1 cup mozzarella cheese over shells. Cover with aluminum foil.

3. Bake at 375°F for 1 hour 45 minutes–2 hours until shells are tender.

Steak and Tomatoes

This hearty, rib-sticking dish tastes delicious served with mashed potatoes. It is a simple dish to prepare, but it tastes like you spent hours in the kitchen.

YIELDS 4 SERVINGS

1 pound top round steak
⅓ cup flour
Salt and pepper to taste
2 tablespoons cooking oil
1 onion, sliced
1 (29-ounce) can chopped tomatoes

Freezing Day

1. Dredge steak in flour; season with salt and pepper.
2. In a heavy skillet over medium-high heat, brown steak for 3–4 minutes per side in cooking oil.
3. Remove steak from the skillet and sauté sliced onion in the same skillet for 3–4 minutes.
4. Return steak to the skillet and add chopped tomatoes, remove from heat, and allow to cool.
5. Freeze steak, onions, and tomatoes in a freezer bag.

Reheating Instructions

Defrost in the refrigerator for 20–24 hours. Cook in a medium saucepan, covered, over medium-low heat, stirring occasionally, for 1 hour or until steak is tender.

Pepper Steak

Flank steak is full of flavor, but it can be tough. Slice it thinly and diagonally across the grain when you cut it into the strips.

> **YIELDS 4–6 SERVINGS**
> 1 (1½-pound) flank steak
> 1 green bell pepper
> 1 yellow bell pepper
> 1 red bell pepper
> 1 large onion
> 1 batch Stir-Fry Sauce (see recipe in Chapter 4)
> Water, as needed (used on reheating day)
> 3 tablespoons cornstarch (used on reheating day)

Freezing Day

1. Cut steak, peppers, and onions into thin strips. Place into a mixing bowl.
2. Add the Stir-Fry Sauce to the bowl and mix well.
3. Put meat, vegetables, and sauce in a freezer bag and freeze.

Reheating Instructions

1. Defrost in the microwave or refrigerator overnight.
2. Put in a heavy skillet and stir-fry over medium-high heat for 7–10 minutes or until meat reaches the desired doneness and the vegetables are tender. Add water as needed. Use cornstarch to thicken sauce if desired.
3. Serve over rice.

How to Thicken Sauce with Cornstarch

Cornstarch is a great solution anytime you have a sauce you want to thicken. Simply mix 3 tablespoons of cornstarch with ¼ cup cold water. Stir until the cornstarch is completely dissolved, and add to sauce. Stir until the sauce thickens. To multiply your sauce, you can also add 1 cup of beef or chicken broth.

Rolled Burgundy Flank Steak

In this recipe you will be making two batches of the marinade. One will be used on cooking day to marinate the flank steak, and the second batch will be frozen and used on the day you cook the steak.

YIELDS 6 SERVINGS

1 (2-pound) flank steak
½ cup Burgundy wine
4 tablespoons Worcestershire sauce
2 teaspoons thyme
1 teaspoon rosemary
2 teaspoons salt
1 teaspoon pepper
1 (6-ounce) box Stove Top Savory Herbs Stuffing Mix
1 cup chopped mushrooms

Freezing Day

1. With a mallet, pound steak to ¼" thickness.

2. Combine wine, Worcestershire sauce, thyme, rosemary, salt, and pepper in a medium bowl. Pour half the marinade into a quart-size freezer bag and freeze. Pour the other half into a shallow dish. Marinate flank steak in the dish for 3–5 hours in the refrigerator, turning twice. Discard marinade.

3. Prepare the stuffing according to directions on the box. Stir in mushrooms.

4. Lay flank steak out on the counter and spread stuffing mixture over the top.

5. Starting at one long side, tightly roll the steak up like a jellyroll and secure it with string.

6. Tightly wrap the rolled steak with a layer of plastic wrap, followed by a layer of aluminum foil. Freeze.

Reheating Instructions

1. Defrost the rolled steak in the refrigerator for a minimum of 24 hours. Defrost the marinade in cold water for about 30 minutes, or in the microwave.

2. Place steak in a 9" × 13" dish and pour marinade in the bottom of the pan. Baste the steak with the marinade.

3. Cook steak in a 400°F oven for 50–60 minutes (until a meat thermometer reaches 160°F). Baste frequently.

Easy Marinating

A simple way to marinate is to put the meat and the marinade in a plastic bag, and put the bag in the refrigerator. Turning the meat is easy, just flip over the bag. And cleanup takes no time at all—just throw away the plastic bag!

Skillet Beef with Black Beans

Worcestershire sauce is so named because it was first made in Worcester, England. It is a popular condiment made up of vinegar, molasses, various spices, and anchovies.

YIELDS 4–6 SERVINGS

1 pound ground beef

1 small onion, chopped

1 green pepper, chopped

1 clove garlic, minced

2 teaspoons lemon juice

2 teaspoons yellow mustard

2 tablespoons Worcestershire sauce

½ teaspoon cumin

1 cup tomato sauce

1 (16-ounce) can black beans

Freezing Day

1. In a heavy skillet over medium heat, brown ground beef, onion, green pepper, and garlic.

2. Add the remaining ingredients except black beans. Mix well.

3. Gently stir in black beans.

4. Freeze in a freezer bag.

Reheating Instructions

1. Defrost in the refrigerator overnight.

2. Heat in a medium skillet over medium-low heat for 20 minutes, or until desired temperature is reached, and serve over rice.

Lemon Pepper Grilled Steak

Instead of grilling, you may prefer to broil the steak. Preheat the broiler, and then place the steak on a broiler pan 6" from the heat. Broil for 10 minutes, turn, and broil an additional 10–15 minutes until steak reaches the desired doneness.

YIELDS 4–6 SERVINGS

1 (2-pound) top round steak
2 cloves garlic, sliced thin
2 tablespoons lemon zest
1 tablespoon butter, room temperature
1 teaspoon black pepper
1 teaspoon salt

Freezing Day

1. Cut small slits on both sides of the steak. Push a thin slice of garlic into each slit.

2. In a medium bowl, mix lemon zest, butter, black pepper, and salt.

3. Spread the mixture over all sides of the steak. Freeze in a freezer bag. If you do not have a freezer bag large enough, wrap steak with a layer of plastic wrap followed by a layer of aluminum foil.

Reheating Instructions

Defrost steak in the refrigerator for up to 24 hours. Grill over medium heat until the desired doneness is reached.

Grilled Corn on the Cob

While the grill is hot, grill corn on the cob for the perfect complement to your steak. Remove excess silk strands from the end of the cob. Soak the corn in water for 1 hour. Shake out excess water and grill over medium heat for 20 minutes, turning frequently. The husk will start to char. When it steams, the corn is done.

Chestnut-Stuffed Cube Steaks with Mushroom Gravy

Chestnuts have a sweet, nutty flavor, and although they can be eaten raw, they taste better when boiled or roasted. They are a seasonal nut and are most often available October through December.

YIELDS 4 SERVINGS

¾ pound chestnuts
4 tablespoons butter
½ onion, chopped
1 rib celery, chopped
½ pound mushrooms, sliced
¼ cup cream sherry
4 cups soft bread cubes (5 or 6 slices bread, toasted)
1 teaspoon sage
½ teaspoon thyme
1–1½ cups chicken broth
4 cube steaks
1 (12-ounce) jar mushroom gravy (used on reheating day)

Freezing Day

1. In a small saucepan, cover chestnuts with water and heat to boiling. Reduce heat to medium and cook for 10 minutes. Remove 3 chestnuts at a time from the water, cut in half lengthwise, and peel each one.

2. In a medium skillet over medium heat, melt butter and sauté onions and celery. Add mushrooms and sherry. Cook over medium-low heat for 10 minutes.

3. In a large bowl, combine vegetables with bread cubes and herbs. Add chestnuts and mix well. Moisten the stuffing with chicken broth, adding a little at a time, until the desired consistency is reached.

4. Lay out steaks and cover each with stuffing. Fold steak over the stuffing, and secure with a toothpick. Flash freeze on a cookie sheet lined with wax paper. Transfer to a freezer bag.

Reheating Instructions

1. Defrost steak in the refrigerator for 24 hours. Place in a baking dish and pour mushroom gravy over the top. Cover with aluminum foil.

2. Bake at 350°F for 30–45 minutes, or until steaks are tender.

Stuffed Peppers with Sunflower Seeds

Stuffed peppers is a dish that can be found around the globe, with each country having its own version. The classic American stuffed peppers contain meat and rice and are served with a tomato sauce, although there are quite a few variations.

YIELDS 8 SERVINGS

2 pounds ground beef

1 batch Ground Beef Seasoning Mix (see recipe in Chapter 4)

2 (15-ounce) cans tomato sauce

2 cups cooked rice (not minute rice)

½ cup sunflower seeds

8 green peppers

1 (15-ounce) can seasoned diced tomatoes (used on reheating day)

Freezing Day

1. In a medium skillet over medium heat, brown ground beef with the Ground Beef Seasoning Mix. Stir in the 2 cans of tomato sauce. Let simmer for 10 minutes. Stir in rice and sunflower seeds.

2. Cut each pepper in half lengthwise, and remove the stem and seeds. Steam peppers by placing them, cut-side up, in ½" of water. Bring to a boil, cover, and simmer for 5 minutes. Remove from heat.

3. Lay each pepper half on a baking sheet and fill with meat filling.

4. Flash freeze and transfer to a freezer bag.

Reheating Instructions

1. Defrost peppers in the refrigerator for 24 hours and lay them in a baking dish. Pour the diced tomatoes over the top of the peppers and around the bottom of the pan.

2. Bake at 350°F for 30–45 minutes until the peppers are hot and start to brown.

How to Freeze Green Peppers

Many vegetables need to be blanched before they can be frozen, but not green peppers. So before you throw away another rotten pepper from your crisper drawer, freeze it instead. Simply cut the peppers in half, and then remove the membrane, seeds, and stem. You can chop them or cut into strips. Flash freeze on a baking sheet, and transfer to a freezer bag.

Glazed Meatloaf

When you bake your meatloaf, put 2 pieces of bread underneath it to soak up the grease while it cooks. When you are ready to serve, simply throw the pieces of bread away.

YIELDS 4–6 SERVINGS

2 pounds lean ground beef

4 eggs, lightly beaten

1 onion, chopped

¼ cup celery, chopped

2 teaspoons seasoning salt

1 teaspoon pepper

1 cup saltine crackers, finely crumbled

2 cups ketchup

⅔ cup ketchup (used on reheating day)

½ cup brown sugar (used on reheating day)

1½ teaspoons prepared yellow mustard (used on reheating day)

Freezing Day

1. In a large bowl, combine beef and eggs. Blend in onions, celery, seasoning salt, pepper, cracker crumbs, and ketchup. Mixture should be smooth and moist.

2. Flash freeze meatloaf in a 9" × 5" loaf pan. Once frozen, remove meatloaf from the pan, wrap well, and return to the freezer.

Reheating Instructions

1. Defrost meatloaf in the refrigerator for 24 hours. Cook at 350°F for 1 hour–1 hour 10 minutes.

2. While meatloaf is baking, prepare the glaze. In a small bowl, mix ketchup, brown sugar, and mustard. Spread on the meatloaf during the last 20 minutes of cooking time.

Tomato Sauce for Meatloaf

If you'd rather have a savory sauce instead of a sweet glaze on your meatloaf, combine the following in a saucepan: 1 (14-ounce) can stewed tomatoes, ½ cup ketchup, 2 tablespoons minced onion, 2 tablespoons finely chopped celery, and 2 tablespoons sugar. Heat over medium heat and serve with the meatloaf.

South of the Border Lasagna

This is a variation of a traditional recipe that has a Mexican flair. Try changing up the dish by adding a layer of black beans, corn, and cilantro; or a layer of salsa, jalapeño peppers, and Spicy Refried Beans (see recipe in Chapter 6).

YIELDS 6–8 SERVINGS

- 2 pounds ground beef
- 1 onion, diced
- 1 clove garlic, minced
- 1 batch Taco Seasoning Mix (see recipe in Chapter 4)
- 1 cup water
- 2 (14.5-ounce) cans diced tomatoes, drained
- 1 (4-ounce) can green chili peppers, drained
- 3 cups Cheddar cheese, shredded
- 3 cups Monterey jack cheese, shredded
- 2 eggs
- 1 pint ricotta cheese
- 1 (10-ounce) can enchilada sauce
- 24 corn tortillas

Freezing Day

1. In a medium skillet over medium heat, brown ground beef and onion 7–10 minutes or until meat is fully cooked. Add garlic and cook an additional minute. Drain. Add the Taco Seasoning Mix and 1 cup water. Bring to a gentle boil and cook 15 minutes over medium-low heat.

2. To the skillet add the diced tomatoes and green chili peppers. Mix well.

3. In a large bowl, mix the Cheddar cheese with the Monterey jack cheese.

4. In a separate medium bowl, beat eggs and mix fully with ricotta cheese.

5. Prepare a 9" × 13" casserole dish for freezing. See the instructions for the Casserole Method in Chapter 1, or use an aluminum pan. In the bottom of the dish, pour a thin layer of enchilada sauce followed by a layer of tortillas.

6. Add a layer of meat, followed by a layer of shredded cheese mixture.

7. Add a layer of tortillas, followed by all of the ricotta cheese mixture.

8. Continue layering the lasagna and top with a layer of shredded cheese. Pour enough enchilada sauce to cover the top of the lasagna.

9. Wrap well. Follow the instructions in Chapter 1 for freezing a casserole.

Reheating Instructions

1. Unwrap frozen lasagna and put in the original casserole dish. Cover loosely with aluminum foil.

2. Bake frozen lasagna at 350°F for 1 hour 15 minutes–1 hour 45 minutes, or until it is fully heated. Remove foil during the last 15–30 minutes.

3. Bake defrosted lasagna at 350°F for 30–45 minutes.

Beef and Green Chilies Mexican Casserole

This casserole is served spooned over Sweet Cornbread (see recipe in Chapter 6). Try it with picante sauce, sour cream, and extra Cheddar cheese on the side.

YIELDS 6–8 SERVINGS

1½ pounds ground beef

1 onion, chopped

1 green pepper, chopped

1 clove garlic, minced

1 (15-ounce) can kidney beans, drained

1 (16-ounce) can chopped tomatoes, drained

1 (10-ounce) can Ro-Tel diced tomatoes

1 (4.5-ounce) can green chilies, drained

3 tablespoons chili sauce

½ cup shredded Cheddar cheese

½ teaspoon salt, or to taste

1 cup shredded Cheddar cheese (used on reheating day)

1 batch Sweet Cornbread (see recipe in Chapter 6) (used on reheating day)

Freezing Day

1. In a large skillet over medium heat, brown the ground beef. After 4 minutes of browning, add the onion and green pepper. Cook an additional 3–6 minutes until meat is fully browned and vegetables are tender. Add garlic and cook 1 more minute. Drain pan.

2. Stir in kidney beans, tomatoes, Ro-Tel tomatoes, green chilies, chili sauce, ½ cup Cheddar cheese, and salt.

3. Mix well, and remove from heat to cool. Freeze in a freezer bag.

Reheating Instructions

1. Defrost meat mixture in the refrigerator overnight and spread it in the bottom of a casserole dish. Top with 1 cup Cheddar cheese and bake at 350°F for 30 minutes.

2. Prepare Sweet Cornbread according to recipe.

3. To serve, slice each piece of cornbread in half from side to side.

4. Spoon the meat mixture on top of each half of cornbread. Top with additional cheese and sour cream, if desired.

Hamburger Casserole

The Ground Beef Seasoning Mix (see recipe in Chapter 4) has a bit of cayenne pepper in it, but just enough for a little zing rather than a lot of heat. This dish would taste delicious with a spicy twist, so if that is your pleasure, add more cayenne.

YIELDS 6–8 SERVINGS

2 pounds ground beef

1 onion, chopped

2 green bell peppers, chopped

1 batch Ground Beef Seasoning Mix (see recipe in Chapter 4)

4 eggs, beaten

4 cups whole-kernel corn (canned or frozen)

4 tomatoes, sliced

2 cups crushed cornflakes (used on reheating day)

1 stick butter, melted (used on reheating day)

Freezing Day

1. In a medium skillet over medium heat, brown ground beef, onion, and green peppers 7–10 minutes until ground beef is fully cooked. Drain. Stir in Ground Beef Seasoning Mix. Add eggs and mix well. Remove from heat.

2. Prepare a 9" × 13" casserole dish for freezing. See the instructions for the Casserole Method in Chapter 1, or use an aluminum pan.

3. Layer the bottom of the casserole dish with 2 cups of corn. Add half of the meat mixture on top of the corn, followed by a layer of sliced tomatoes. Repeat the layers.

4. Wrap well according to the Casserole Method and freeze.

Reheating Instructions

1. Following the Casserole Method, defrost casserole in the refrigerator overnight. Top with crushed cornflakes, and pour melted butter over the top of the cornflakes.

2. Bake at 350°F for 45 minutes.

How to Freeze Whole-Kernel Corn

When corn is in season, buy it cheap and freeze it for the whole year. Husk the corn and remove the silk. Blanch in boiling water for 4–6 minutes, then put it in a bowl of ice water for 4–6 minutes. Drain, then cut the kernels off the cob. Put kernels in a freezer bag, separate the kernels from each other, and freeze.

Teriyaki Beef and Vegetable Kabobs

Fresh grilled pineapple is delicious when paired with the teriyaki-marinated sirloin steak and vegetables. Serve the kabobs over rice.

YIELDS 6–8 SERVINGS

1 cup Teriyaki Marinade (see recipe in Chapter 4)

2 pounds sirloin steak cut into 1½" cubes

2 green bell peppers, cut into 2" pieces

1 sweet onion, cut into 2" pieces

Skewers (used on reheating day)

1 fresh pineapple, cut into 2" pieces (used on reheating day)

½ cup Teriyaki Marinade (see recipe in Chapter 4) (used on reheating day)

Freezing Day

1. Prepare a double batch of Teriyaki Marinade, or defrost it if it is already prepared.

2. Put steak, peppers, and onions in a freezer bag. Pour the marinade over the top and freeze.

Reheating Instructions

1. Defrost steak, peppers, and onions in the refrigerator overnight, or in the microwave, and discard the marinade.

2. Prepare the skewers by threading on each a combination of steak, peppers, onions, and pineapple.

3. Prepare a batch of Teriyaki Marinade. This will be used for basting during grilling.

4. Grill the skewers over high heat for approximately 10 minutes. Baste with Teriyaki Marinade.

Beef and Broccoli Stir-Fry

Sirloin is the preferred choice of beef for this dish because it is tender when cooked. If you use a tougher cut of steak, be sure to cut it thinly and tenderize it with a meat mallet before freezing.

4 cups fresh broccoli, chopped

6 cups water

2 cloves garlic, minced

3 cups beef bouillon

2 tablespoons sugar

4 tablespoons soy sauce

½ teaspoon ground ginger

1 teaspoon oyster sauce

¼–½ teaspoon red pepper, to taste

1 pound beef sirloin, sliced thinly across the grain

3 tablespoons oil (used on reheating day)

1 green onion, sliced (used on reheating day)

1 tablespoon cornstarch (used on reheating day)

2 tablespoons cold water (used on reheating day)

Freezing Day

1. Blanch the broccoli: Bring 6 cups of water to a boil, and prepare a large bowl filled with ice and water. Put the broccoli in the boiling water for 3 minutes. Remove and put in the ice water for 3 minutes. Drain well and put in a freezer bag. Set aside.

2. In a mixing bowl, whisk together garlic, beef bouillon, sugar, soy sauce, ginger, oyster sauce, and red pepper.

3. Put sliced beef in a freezer bag and pour the sauce over the top. Freeze with the bag of broccoli.

Reheating Instructions

1. Defrost the bag of beef with sauce and the bag of broccoli in the refrigerator overnight.

2. Pour the sauce into a small saucepan. Bring to a boil for 1 minute, then reduce heat to medium-low for 2–3 minutes.

3. Heat a heavy skillet over high heat. Add oil and arrange the sirloin in the skillet in a single layer. Cook for 1 minute and turn the beef over. Cook on the second side for 1 minute.

4. Add onions and sauce to the skillet and bring to a low boil. Add the broccoli and cook for 1 minute, stirring constantly.

5. Mix the cornstarch with 2 tablespoons of cold water. Add to the skillet and stir for 1–2 minutes, or until the sauce thickens. Serve over rice.

Why Blanch the Broccoli?

There are two reasons broccoli is blanched. First, fresh broccoli must be blanched before freezing because without blanching it will continue to ripen while frozen, which could alter its taste, texture, and appearance. The second reason is that blanching shortens the time the broccoli needs to cook with the steak in the skillet, which protects the steak from overcooking.

Spicy Beef and Penne Pasta

This hearty stew is a great choice when you have a crowd to feed. It is popular with the kids, and it goes well with a loaf of crunchy French bread.

1 pound ground beef
2 tablespoons minced onion
1 clove garlic, minced
1 teaspoon red pepper flakes
6 cups plus ¾ cup water, separated
5 beef bouillon cubes
9 tablespoons cornstarch
1 (16-ounce) bag frozen corn
1 (16-ounce) box penne pasta (used on reheating day)

Freezing Day

1. In a large skillet over medium heat, brown ground beef. Add minced onion, garlic, and red pepper flakes. Cook until all the pan juices have evaporated, approximately 10 minutes.

2. In a separate saucepan, bring 6 cups of water to a boil. Dissolve bouillon cubes in boiling water. Add to ground beef.

3. In a measuring cup, mix ¾ cup water with cornstarch. Mix well.

4. Add cornstarch mixture to the skillet. Cook over medium heat 10–12 minutes, stirring frequently, until mixture thickens. Add corn. Remove from heat and cool.

5. Freeze in a freezer bag.

Reheating Instructions

1. In a large pot, defrost the beef mixture and heat over medium-low heat for 30 minutes until it is fully heated.

2. Cook penne pasta according to package directions. Drain and add to the beef mixture. Serve.

Sausage and Peppers

Sausage and Peppers tastes wonderful served as a sub on a toasted, crunchy roll, or it can be served over your favorite pasta.

YIELDS 4 OR 5 SERVINGS

4 tablespoons olive oil, divided

2 cloves garlic, minced

⅛ teaspoon salt

⅛ teaspoon pepper

4 large leaves fresh basil, minced

1 (15-ounce) can diced tomatoes, drained

1½ pounds sweet (or hot) Italian sausage links, diagonally sliced

1 large green bell pepper, sliced

1 large red bell pepper, sliced

1 large yellow bell pepper, sliced

2 large sweet onions, thinly sliced

Freezing Day

1. Heat a medium skillet over medium heat. Add 2 tablespoons olive oil, garlic, salt, and pepper to the hot skillet. Sauté garlic 1–2 minutes until it becomes golden brown. Add basil and tomatoes. Cook over medium-high heat, stirring, for about 5 minutes. Transfer everything from the skillet to a medium bowl and allow to cool.

2. In the same skillet, brown sausage over medium-high heat for about 5 minutes. Remove sausage from the skillet and set aside to cool.

3. Add the remaining 2 tablespoons olive oil to the skillet and cook peppers and onions 5–10 minutes over medium-high heat until the vegetables are tender. Set aside to cool.

4. Put all parts of the meal (tomatoes, sausage, peppers, and onions) into a freezer bag. Freeze.

Reheating Instructions

Defrost Sausage and Peppers in the refrigerator for 24 hours. Put into a large skillet over medium heat, cover, and simmer for approximately 15 minutes until the sausage is fully cooked.

Baked Barbecue Pork Chops

Want to take a shortcut with this recipe? Instead of making the sauce, use your favorite bottled barbecue sauce and pour it over the pork chops in the freezer bag.

YIELDS 4–6 SERVINGS

2 pounds pork chops
Salt and pepper to taste
2 tablespoons olive oil
1 onion, finely chopped
2 ribs celery, finely chopped
2 cups water
1 tablespoon lemon juice
¼ cup Worcestershire sauce
½ cup ketchup
½ cup barbecue sauce
¼ cup vinegar
¼ cup brown sugar
1 teaspoon chili powder
1 teaspoon salt

Freezing Day

1. Season the pork chops on both sides with salt and pepper. In a large skillet over medium-high heat, brown the chops 3–4 minutes on both sides in olive oil. Remove from heat to cool.

2. In a large saucepan, mix the remaining ingredients. Bring to a boil, reduce heat, and simmer for 10 minutes. Remove from heat to cool.

3. Place pork chops in a freezer bag and pour the sauce over the top. Freeze.

Reheating Instructions

1. Defrost pork chops and sauce in the refrigerator for 12–24 hours and put in a baking dish.

2. Bake at 350°F for 1 hour or until the chops are fully cooked.

The Picky Eater

Is someone in your home a picky eater? Dinnertime can be a time of frustration for someone who is hungry but doesn't like what is being served. Consider keeping a few backup meals in the freezer that can be quickly cooked in the microwave. It may be a single serving of macaroni and cheese or a cup of soup.

Pork Ragout

Ragout *(pronounced ra-GOO) is a French term that refers to a stew that is slowly cooked over a low heat. It can contain a wide variety of meat and vegetables that are often heavily seasoned.*

2 tablespoons olive oil

1 large onion, sliced

1 clove garlic, minced

Salt and pepper to taste

1½ pounds pork, cubed

Flour for dredging pork

1 (16-ounce) can diced tomatoes

1½ cups fresh mushrooms, sliced

4 medium carrots, sliced

¼ cup port wine

Freezing Day

1. In a large stockpot or Dutch oven, heat oil over medium heat. Sauté onions 5–10 minutes until tender, add garlic and sauté 1 more minute, then remove from heat.

2. Salt and pepper the pork, then dredge it in flour. Brown the pork for 5–10 minutes in the stockpot where the onions were cooked. Add more olive oil if necessary.

3. Return onions to the stockpot and add all the remaining ingredients.

4. Put ragout into a freezer bag and freeze.

Reheating Instructions

Defrost ragout in the refrigerator for 12–24 hours and cook in a large saucepan over medium-low heat for 45 minutes–1 hour.

Honey Mustard Baked Pork Chops

These pork chops are perfect for the tarragon lover! If you don't have access to fresh tarragon, you may substitute 1 teaspoon dried tarragon for 1 tablespoon fresh tarragon.

YIELDS 4 SERVINGS

2 tablespoons honey
2 tablespoons Dijon mustard
1 tablespoon fresh tarragon
4 pork chops

Freezing Day

1. In a bowl, mix honey, mustard, and tarragon.
2. Brush mixture on both sides of pork chops and flash freeze on a baking sheet lined with wax paper. Transfer to a freezer bag.

Reheating Instructions

1. To cook defrosted pork chops, bake 45 minutes–1 hour at 350°F or until pork chops reach an internal temperature of 170°F. Cooking time will depend upon the thickness of the pork chops. Turn halfway through cooking time.
2. To cook frozen pork chops, bake 1 hour–1 hour 15 minutes at 350°F or until pork chops reach an internal temperature of 170°F. Turn halfway through cooking time.

Pan-Fry Your Pork Chops

If you like a nice sear on the outside of your pork chops, use a combination of skillet and oven. Heat a cast-iron skillet over medium-high heat with 1 tablespoon of oil. Fry seasoned chops 5 minutes on one side (do not move it!), then 5 minutes on the other side. Put the skillet in an oven preheated to 400°F for 5 minutes, or until pork reaches 170°F.

Pork Tenderloin with Bacon

The juices made from deglazing the pan with the sherry and cola after searing the pork are absolutely delicious. Serve with any leftover juices for pouring on meat.

YIELDS 8–10 SERVINGS

3 tablespoons Italian seasoning
3 tablespoons paprika
1 teaspoon salt
1 (4–5-pound) pork tenderloin
4 tablespoons olive oil
¼ cup cooking sherry
½ cup cola
¾ pound bacon

Freezing Day

1. Mix Italian seasoning, paprika, and salt. Rub seasoning around the outside of the pork.

2. Preheat the oven to 375°F. Heat the oil in a medium skillet over medium-high heat. Sear the pork on each side for 3–4 minutes until it is golden brown and crispy all around. Remove pork from the skillet and put in a roasting pan.

3. Deglaze the skillet with the sherry and cola over high heat, stirring up the brown bits on the bottom of the skillet. Pour over the roast.

4. Lay strips of bacon across the pork (perpendicular to the length), slightly overlapping. Tuck ends under the pork. Wrap the pan tightly with aluminum foil, tenting it so it does not touch the bacon.

5. Cook the roast for 30 minutes per pound.

6. Remove pork from the oven, and pour the juices into a bowl to cool. Double wrap the pork tightly with foil and freeze. Put the juice in a freezer bag and freeze.

Reheating Instructions

1. Remove a layer of foil from the roast, keep the second layer around the roast, and defrost in the refrigerator for approximately 24 hours.

2. Once defrosted, put the foil-wrapped pork in a roasting pan and heat for 45 minutes at 325°F, or until it reaches an internal temperature of 170°F.

3. Unwrap the pork and broil on the middle rack for about 5 minutes until the bacon is crisped and browned. Let rest for 10–15 minutes before slicing.

4. Heat up the juices in a small saucepan over medium heat for 5–10 minutes, or until the desired temperature is reached. Pour over the meat, then serve.

Pot Stickers with Sesame Ginger Dipping Sauce

A pot sticker is a Chinese dumpling that can be stuffed with a variety of ground meats and vegetables. When cooked, the dumpling is browned on one side, then simmered in a liquid.

YIELDS 4–6 SERVINGS

1 pound ground pork

½ head cabbage, finely chopped

¼ cup finely chopped green onion

1 tablespoon soy sauce

2 teaspoons sesame oil

1 teaspoon sugar

½ teaspoon fresh gingerroot, minced

2 (14-ounce) packages round pot sticker wrappers (wonton wrappers)

2 tablespoons cooking oil (used on reheating day)

½ cup chicken broth (used on reheating day)

1 batch Sesame Ginger Dipping Sauce (see recipe in Chapter 4) (used on reheating day)

Freezing Day

1. In a medium skillet over medium heat, brown the ground pork. Drain and crumble the pork so it is in very small pieces.

2. In a mixing bowl, mix the cooked pork, cabbage, green onion, soy sauce, sesame oil, sugar, and ginger. Mix thoroughly.

3. Line a baking sheet with wax paper. To make the pot stickers, lay a wrapper flat and put about a teaspoon of filling on it. Wet the edges, fold it over, and seal tightly.

4. Flash freeze the pot stickers, and then transfer to a freezer bag.

Reheating Instructions

1. Add 2 tablespoons oil to a medium skillet and heat over medium heat. Put frozen pot stickers in the skillet (12 at a time) and cook 5 minutes on one side until golden brown.

2. Reduce the heat to low, add chicken broth, and cover. Let them steam until they soak up most of the chicken broth, about 10 minutes.

3. Uncover and cook an additional 2–3 minutes until the wrappers have shrunk down over the filling. Serve with Sesame Ginger Dipping Sauce.

Braised Apple–Stuffed Pork Chops

The fruity apple flavor complements the pork chops wonderfully. Serve this with Creamy Leek Soup (see recipe in Chapter 5) and Dinner Rolls (see recipe in Chapter 6).

YIELDS 2–4 SERVINGS

4 apples
4 thick center-cut pork chops
1 teaspoon cumin
1 teaspoon salt
½ teaspoon pepper
6 tablespoons olive oil
1 tablespoon butter, divided
1 cup apple juice, divided
½ teaspoon cinnamon
2 teaspoons dark brown sugar

Freezing Day

1. Core, peel, and slice the apples into eighths. Set aside. In the side opposite the bone, cut a pocket in each pork chop large enough for 3 apple slices.

2. Season pork chops with cumin, salt, and pepper.

3. In a large skillet over medium-high heat, add the oil, ½ tablespoon butter, and the pork chops and sear the chops for 3–4 minutes on each side until well browned.

4. Remove the chops from the pan and increase the heat to high. Deglaze by adding ½ cup apple juice and scraping loose all the cooked bits that have stuck to the pan and mixing them into the sauce. Add the remaining ½ tablespoon butter.

5. Add apples to the skillet. Cover the apples, turn heat to low, and cook for 5 minutes.

6. Remove half of the apple slices to a plate; add the remaining ½ cup apple juice, cinnamon, and brown sugar to the skillet. Continue to cook the apples and sauce mixture for 2–4 minutes.

7. Stuff 3 slices or more of the reserved apples into each chop. Mash the remaining apples in the sauce.

8. Prepare a casserole dish for the freezer according to the instructions in Chapter 1. Place pork chops in a single layer in a baking dish, pour apple sauce mixture over chops, wrap tightly, and freeze according to casserole dish freezing instructions.

Reheating Instructions

Defrost completely in the refrigerator for 24 hours. Preheat the oven to 350°F. Place chops in the oven and reduce the temperature to 325°F. Cook, tightly covered, for 45 minutes.

Cook Seasonally

Visit your local farmers' market, find out what is in season, and plan your cooking around those foods. Not only will your food be fresh and at the peak of its flavor, but you will able to buy it at a great price and freeze it so you can enjoy it year-round.

Honey Sesame Pork Tenderloin

Use an ovenproof meat thermometer every time you cook, and eliminate the guesswork involved with knowing when your meal is safe to eat. Insert the thermometer into the thickest part of the meat before putting it into the oven. You know pork is ready once the internal temperature reaches 160°F.

YIELDS 4–6 SERVINGS

pounds pork tenderloin
blespoons olive oil
p water
spoons sesame oil
oon ground ginger
arlic, minced
sauce
me seeds

brown sugar
yenne pepper
soy sauce

Freezing Day

1. Preheat the oven to 325°F. Brown pork loin in 4 tablespoons of olive oil in a heavy skillet over medium-high heat for 3–4 minutes per side or until well browned. Reduce to medium-low, add water, and let most of the water cook off.

2. Add sesame oil to the pan. Cook pork loin 90 seconds on each side and remove to a deep baking dish.

3. Mix ginger, garlic, and soy sauce in a cup and brush onto pork loin. Bake pork loin for 20 minutes.

4. Remove the pork from the oven and cool.

5. Reduce the oven temp to 325°F, place sesame seeds in a single layer on a baking sheet, and bake for 15 minutes or until golden brown.

6. In a small mixing bowl, combine honey, brown sugar, cayenne, and soy sauce. Brush on pork and sprinkle with cooked sesame seeds. Put on a baking sheet lined with wax paper and flash freeze. Spray a sheet of plastic wrap with cooking spray and wrap around the frozen pork. Finish wrapping with aluminum foil.

Reheating Instructions

1. Defrost pork in the refrigerator for about 24 hours.

2. Bake, uncovered, at 350°F for about 20–30 minutes or until a meat thermometer reads 160°F. Let stand for at least 10 minutes before slicing.

Sweet and Spicy Pork Chops

The honey adds the sweet and the cayenne pepper adds the spice in this recipe. Need more heat? Up the amount of cayenne pepper in the sauce a pinch at a time. Be careful—the heat can really sneak up on you!

YIELDS 2–4 SERVINGS

2 tablespoons olive oil
4 pork chops
Salt and pepper to taste
1 teaspoon cumin
⅓ cup honey
¼ cup hickory barbecue sauce
4 tablespoons soy sauce
⅓ teaspoon cayenne pepper

Freezing Day

1. Heat olive oil in a large skillet over medium-high heat. Season pork chops with salt, pepper, and cumin. Cook in the hot oil until well browned on both sides, about 4 minutes per side. Remove from pan, cool, and freeze.

2. In a small bowl mix together honey, barbecue sauce, soy sauce, and cayenne pepper. Freeze in a freezer bag or Tupperware.

Reheating Instructions

1. Defrost pork chops and sauce in the refrigerator for 12–24 hours.

2. Place the chops in a casserole dish.

3. Pour the sauce evenly over the chops. Cover the dish with aluminum foil and bake at 325°F for 1 hour.

Walnut Tarragon Pork Cutlets

Fresh tarragon can be used in place of dried tarragon. Use 1 tablespoon of fresh tarragon in place of 1 teaspoon of dried tarragon.

YIELDS 4 SERVINGS

2 teaspoons olive oil

4 boneless pork loin chops

Salt and pepper to taste

½ cup dry white wine

½ cup chopped walnuts

½ teaspoon cinnamon

1 teaspoon dried tarragon

½ cup unsweetened applesauce (used on reheating day)

Freezing Day

1. Heat olive oil in a large skillet over medium-high heat. Season pork chops with salt and pepper, and cook in the hot oil until lightly browned on both sides, about 4 minutes per side.

2. Add the wine, walnuts, cinnamon, and tarragon, and bring to a simmer. Reduce heat to medium-low, cover, and simmer, stirring occasionally, 10–15 minutes, until the pork is no longer pink in the center.

3. Remove the pork chops from the skillet, set aside to cool, and freeze. Freeze the sauce separately.

Reheating Instructions

1. Defrost the chops and sauce overnight in the refrigerator. Place chops in a medium saucepan with the sauce and cook, covered, over medium-low heat for 30 minutes or until the chops are warmed through.

2. Remove the pork chops from the skillet and keep warm. Add applesauce to the sauce and heat an additional 5 minutes. Pour the sauce over the pork chops and serve.

Cranberry Apricot Pork Chops

The flavors of cranberry and apricot beautifully meld into a delicious sauce that perfectly complements the pork chops. Serve with a side of rice and your favorite vegetable.

YIELDS 4 SERVINGS

4 center-cut pork chops
Salt and pepper to taste
2 tablespoons vegetable oil
4 teaspoons honey
1 cup fresh cranberries
½ cup apricot marmalade

Freezing Day

1. Prepare a casserole dish for freezing according to the Casserole Method in Chapter 1.
2. Season pork chops with salt and pepper; then in a large skillet over medium-high heat, brown both sides of chops in vegetable oil for 3–4 minutes.
3. Remove pork chops from the pan and lay them in the bottom of the casserole.
4. Spread 1 teaspoon honey on the top of each pork chop.
5. In a small bowl, mix cranberries with the marmalade. Spoon over the pork chops.
6. Follow the Casserole Method for freezing, wrap well, and freeze.

Reheating Instructions

1. Defrost casserole in the refrigerator for 24 hours, according to the Casserole Method for freezing.
2. Bake at 350°F for 35–45 minutes until pork is fully cooked.

How to Freeze Fresh Cranberries

Fresh cranberries are only available in the fall and early winter. Fortunately, fresh cranberries will freeze very well so you can enjoy this healthy, delicious fruit year-round. Do not wash the berries before freezing. Sealed in an airtight container, fresh cranberries will freeze well for almost a whole year. Freeze in small batches of 1–2 cups, so you'll only have to thaw what you need for a given recipe.

Barbecue Brisket

This brisket turns out moist and tender as it is slowly cooked in the sauce. Serve on sandwich buns or sliced on a platter.

> **YIELDS 15–18 SERVINGS**
> 1 (5-pound) beef brisket (not corned beef)
> 4 teaspoons liquid smoke
> ½ teaspoon salt
> ¼ teaspoon pepper
> 1 cup chili sauce
> ½ cup barbecue sauce

Freezing Day

1. Season the brisket with liquid smoke, salt, and pepper. Place in the slow cooker.
2. Combine chili sauce and barbecue sauce in a small bowl and pour over the brisket.
3. Cover and cook 8–10 hours or until brisket is tender.
4. Thinly slice the meat against the grain and freeze in a freezer bag.
5. Pour the sauce into a large measuring cup and let it sit several minutes. Pour off and discard any oil that rises to the top of the sauce, then freeze the sauce separately in a freezer bag.

Reheating Instructions

1. Defrost brisket and sauce in the refrigerator overnight.
2. Place brisket slices in a baking dish and pour the sauce over the top.
3. Bake at 350°F for 20–25 minutes or until the meat is heated through.

Parmesan-Crusted Pork Chops

The Parmesan, onion, and egg in this recipe make a delicious crusted topping on the pork chop. This dish is so good, it might not make it into your freezer—you'll want to eat it right away!

YIELDS 6 SERVINGS

Salt and pepper to taste
6 pork chops
1 tablespoon vegetable oil
2 tablespoons butter
⅓ cup flour
⅔ cup milk
1 egg
1 small onion, finely chopped
½ cup Parmesan cheese

Freezing Day

1. Salt and pepper pork chops to taste. In a heavy skillet over medium-high heat, brown pork chops in oil, 3–4 minutes per side, then arrange them in a single layer on a baking sheet.

2. In a medium saucepan over medium heat, melt the butter. Gradually stir in flour and milk and mix with a whisk to remove all the lumps.

3. Add the egg and mix well. Cook 5–10 minutes, stirring often, until the mixture turns shiny.

4. Stir in onion and cheese.

5. Spread the mixture over the top of each pork chop. Flash freeze the pork chops, then transfer to a freezer bag.

Reheating Instructions

1. Fully defrost chops in the refrigerator for approximately 24 hours. Bake pork chops at 350°F for 30–45 minutes or until pork chops are fully cooked.

2. To cook pork chops straight from the freezer, bake at 350°F for 1 hour–1 hour 15 minutes or until pork chops are fully cooked. Cooking time will depend upon the thickness of the pork chops.

Portion Control Pork Chops

Pork chops are easy to portion control. Instead of freezing them all together in a casserole dish, flash freeze the pork chops, then transfer the chops to a freezer bag. You may remove as many chops as needed from the bag on reheating night.

Pulled Pork

Serve this pork with Sweet Barbecue Sauce (see recipe in Chapter 4), Dinner Rolls (see recipe in Chapter 6), and a salad for a delicious meal.

> **YIELDS 6–8 SERVINGS**
> 1 (3-pound) lean pork roast
> Salt and pepper to taste
> 1 teaspoon onion powder
> 2 medium onions, sliced
> 3 cloves garlic, minced
> Water to cover

Freezing Day

1. Season pork with salt, pepper, and onion powder and set aside.
2. Lay ⅔ of the sliced onions in the bottom of a slow cooker, and add ½ the minced garlic evenly over onions. Place seasoned pork roast on top of onions, and lay remaining onion and garlic on top of roast.
3. Cover with water.
4. Cook on low for 8 hours and remove to a plate.
5. Remove any fat and pull meat apart using two forks. Freeze using a freezer bag.

Reheating Instructions

Defrost pork in the refrigerator overnight, heat in a medium saucepan over medium heat (or microwave), and serve.

Gravy in the Slow Cooker

Once you remove the pork from the cooker, you can make gravy out of the juices. Remove the onions and set aside. In a small bowl, combine ½ cup cold water with 3 tablespoons cornstarch. Stir until cornstarch is completely dissolved. Pour into the slow cooker and stir until the mixture thickens. Add onions to gravy, cool, and freeze in a plastic container or freezer bag.

Chapter 8

Poultry

Chicken and Mushroom Fettuccine Alfredo

Offer your guests fresh ground pepper with this meal. To add variety, stir in broccoli florets or peas.

YIELDS 8 SERVINGS

1 pound boneless, skinless chicken breasts, cubed

½ teaspoon poultry seasoning

3 tablespoons olive oil

8 ounces fresh mushrooms, sliced

1 clove garlic, minced

1 batch Alfredo Sauce (see recipe in Chapter 4)

1 pound fettuccine pasta (used on reheating day)

Salt and pepper to taste (used on reheating day)

Freezing Day

1. Season the cubed chicken with poultry seasoning. In a large skillet over medium-high heat, add the olive oil and chicken and sauté for 4–5 minutes until the chicken is no longer pink. Add mushrooms and sauté 5–6 minutes. Add garlic and sauté 1 minute. Remove from heat.

2. Prepare Alfredo Sauce and mix with chicken and mushrooms.

3. Freeze in a freezer bag.

Reheating Instructions

1. Defrost Chicken and Mushroom Alfredo in the refrigerator overnight. Heat in a medium saucepan over medium heat for 15–20 minutes or until it reaches the desired temperature.

2. Prepare fettuccine according to package directions.

3. Serve fettuccine on a plate with the sauce and chicken spooned over the top. Season with salt and pepper to taste.

Vacuum Sealer for Freezing

A vacuum sealer is a great way to seal food before freezing, but be careful how you use it. Some of the softer foods like pasta, sauces, some fruits, or rice will need to be flash frozen before being vacuum sealed. When you flash freeze first, you prevent the vacuum sealer from squishing the soft food.

Chicken Cordon Bleu

Cordon bleu *is a French phrase meaning "blue ribbon." The term has come to stand for food or chefs that are distinguished and of the highest quality.*

YIELDS 8 SERVINGS

6 boneless, skinless chicken breasts
6 slices deli ham
¾ pound Swiss cheese, grated
2 eggs
¼ cup milk
¾ cup flour
¾ teaspoon, plus ½ teaspoon salt
1 cup plain bread crumbs
1 cup grated Parmesan cheese
1–2 tablespoons finely chopped fresh basil or dried basil
1 teaspoon garlic powder
½ teaspoon black pepper
4–6 tablespoons olive oil, as needed
2 cups chicken broth (used on reheating day)

Freezing Day

1. Lay each piece of chicken between 2 sheets of plastic wrap. With a meat mallet, flatten the chicken until it is ¼" thick.

2. Cover each piece of chicken with a slice of ham, and sprinkle the Swiss cheese on top of the ham. Fold each long side of the chicken breast in, begin at a short end, and roll it up jellyroll style. Secure with a toothpick.

3. In a small bowl, mix eggs and milk. Set aside.

4. In a shallow plate, mix flour and ¾ teaspoon salt. Set aside.

5. In a separate shallow plate, mix bread crumbs, Parmesan cheese, basil, garlic powder, ½ teaspoon salt, and pepper.

6. Dip chicken pieces in flour mixture to coat. Next dip in egg mixture to coat. Lastly, dredge in bread crumb mixture.

7. Heat oil in a large skillet over medium heat. Brown chicken for 2–3 minutes on all sides until golden brown. Drain on paper towels.

8. Lay the chicken on a baking sheet lined with wax paper and flash freeze. Once frozen, transfer to a freezer bag.

Reheating Instructions

1. Defrost chicken in the refrigerator for 24 hours and put in a 9" × 13" baking dish. Pour 2 cups chicken broth into the pan.

2. Bake chicken at 400°F for 30–40 minutes until chicken is fully cooked.

Chicken Cordon Bleu Sauce

Put this sauce in a gravy boat on the table so it can be poured over the chicken on individual plates. To make, melt 1 tablespoon butter. Whisk in 1 tablespoon flour. Slowly stir in 1 cup milk and continue to whisk until sauce thickens. Stir in ½ cup shredded Swiss cheese and 3 tablespoons chicken broth. Heat until cheese melts.

Grilled Citrus Chicken

This chicken may be broiled instead of grilled, although you won't get the smoky flavor that comes from grilling if you choose that route. To broil, place chicken on a broiler pan in a pre-heated oven with the chicken 6" from the heat. Broil on both sides until the chicken reaches 170°F.

Freezing Day

1. Place chicken in a gallon-size freezer bag.

2. In a mixing bowl, whisk together the remaining ingredients. Divide the marinade in half. Pour half of the marinade over chicken and freeze. Pour the other half of the marinade in a quart-size freezer bag and freeze.

Reheating Instructions

1. Defrost chicken in the refrigerator overnight, in the microwave, or in cold water, and discard included marinade. Defrost quart-size bag of marinade. This will be used to brush over chicken during grilling.

2. Over medium heat, grill chicken breasts 12–15 minutes or until no longer pink. Brush chicken with marinade throughout cooking.

Apricot Walnut–Stuffed Chicken

Basmati rice is grown in India and gets its name from a Hindu word meaning "full of aroma." It has a sweet and slightly nutty flavor, and it goes well with many savory dishes.

YIELDS 4 SERVINGS

¾ cup dried apricots
1 cup chicken broth
1 sprig fresh thyme
½ cup uncooked basmati rice
¼ cup walnuts, chopped
¼ teaspoon cinnamon
4 boneless, skinless chicken breast halves
1 tablespoon butter (used on reheating day)
⅓ cup apricot preserves (used on reheating day)
¼ teaspoon salt (used on reheating day)
¼ cup flour (used on reheating day)
4 tablespoons vegetable oil (used on reheating day)

Freezing Day

1. Place dried apricots in a medium saucepan with the chicken broth and thyme. Bring to a gentle boil. Turn heat down to medium-low and cover for 10–15 minutes until apricots are soft.

2. Cook the rice in a separate saucepan according to package directions.

3. When apricots are soft, remove from the pan and discard broth and thyme. Chop apricots and place in a large bowl. Add cooked rice, walnuts, and cinnamon. Mix well.

4. Cut a slit in the side of each chicken breast, and widen it to make a pouch.

5. Stuff each breast with the apricot-walnut mixture. Secure the breast closed with a toothpick. Flash freeze and transfer to a freezer bag.

Reheating Instructions

1. Defrost chicken breasts in the refrigerator for 24 hours.

2. In a shallow dish, melt butter in the microwave. Stir in the apricot preserves and salt.

3. Put flour in a second shallow dish.

4. Dip each chicken breast in the apricot preserves, then the flour.

5. In a large skillet over medium heat, sauté the chicken in oil until fully cooked, approximately 10 minutes per side.

6. For an alternative to frying, bake chicken at 375°F for 40 minutes, or until juices run clear.

Turkey Fricassee in Mushroom and Wine Sauce

Fricassee is a French term that refers to a process of cooking. It involves browning white meat in butter, adding flour, and then adding liquids to make a sauce. The end result is often compared to a stew.

YIELDS 4 SERVINGS

1 pound boneless, skinless turkey breast
8–10 tablespoons butter, divided
8 ounces fresh mushrooms, sliced
1 small onion, diced
1 clove garlic, minced
3 tablespoons flour
1 cup chicken broth
½ cup dry white wine (used on reheating day)
¾ cup sour cream (used on reheating day)

Freezing Day

1. Cut the turkey breast into bite-size cubes. In a medium skillet, melt 4 tablespoons butter over medium-high heat, being careful not to burn it. Add the turkey and cook 4–6 minutes until golden brown on all sides. Remove turkey from the skillet and set aside on a plate.

2. Add more butter to the skillet if necessary and sauté mushrooms and onion over medium heat for 5 minutes. Add garlic and sauté 1 more minute. Remove the vegetables from the skillet and place on the plate with the turkey.

3. In a clean skillet, melt 4 tablespoons butter. Stir in 3 tablespoons flour and mix.

4. Add the chicken broth to the skillet and stir until mixture begins to thicken, approximately 3–5 minutes. Add the turkey and vegetables to the skillet, mix well, and immediately remove from heat to cool.

5. Put the turkey and sauce into a freezer bag and freeze.

Reheating Instructions

1. Defrost turkey in the refrigerator overnight, in the microwave, or in cold water, and put into a medium skillet. Stir in the wine and sour cream.

2. Cover and cook on medium for 10 minutes.

Broiled Garlic and Tarragon Chicken Breasts

Tarragon vinegar is easy to make and enhances the flavor of vegetables, as well as poultry and fish dishes. To make it, place a sprig of tarragon in a jar with distilled white vinegar. Steep for a few days, and then remove the sprig.

YIELDS 4 SERVINGS

4 boneless, skinless chicken breast halves
1 clove garlic, sliced thin
5 tablespoons olive oil
4 teaspoons dried tarragon, crushed
¼ teaspoon pepper
¼ teaspoon salt

Freezing Day

1. Using a paring knife, cut 2 small slits in the top of each chicken breast. Insert a slice of garlic in each slit.
2. In a small saucepan, combine the olive oil, tarragon, pepper, and salt and heat on medium-low for 5 minutes.
3. Brush the olive oil mixture on all sides of each chicken breast and freeze in a freezer bag.

Reheating Instructions

1. Defrost chicken breasts in the refrigerator overnight and place on a broiler pan.
2. Broil about 6" from heat for 7–8 minutes. Turn chicken and broil another 7–10 minutes or until chicken is fully cooked.

How to Flash Freeze Herbs

One method for freezing fresh herbs is accomplished by freezing the entire sprig of leaves. First wash the herbs, then fully dry them and remove all the moisture. Lay the herbs out on a baking sheet and flash freeze. Transfer them into a small freezer bag. To use, simply crumble frozen herbs into your dish.

Braised Italian Chicken

Braising is a method of cooking in which meat is first seared in a hot skillet, then finishes cooking in liquid in a covered pan. It works well for cuts of meat that tend to be tough because the process tenderizes the meat.

YIELDS 6 SERVINGS

1½ pounds boneless chicken thighs

2 tablespoons oregano

½ teaspoon garlic powder

¼–½ teaspoon black pepper, according to taste

½ teaspoon salt

2 tablespoons olive oil

1 seasoning packet from chicken-flavored Ramen noodles

2 cups hot water

1 (6-ounce) can tomato paste

1 tablespoon minced onion

1 large zucchini, sliced

Freezing Day

1. Season both sides of the chicken with oregano, garlic, pepper, and salt.

2. Heat olive oil in a large skillet over medium-high heat. Brown the chicken thighs, 3–4 minutes per side. During the browning time, do not move the thighs or scrape underneath them. You want the yummy brown crunchies to cook under the chicken. Once thighs are browned, remove them to a platter.

3. In a medium bowl, add the seasoning packet to the water, mix, and add to the skillet. Bring to a boil. Use a spatula to scrape the bottom of the skillet and mix everything. Add tomato paste and minced onion. Mix well.

4. Return thighs to the sauce, add sliced zucchini, and remove from heat to cool. Freeze the meal in a freezer bag.

Reheating Instructions

Defrost chicken and sauce in the refrigerator for 24 hours. Put in a medium skillet over medium-low heat, cover, and cook for 1 hour. Turn chicken halfway through cooking time.

The Secret to Braising

When browning meat for braising recipes, don't be afraid to turn up the heat. You want a good dark brown sear that can only come from medium-high heat. You also want to get some well-cooked bits that stay in the pan that will deglaze into a nice sauce, so don't be too quick to turn the meat.

Grilled Hawaiian Chicken

Give each of your dinner guests a small bowl filled with Sweet-and-Sour Sauce (see recipe in Chapter 4) for dipping chicken. Serve with grilled pineapple slices and rice for a meal everyone will love.

YIELDS 4 SERVINGS

1⅓ cups butter
1 cup pineapple juice
6 tablespoons honey
½ cup soy sauce
1 teaspoon ginger
4 split chicken breasts
1 batch Sweet-and-Sour Sauce (see recipe in Chapter 4) (used on reheating day)

Freezing Day

1. In a medium saucepan over medium heat, melt butter. Add pineapple juice, honey, soy sauce, and ginger. Divide sauce into 2 equal parts.

2. Put chicken into a freezer bag. Pour half of the sauce over the chicken and freeze. Pour the other half of the sauce into a quart-size freezer bag and freeze separately.

Reheating Instructions

1. Defrost the chicken and the separate marinade bag in the refrigerator for 24 hours. The separate bag of marinade is to baste the chicken during grilling.

2. Grill the chicken over medium heat for 30 minutes with the bone-side down, and 15–20 minutes on the other side, or until the breast reaches 165°F. Baste with the reserved marinade during the last 15 minutes of grilling only.

Chicken Breast with Creamy Tarragon Sauce

Not only does tarragon taste delicious, but it can help your body as well. It is healthy for your digestive system, eases stomach cramps, and even stimulates your appetite. And if you have high blood pressure, try substituting tarragon for salt!

YIELDS 6 SERVINGS

6 boneless, skinless chicken breast halves
½ teaspoon salt
¼ teaspoon pepper
¼ cup flour plus 2 tablespoons flour, divided
3 tablespoons olive oil
½ small onion, chopped
½ cup dry white wine
2 teaspoons tarragon
½ cup chicken broth
½ cup heavy cream (used on reheating day)
2 tablespoons butter (used on reheating day)

Freezing Day

1. Sprinkle the chicken breasts with salt and pepper, and coat them in ¼ cup of flour.

2. In a large skillet, heat the olive oil over medium-high heat. Add the chicken and brown 3 minutes on both sides. Remove chicken from the skillet to cool.

3. Sauté onions in the skillet 5–10 minutes until the onion is translucent.

4. Over high heat, deglaze the skillet with the wine. Add 2 tablespoons flour and mix well. A thick paste should form. Add tarragon and chicken broth, mix well, and immediately remove from heat to cool.

5. Put chicken in a freezer bag and pour the skillet ingredients over the chicken. Freeze.

Reheating Instructions

1. Defrost the chicken and sauce in the refrigerator overnight and put in a large skillet. Cover. Cook approximately 30 minutes over medium heat until the chicken is fully cooked. Remove chicken from the skillet.

2. Add the heavy cream and 2 tablespoons butter to the skillet. Stir 5–7 minutes until the sauce is fully heated. Serve chicken with the sauce spooned over the top.

How to Deglaze

This recipe calls for you to deglaze the skillet. "Deglaze" is a culinary term that means to remove the brown pieces and drippings that stuck to the bottom of the skillet during browning. A liquid such as wine is poured into the skillet and, over high heat, the bottom of the skillet is scraped so the browned pieces can flavor the sauce.

Braised Southwestern Chicken

This hearty chicken dish is best served over rice. If you want to add heat to your dish, include chopped jalapeño peppers, or put a bottle of hot sauce on the table and season to taste.

Freezing Day

1. In a large skillet, brown chicken 2–3 minutes per side, in olive oil, over medium-high heat.

2. Add the wine and deglaze the pan over high heat by stirring to remove the brown bits stuck to the bottom of the pan.

3. Stir in remaining ingredients and immediately remove from heat.

4. Pour into a freezer bag and freeze.

Reheating Instructions

Defrost chicken and sauce in the refrigerator overnight. Put into a large saucepan and bring to a low boil. Cover pan, turn down heat, and simmer for 20–30 minutes until chicken is fully cooked.

Raspberry-Glazed Chicken Breasts

This dish uses only five ingredients and is simple to put together. Vary the cooking method by cooking in a covered skillet over medium heat.

YIELDS 4–6 SERVINGS

1½ cups raspberry preserves
½ cup balsamic vinegar
½ cup soy sauce
2 cloves garlic, minced
2 pounds boneless, skinless chicken breast

Freezing Day

1. In a medium saucepan, combine all the ingredients except the chicken. Bring to a boil, reduce heat, and simmer for 10 minutes. Cool.

2. Put chicken breasts in a freezer bag and pour the sauce over the chicken. Freeze.

Reheating Instructions

Defrost chicken in the refrigerator overnight. Put the chicken and sauce into a baking dish. Bake chicken at 350°F, covered, for 30–40 minutes or until chicken is fully cooked.

Mini Turkey Meatballs

These minimeatballs taste wonderful on rolls with red sauce and mozzarella cheese, or with Alfredo Sauce (see recipe in Chapter 4) and served over noodles.

YIELDS 4 SERVINGS

1 pound ground turkey
½ cup Italian bread crumbs
1 clove garlic, minced
1 egg
½ teaspoon Italian seasoning
1 tablespoon Worcestershire sauce
1 tablespoon olive oil

Freezing Day

1. Preheat the oven to 350°F. In a large mixing bowl, combine all the ingredients except olive oil. Mix well and form into small meatballs.

2. Place meatballs in a pan and bake for 20–30 minutes, or until they are fully cooked. Flash freeze and transfer to a freezer bag.

Reheating Instructions

Defrost meatballs in the refrigerator for 24 hours. Put meatballs in a saucepan with your favorite sauce and warm over medium heat for 30 minutes or until the desired temperature is reached.

Grilled Honey Mustard Chicken

The honey mustard sauce in this recipe tastes delicious on hamburgers, and you can use it with pork chops or sliced ham.

YIELDS 6 SERVINGS

6 boneless, skinless split chicken breasts
1 cup honey
½ cup Dijon mustard
2 tablespoons Worcestershire sauce

Freezing Day

1. Place the chicken breasts in a freezer bag.
2. In a food processor, mix honey, Dijon mustard, and Worcestershire sauce until a smooth consistency is reached.
3. Put ⅓ of honey mustard sauce in a small freezer bag or plastic container.
4. Pour remaining ⅔ of sauce over chicken and seal the bag. With your hands on the outside of the bag, move chicken around so it is coated with sauce. Freeze.

Reheating Instructions

1. Defrost chicken and the separate container of sauce in the refrigerator overnight.
2. Over high heat, grill chicken 2 minutes per side. Decrease grill temperature to medium-low and cook an additional 5–10 minutes until chicken reaches an internal temperature of 165°F. Use the separate container of sauce to baste chicken during the last few minutes of cooking.

Use Tongs When Grilling

When you are grilling chicken or steak and it is time to turn the meat, use a pair of tongs instead of a fork that will pierce the meat. The delicious juices inside the meat can escape through the puncture and cause the meat to be dry and chewy.

Curried Chicken

Made from the meat of the coconut, coconut milk is created through a multistep process of steeping grated coconut in hot water, straining out the pulp, and repeating this process up to three times. Thankfully, canned coconut milk is readily available in grocery stores.

YIELDS 4–6 SERVINGS

1 whole chicken, cooked
1 onion, chopped
2 tablespoons butter
2 tablespoons flour
1 teaspoon curry powder (or to taste)
1 (14-ounce) can coconut milk
4 drops hot sauce (or to taste)

Freezing Day

1. Remove cooked chicken from the bone and set aside.

2. In a medium saucepan over medium-high heat, sauté onions in butter for 5–10 minutes until onions are soft and translucent. Stir in flour and curry powder.

3. Slowly pour in coconut milk, stirring until the mixture thickens. Add hot sauce and mix well. Simmer for 10 minutes.

4. Add chicken to the sauce, mix, and immediately remove from heat to cool. Freeze in a freezer bag.

Reheating Instructions

Defrost chicken mixture in the refrigerator overnight, in the microwave, or in cold water. Heat in a large saucepan over medium heat for 15–20 minutes or until the desired temperature is reached. Serve over rice.

Turkey Breast with Buttery Citrus Sauce

Make a second batch of the buttery citrus sauce to serve with the turkey on reheating day, and pour over the cutlets before serving.

YIELDS 2–4 SERVINGS

1 pound boneless, skinless turkey breast
Salt and pepper to taste
½ cup scallions, minced
½ cup orange juice
1 teaspoon orange zest
1 tablespoon lemon juice
½ cup butter, softened

Freezing Day

1. With a meat mallet, flatten turkey breast. Season with salt and pepper on each side.
2. In a medium saucepan over medium-low, heat scallions and orange juice for 5 minutes.
3. In a food processor, add orange zest, lemon juice, and butter. Slowly pour in orange juice and scallions and process until smooth.
4. Put turkey breast in a freezer bag and add the butter mixture. Seal the bag, and squish it with your hands to cover turkey with butter sauce. Freeze.

Reheating Instructions

Defrost turkey in the refrigerator overnight. Discard marinade. In a medium skillet over medium-high heat, brown the turkey approximately 3 minutes on each side until fully cooked.

Rosemary and Pineapple Chicken

Rosemary is brain food. Did you know that studies show rosemary can increase the blood flow to your brain increasing concentration? Now that is something to think about!

Freezing Day

1. Sprinkle one side of the chicken breasts with salt, pepper, and rosemary.

2. Add olive oil to a large skillet. Brown the chicken over medium-high heat, with the rosemary-side down first. Brown each side approximately 3 minutes, then remove chicken from the skillet.

3. Add the chicken broth to the empty skillet. Scrape the browned pieces off the bottom of the skillet. Add the pineapple chunks and juice from the can to the skillet. Mix with broth and set aside to cool.

4. Put chicken pieces in a freezer bag, and pour the broth and pineapple chunks over the chicken. Freeze.

Reheating Instructions

1. Defrost chicken mixture in the refrigerator overnight. Put the mixture into a large skillet and cook, covered, over medium to medium-low heat for 30 minutes or until chicken is fully cooked. Add sliced apples during the last 5 minutes of cooking time.

2. Remove chicken and fruit from the skillet.

3. In a small bowl, mix cornstarch with ¼ cup cold water.

4. Add the cornstarch mixture, milk, and butter to the sauce in the skillet. Stir over medium heat until the sauce thickens, 5–10 minutes.

5. Serve sauce spooned over chicken.

Getting the Most Flavor During Browning

When browning the chicken breasts, it may be tempting to peek under the chicken to see how it is doing or scoot it around inside the skillet. Resist the urge to move it at all. You will get a better flavor in the skillet for your sauce if you allow the chicken to stay in one place and brown.

Paprika Chicken

Paprika is a spice most often associated with Hungary, where in Kalocsa you can visit the Paprika Museum or enter the cooking contest at the annual Paprika Days Festival. Paprika is sometimes used as a garnish to add color to a dish, but the flavor is not released until the paprika is heated.

YIELDS 2–4 SERVINGS

⅛ teaspoon garlic powder

1 cup chicken stock

¼ cup white wine

1 pound boneless, skinless chicken breasts

1 cup fresh mushrooms, sliced (used on reheating day)

1 teaspoon salt (used on reheating day)

1 teaspoon paprika, or according to taste (used on reheating day)

1½ cups sour cream (used on reheating day)

Freezing Day

1. In a medium bowl, mix garlic powder, chicken stock, and white wine.
2. Put chicken breasts in the bottom of a freezer bag. Pour the liquid over the top. Freeze.

Reheating Instructions

1. Defrost chicken in the refrigerator overnight. Pour chicken and liquid into a medium pot. Add the mushrooms. Simmer for 45 minutes or until chicken is fully cooked and tender.
2. Stir in salt, paprika, and sour cream. Heat the chicken and sauce for 5–10 minutes. Serve over rice.

Homemade Dumplings

Paprika Chicken can be served with dumplings instead of rice. To make dumplings, combine 2½ cups flour, 3 eggs, and ⅓ cup water. Mix well. Start a pot of water boiling. Add 1–2 teaspoons of salt to the water. Once boiling, fill a teaspoon with batter and drop it into the water. Once the dumpling floats to the top, remove it from the water.

Chicken Tacos

Add toppings to these soft tacos such as Monterey jack cheese, diced tomatoes and onions, lettuce, guacamole, sour cream, and Pico de Gallo (see recipe in Chapter 4).

YIELDS 4 OR 5 SERVINGS

Juice of 1 lime
1 teaspoon lime zest
½ cup apple cider vinegar
1 teaspoon sugar
½ teaspoon salt
½ teaspoon black pepper
3 tablespoons fresh cilantro
1½ pounds chicken breasts, cut into strips
10 flour tortillas (used on reheating day)

Freezing Day

1. In a food processor, combine lime juice, lime zest, apple cider vinegar, sugar, salt, pepper, and cilantro. Process until smooth.

2. Put strips of chicken in a freezer bag. Pour the marinade over the chicken and freeze.

Reheating Instructions

1. Defrost chicken in the refrigerator overnight and discard marinade. Sauté chicken in a large skillet for 5–6 minutes over medium-high heat, or until fully cooked.

2. Heat flour tortillas according to package directions. Fill each tortilla with chicken and add your favorite toppings.

Stuffed Turkey Tenderloins

The unusual sweet and spicy filling that stuffs these tenderloins is delicious. To serve without freezing, just serve the rolls after they are thoroughly cooked.

Freezing Day

1. Cut turkey tenderloins in half crosswise to make 4 pieces. Cut a slit in the side of each piece and spread turkey pieces open. Sprinkle with salt and pepper. In a small bowl combine raisins, dried fruit, cream cheese, and honey mustard and mix well. Divide this mixture among turkey pieces and fold to enclose filling. Use toothpicks to secure edges.

2. Preheat the oven to 400°F. Coat tenderloins with honey and roll in bread crumbs. Place in a 9" × 13" baking pan and bake for 40–45 minutes, turning once, until internal temperature registers 170°F. Cool rolls in the refrigerator, then wrap individually in freezer wrap and place in ziplock bags. Label, seal, and freeze.

Reheating Instructions

Thaw overnight in the refrigerator. Preheat the oven to 400°F. Place turkey rolls in a 9" × 13" baking pan and bake for 18–25 minutes or until thoroughly heated and bread crumb coating is crisp.

Orange Chicken

Serve this chicken and sauce over a bed of rice. You can also pair it with a salad containing mandarin oranges and almonds, finished off with a vinaigrette dressing.

YIELDS 2–4 SERVINGS

1 pound boneless, skinless chicken breasts
3 tablespoons soy sauce
2 tablespoons honey
¼ cup orange juice concentrate
¼ cup orange juice
1 clove garlic, minced
1 package onion soup mix

Freezing Day

1. Put chicken in a freezer bag.
2. In a food processor, mix the remaining ingredients. Process until smooth. Pour over chicken and freeze.

Reheating Instructions

Defrost chicken and sauce in the refrigerator overnight. Put in a 9" × 13" baking dish. Bake at 350°F, uncovered, for 1 hour or until chicken is fully cooked.

Cubing Juice Concentrate

It is often more economical to buy juice concentrate in a large container, but you don't always need to use it all at once. To solve the problem, spoon the leftover concentrate into ice-cube trays and freeze. Once frozen, transfer to a freezer bag. The cubes also make beautiful ice cubes when put in drinks such as lemonade!

Mustard Chicken

Not only can you bake this chicken, but you can grill it or even bread and fry it. It is really easy to prepare and proves to be very elegant.

YIELDS 6–8 SERVINGS

1 (8-ounce) jar Grey Poupon
2 cups heavy cream
2 dashes balsamic vinegar
4 tablespoons dried tarragon
Salt and pepper to taste
2 pounds boneless chicken breasts

Freezing Day

1. In a medium bowl, mix the mustard, cream, vinegar, tarragon, salt, and pepper.
2. Put chicken into a freezer bag and pour the sauce over the top of it. Freeze.

Reheating Instructions

1. Defrost chicken in the refrigerator overnight and put in a baking dish with the sauce.
2. Bake at 350°F for 1 hour or until chicken is fully cooked.

Just How Much Is a Dash?

If you are not the type of cook who likes to dash and pinch and needs more precise measurements, the consensus is that a dash equals ⅛ of a teaspoon. In other words, there are 8 dashes in a teaspoon. A pinch is smaller than a dash. A pinch is half of a dash, or 1/16 of a teaspoon.

Breaded Chicken Breast with Muenster Cheese Bake

This is a great choice for serving to guests for dinner. The chicken is moist and full of flavor, and the Muenster cheese is the perfect topping.

YIELDS 6 SERVINGS

2 eggs

¼ cup milk

¾ cup flour

¾ teaspoon, plus ½ teaspoon salt

1 cup plain bread crumbs

1 cup grated Parmesan cheese

1–2 tablespoons finely chopped fresh basil or dried basil

1 teaspoon garlic powder

½ teaspoon black pepper

6 boneless chicken breasts, cut into 2 or 3 pieces

½ cup olive oil for frying

Slices of Muenster cheese; ½ slice for each piece of chicken

1–2 cups chicken broth (used on reheating day)

Freezing Day

1. In a small bowl, mix eggs and milk. Set aside.

2. In a shallow plate, mix flour and ¾ teaspoon salt. Set aside.

3. In a separate shallow plate, mix bread crumbs, Parmesan cheese, basil, garlic powder, ½ teaspoon salt, and pepper.

4. Dip chicken pieces in flour mixture to coat. Next dip in egg mixture to coat. Lastly dredge in bread crumb mixture.

5. Heat oil in a large skillet over medium heat. Fry chicken for 2–3 minutes on each side until golden brown. Drain on paper towels.

6. Top each piece of chicken with ½ slice Muenster cheese. Flash freeze the chicken, then transfer to a freezer bag.

Reheating Instructions

1. Defrost chicken in the refrigerator overnight. Lay chicken pieces in a 9" × 13" baking dish.

2. Pour 1–2 cups of chicken broth over the chicken. Use enough broth so it comes halfway up the sides of the chicken breasts. Broth should not cover chicken. Bake at 425°F for 20 minutes until cheese melts.

Sweet-and-Sour Chicken

This recipe calls for a fryer, but you can use the pieces you like best. Try chicken breasts only, or boneless chicken thighs. Suit it to whatever you have on hand!

YIELDS 4–6 SERVINGS

1 (2½-pound) fryer, cut into pieces
2 tablespoons cornstarch
3 tablespoons cold water
1 cup brown sugar
1 cup soy sauce
½ cup apple cider vinegar
2 cloves garlic, minced
1 teaspoon ginger
¼–½ teaspoon red pepper flakes, to taste
1 (20-ounce) can pineapple rings (used on reheating day)

Freezing Day

1. Put chicken pieces in the bottom of a freezer bag.
2. In a small bowl, mix the cornstarch and water until the cornstarch is completely dissolved.
3. In a medium saucepan, add brown sugar, soy sauce, vinegar, garlic, ginger, and pepper flakes. Stir in the cornstarch and water.
4. Bring sauce to a boil, stirring constantly for 3–5 minutes. Once mixture thickens, remove from heat and let cool. Pour half the sauce over chicken in a freezer bag and freeze. Pour the other half of the sauce in a separate freezer bag and freeze.

Reheating Instructions

1. Defrost chicken in the refrigerator for at least 24 hours and discard the marinade. Defrost the bag of extra sauce—this is used for basting during cooking.
2. Bake chicken in a greased casserole dish for 1 hour (or until chicken is fully cooked) at 400°F, turning halfway through cooking time. Baste chicken with extra sauce every 15 minutes.
3. Add pineapple rings to the top of chicken during the last 10 minutes of baking.

Glazed Turkey Breast

To serve without freezing, roast the turkey as directed. When the internal temperature reaches 180°F, let the turkey stand, covered, for 10 minutes before slicing. Serve with cooked rice.

YIELDS 6–8 SERVINGS

1 (5-pound) boneless turkey breast
1 teaspoon salt
⅛ teaspoon white pepper
⅓ cup honey
1 cup orange juice
3 tablespoons lime juice
2 teaspoons dried basil

YIELDS 18–24 SERVINGS

3 (5-pound) boneless turkey breasts
1 tablespoon salt
⅜ teaspoon white pepper
1 cup honey
3 cups orange juice
9 tablespoons lime juice
2 tablespoons dried basil

Freezing Day

1. Preheat the oven to 325°F. Loosen skin from turkey breast. In a small bowl, combine the remaining ingredients. Brush some of this mixture on the flesh under the skin. Gently smooth skin back into place and brush entire turkey breast with this mixture.

2. Coat a roasting pan with nonstick cooking spray. Place breast in the roasting pan, with the skin-side down, and pour half the sauce over. Roast for 1 hour. Turn turkey over and cover with the remaining sauce. Continue roasting for 60–90 minutes, basting occasionally with pan juices, until turkey registers 180°F on an instant-read thermometer. Cool turkey in the refrigerator and slice. Place slices in ziplock bags and pour pan juices over turkey; freeze.

Reheating Instructions

Thaw overnight in the refrigerator. Place turkey slices and pan juices in a heavy skillet. Heat turkey over medium heat for 8–12 minutes, shaking the pan occasionally, until slices are thoroughly heated and juices boil.

Chicken Cacciatore

Chicken Cacciatore is an Italian dish that was once called hunter's stew because it was something hunters could easily make in the field. Try using boneless chicken thighs for an even richer taste.

1½ pounds boneless, skinless chicken breasts

1 onion, sliced into rings

1 green bell pepper, sliced

½ pound mushrooms, sliced

2 cloves garlic, minced

2 (6-ounce) cans tomato paste

¼ cup red wine

1 cup water

1 (14.5-ounce) can stewed tomatoes with liquid

1 teaspoon dried oregano

½ teaspoon dried basil

½ teaspoon salt

¼ teaspoon pepper

Freezing Day

Put chicken, onions, peppers, and mushrooms in a freezer bag. In a separate bowl mix the remaining ingredients and pour over the chicken. Freeze.

Reheating Instructions

Defrost chicken in the refrigerator overnight. Put in a slow cooker and cook 7–9 hours on low. Add additional water if needed.

Lemon Basil Grilled Chicken

Have a supply of these marinated chicken breasts on hand for quick and easy meals. Throw one on the grill for a fresh, delicious lunch. Enjoy it on a kaiser roll, or slice it up and lay the chicken on top of a garden salad.

YIELDS 6 SERVINGS

6 boneless, skinless chicken breasts

2 tablespoons olive oil

¼ cup white wine

3 tablespoons fresh basil, chopped

¼ teaspoon salt

½ cup lemon juice

Lemon pepper to taste (used on reheating day)

Freezing Day

1. Put chicken breasts in the bottom of a freezer bag.
2. In a mixing bowl, combine the oil, wine, basil, salt, and lemon juice. Pour over chicken and freeze. If you want to freeze each breast separately, put each piece in its own freezer bag, divide the marinade into 6 equal parts, and pour over chicken.

Reheating Instructions

Defrost chicken in the refrigerator overnight. Season with lemon pepper, then grill chicken over medium heat 12–15 minutes or until no longer pink.

Grilling Tip for Best Flavor

When grilling, the best flavor will result from using natural wood charcoal instead of charcoal briquettes. Briquettes have lots of filler and often are infused with lighter fluid to make them easier to light. Always use a charcoal chimney to start your charcoal instead of lighter fluid. Lighter fluid leaves a distinctive taste that is best avoided.

Chicken Fajitas

Have toppings like shredded Cheddar cheese, sour cream, and jalapeño peppers available for the fajitas. They also taste great with Pico de Gallo (see recipe in Chapter 4).

YIELDS 6 SERVINGS

2 pounds boneless chicken, sliced thin

2 tablespoons cilantro, chopped

¼ cup olive oil

¼ cup balsamic vinegar

¼ cup Worcestershire sauce

4 tablespoons lime juice

1 clove garlic, minced

1 teaspoon Mrs. Dash

6 drops hot sauce

3 tablespoons olive oil (used on reheating day)

1 onion, cut into rings (used on reheating day)

1 green bell pepper, thinly sliced (used on reheating day)

10–12 flour tortillas (used on reheating day)

Freezing Day

1. Put sliced chicken and cilantro in the bottom of a freezer bag.

2. In a food processor, combine olive oil, balsamic vinegar, Worcestershire sauce, lime juice, garlic, Mrs. Dash, and hot sauce. Pour marinade over the chicken. Freeze.

Reheating Instructions

1. Defrost chicken in the refrigerator overnight and discard marinade. Heat a large skillet over high heat; add oil and chicken. Stir-fry chicken, onions, and green peppers 5–10 minutes until chicken is fully cooked and vegetables are to desired tenderness.

2. Wrap the flour tortillas in moist paper towels and heat in the microwave for 1 minute.

3. To serve, fill each tortilla with chicken, vegetables, and any other desired toppings and wrap burrito style.

Save the Citrus!

After you have squeezed your oranges, lemons, and limes, save the peel to make zest. Wash the peel well and dry it. Put the peel into a freezer bag and freeze for up to 3 months. The next time a recipe calls for zest, you can go right to your frozen rind and grate the amount needed.

Baked Chicken with Broccoli

The light tarragon sauce is a delicious accompaniment to the chicken and broccoli. Try substituting cauliflower or green beans for the broccoli, or even a medley of vegetables.

YIELDS 6–8 SERVINGS

8 ounces bacon

3 tablespoons bacon drippings

3 tablespoons flour

2¾ cups chicken broth

1½ teaspoons tarragon

1½ teaspoons basil

¾ teaspoon salt

4 teaspoons minced onion

¾ teaspoon garlic powder

2½ teaspoons lime juice

2½ pounds chicken tender fillets

1 (24-ounce) bag frozen broccoli florets

2 cups Cheddar cheese

Freezing Day

1. Chop bacon into bite-size pieces and fry in a medium skillet over medium heat until cooked through. Remove bacon from the pan and set aside. Remove all but 3 tablespoons of bacon drippings from the skillet. Add 3 tablespoons flour to the bacon drippings and mix over heat to form a roux.

2. Add chicken broth to the skillet and stir 4–5 minutes until sauce thickens.

3. Add tarragon, basil, salt, minced onion, garlic powder, and lime juice to the sauce. Bring to a boil, and then reduce heat. Simmer for 10 minutes.

4. Prepare a 9" × 13" casserole dish for freezing. See instructions for the Casserole Method in Chapter 1, or use an aluminum pan. Layer the bottom of the dish with the chicken, and top with frozen broccoli. Pour sauce over the broccoli and chicken.

5. Top with bacon, then cheese. Freeze using casserole freezing method.

Reheating Instructions

1. Following the Casserole Method, defrost the casserole in the refrigerator overnight, cover, and cook at 350°F for 1 hour–1 hour 15 minutes until chicken is fully cooked.

2. To cook casserole frozen, cover and cook 2 hours–2 hours 15 minutes at 350°F.

A Bit about Tarragon

Tarragon is an aromatic herb also commonly referred to as dragon herb or dragon's wort. It is one of the four "fines herbes" of French and Mediterranean cooking, along with parsley, chives, and chervil. It is commonly used in chicken, fish, and egg dishes.

Chicken and Mashed Potato Pie

Flash freeze this dish before wrapping it. Place the pie on a baking sheet and put in the freezer for 2–3 hours. Once frozen, wrap well with plastic wrap and remove the plastic before defrosting. By following these tips, the potatoes will not stick to the plastic wrap.

YIELDS 6 SERVINGS

1 Easy Pie Crust (see recipe in Chapter 12)

1 batch Mashed Potatoes (see recipe in Chapter 6)

2 pounds boneless chicken breasts, cubed

Poultry seasoning, as desired

1 (10.75-ounce) can condensed cream of chicken soup

¼ cup milk

1 (14.5-ounce) can mixed vegetables, drained

Salt and pepper to taste

½ cup freshly grated Parmesan cheese (used on reheating day)

Freezing Day

1. Prepare pie crust and Mashed Potatoes.

2. Put chicken in a large saucepan and cover with water. Add poultry seasoning to the water. Simmer for 30–40 minutes until fully cooked.

3. In a large bowl, mix cooked chicken, cream of chicken soup, milk, mixed vegetables, salt, and pepper. Add ¼ cup more milk if needed.

4. Put chicken and vegetables in the pie crust.

5. Spoon Mashed Potatoes over the chicken and vegetables, covering completely. Flash freeze, then wrap well.

Reheating Instructions

1. Defrost fully in the refrigerator overnight. Bake at 375°F for 30–35 minutes until fully heated through.

2. Sprinkle Parmesan cheese over pie during the last 10 minutes of cooking.

Turkey Spinach Casserole

To serve this casserole without freezing, combine Parmesan cheese and bread crumbs and sprinkle over the turkey mixture. Bake at 375°F for 20–25 minutes, until the casserole bubbles and the cheese browns.

YIELDS 4-6 SERVINGS

1 onion, chopped

2 cloves garlic, minced

1 cup sliced carrots

2 tablespoons olive oil

2 cups cooked, cubed turkey

1 (14-ounce) jar pasta sauce

2 cups frozen cut-leaf spinach, thawed

1 cup ricotta cheese

1 egg

1 cup grated mozzarella cheese

1 cup grated Parmesan cheese

¼ cup dried Italian bread crumbs

YIELDS 12-18 SERVINGS

3 onions, chopped

6 cloves garlic, minced

3 cups sliced carrots

6 tablespoons olive oil

6 cups cooked, cubed turkey

3 (14-ounce) jars pasta sauce

6 cups frozen cut-leaf spinach, thawed

3 cups ricotta cheese

3 eggs

3 cups grated mozzarella cheese

3 cups grated Parmesan cheese

¾ cup dried Italian bread crumbs

Freezing Day

1. In a heavy skillet over medium heat, sauté onion, garlic, and carrots in olive oil until crisp-tender. Add turkey and pasta sauce and simmer for 5 minutes.

2. Meanwhile, thoroughly drain spinach and combine in a medium bowl with ricotta, egg, and mozzarella. Place spinach mixture in a 2-quart casserole and top with turkey mixture. Cool in an ice-water bath or the refrigerator; then wrap, label, attach a small freezer bag with Parmesan cheese and bread crumbs, and freeze.

Reheating Instructions

Thaw casserole overnight in the refrigerator. Sprinkle with Parmesan cheese and bread crumb mixture and bake in a preheated 375°F oven for 30–40 minutes, until bubbly and thoroughly heated.

Chapter 9

Seafood

Shrimp Creole

Bacon drippings add instant flavor to your dishes. After cooking bacon, pour the grease into a jar, secure the lid, and store in the refrigerator. Now you'll have bacon drippings available anytime you need them.

YIELDS 6 SERVINGS

- 1 small onion, chopped
- 1 small bell pepper, chopped
- 3 tablespoons bacon drippings (or vegetable oil)
- 2 cloves garlic, minced
- 1½ teaspoons chopped parsley
- 2 teaspoons sugar
- 2 teaspoons seasoned salt
- ¼ teaspoon pepper
- 1 (14-ounce) can seasoned diced tomatoes
- 1 (8-ounce) can tomato paste
- 1 tablespoon hot sauce
- 2 pounds cooked shrimp

Freezing Day

In a medium skillet over medium heat, sauté onion and bell pepper in bacon drippings for 8–10 minutes until vegetables are soft. Add garlic and sauté 1 minute. Add the remaining ingredients, mix, and immediately remove from heat. Pour into a freezer bag and freeze.

Reheating Instructions

Defrost in the refrigerator for 12–24 hours and put into a medium saucepan. Simmer over medium heat for 20 minutes. Serve over rice.

How to Cook Shrimp

Begin by removing the shell and tail, and deveining the shrimp. Next, put the shrimp in boiling hot water with 1 teaspoon salt and the juice of ½ lemon. Remove the pan from the heat and leave the shrimp in the water for about 5 minutes, or until the shrimp are fully cooked and opaque in color.

Marinated Red Snapper

When you purchase red snapper, make sure you ask for fillets with the skin. The skin helps to hold in the flavor of the fish, and also holds the fillet together so it doesn't fall apart during cooking.

YIELDS 4 SERVINGS

- 2 tablespoons teriyaki sauce
- 4 tablespoons olive oil
- 4 tablespoons lime juice
- 4 red snapper fillets

Freezing Day

1. In a food processor, mix teriyaki sauce, olive oil, and lime juice.
2. Place snapper fillets in a freezer bag. Pour marinade over top and freeze.

Reheating Instructions

1. Fully defrost fish in the refrigerator overnight and discard marinade.
2. Place snapper, skin-side down, on a broiler pan. Broil 6" from heat 8–10 minutes until the fish is done cooking, or starts to flake.

Grilled Curry Shrimp

Shrimp can be grilled individually, or you can put them on skewers. Threading the shrimp on skewers makes them easier to turn and control on the grill.

YIELDS 6 SERVINGS

2 pounds large shrimp, peeled and deveined with tails attached

2 tablespoons butter

¼ cup green onions, minced

½ teaspoon salt

2½ teaspoons curry powder

1 teaspoon sugar

⅛ teaspoon ginger

⅛ teaspoon cinnamon

2 tablespoons flour

1 cup half-and-half

Skewers (used on reheating day)

Freezing Day

1. Put shrimp in a freezer bag.

2. In a medium skillet, melt butter over medium-high heat and sauté the green onions for 5–10 minutes until tender. Add the salt, curry powder, sugar, ginger, and cinnamon.

3. Stir the flour into the skillet, mixing it well with onions and spices. Pour in the half-and-half. Stir 5–10 minutes until mixture thickens.

4. Pour curry sauce over shrimp and freeze.

Reheating Instructions

1. Defrost shrimp in the refrigerator overnight. Thread shrimp onto skewers.

2. Lightly oil the grill. Over high heat, grill the shrimp for 2–3 minutes per side.

How to Devein Shrimp

To devein a shrimp, remove the outer shell and legs from the shrimp. Next, make a long cut along the back of the shrimp to expose the vein. Flare out the shrimp on each side, further exposing the vein. Drag your finger along the vein, removing it completely, and rinse the shrimp with water.

Shrimp Pesto

Most Italian chefs consider putting Parmesan cheese on seafood pastas a faux pas. But you have permission to do so, because it is delicious over this Shrimp Pesto! You may also substitute chicken for the shrimp if you have a shellfish allergy.

YIELDS 2–4 SERVINGS

1 (16-ounce) box rotini or farfalle pasta

½ pound shrimp, shells and tails removed

1 onion, chopped

2 tablespoons olive oil

3 cloves garlic, diced

1 tomato, diced

3–4 tablespoons Basil and Pine Nut Pesto, to taste (see recipe in Chapter 4)

Freshly grated Parmesan cheese (used on reheating day)

Butter (if needed, used on reheating day)

Freezing Day

1. Start water boiling for pasta.

2. Cut shrimp into pieces. In a medium skillet over medium heat, sauté the onion in olive oil for 5–10 minutes until onions are translucent. Add garlic and sauté 1 minute. Add shrimp and sauté 2 minutes on each side or until shrimp turns pink.

3. Cook pasta al dente; be careful not to overcook the pasta.

4. Drain pasta and put in a large mixing bowl. Add the shrimp, onion, garlic, and tomatoes to the pasta. Add enough pesto to lightly cover the pasta. Toss together and freeze in a freezer bag.

Reheating Instructions

Defrost pasta in the refrigerator overnight and heat in a medium saucepan over medium low until it is heated through, approximately 15–20 minutes or until the desired temperature is reached. If desired, add more pesto or butter to the dish. Sprinkle with Parmesan cheese to taste.

Hot and Spicy Shrimp Kabobs

Vary this recipe by adding pieces of chicken with the vegetables on some kabobs, and pieces of pork on other kabobs!

> **YIELDS 4–6 SERVINGS**
>
> 2 pounds jumbo shrimp
> 2 large sweet onions
> Skewers
> 16 large fresh mushrooms
> 4 large banana peppers, cut into 1½" pieces
> 16 cherry tomatoes
> ⅛ cup soy (used on reheating day)
> ½ cup honey (used on reheating day)
> 1 tablespoon red pepper flakes (used on reheating day)

Freezing Day

1. Peel and devein the shrimp. Cut each onion into 8 wedges.
2. On 8 metal or soaked wooden skewers, alternately thread the shrimp and vegetables.
3. Grill kabobs, covered, over medium heat for 3 minutes on each side or until shrimp begin to get pink. Remove from heat, cool, and freeze on the skewers by wrapping kabobs in plastic wrap first, followed by aluminum foil.

Reheating Instructions

1. Defrost shrimp kabobs in the refrigerator overnight.
2. In a small bowl, mix soy, honey, and red pepper flakes to make a glaze.
3. Place kabobs on a foil-lined tray and coat well with glaze, using all the sauce.
4. Cook for 10 minutes at 375°F. Remove, spoon extra sauce over kabobs, and serve warm.

Tips for Grilling Kabobs

When cooking kabobs, try to cut all the ingredients about the same size so they cook evenly. If using bamboo skewers, make sure to soak them in water for 30 minutes prior to use. For foods (like shrimp) that can curl on the skewer, it will help to use two skewers inserted parallel to each other.

Grilled Orange Salmon

When selecting salmon, purchase the freshest fish available. The salmon should smell like the ocean, and it should not have a fishy smell.

> **YIELDS 6 SERVINGS**
> ½ cup orange juice
> 2 teaspoons orange zest
> ½ cup honey
> 1 tablespoon teriyaki sauce
> 2½ pounds salmon fillets

Freezing Day

1. In a small bowl, mix orange juice, zest, honey, and teriyaki sauce.
2. Put salmon in a freezer bag and pour in marinade. Freeze.

Reheating Instructions

Defrost salmon in the refrigerator overnight and discard marinade. Grill over medium heat, skin-side down, just until it flakes.

How to Avoid Overcooking on the Grill

Salmon, like any other meat, will continue to cook after being removed from the grill. Cook salmon until the meat begins to change color and becomes flaky. When the salmon appears opaque and flaky in the thickest part of the meat, immediately remove from heat. If you are not serving immediately, wrap in foil to keep moist.

Clam Spaghetti

Want to spice it up? Add ½ teaspoon red pepper flakes to the sauce to add a bit of a kick.

YIELDS 4–6 SERVINGS
¼ cup butter or margarine
3 tablespoons flour
3 cloves garlic, minced
1 tablespoon dried parsley
¼ teaspoon dried oregano
¼ teaspoon dried basil
¼ teaspoon ground black pepper
3 tablespoons olive oil
¼ cup white wine plus 1 tablespoon
2 (6.5-ounce) cans minced clams, with juice
1 pound linguine (used on reheating day)
Grated Parmesan cheese, to taste (used on reheating day)

Freezing Day

1. In a medium saucepan over medium heat, melt butter. Stir in flour making a paste.
2. Add garlic, herbs, pepper, olive oil, wine, and juice from the clams. Stir continually for 5 minutes over medium-low heat. Remove from heat and stir in clams.
3. Transfer to a freezer bag and freeze.

Reheating Instructions

1. Defrost clams and sauce in the refrigerator overnight. Heat in a medium saucepan over medium-low heat 5–10 minutes until it reaches desired temperature.
2. Cook linguine according to package directions.
3. Toss the linguine with the clam sauce. Serve with grated Parmesan cheese.

Red Clam Sauce

For a variation of this meal, turn your white sauce into red sauce. Make the white sauce according to the recipe. In a separate saucepan, combine 1 (28-ounce) can crushed tomatoes, 1 (14.5-ounce) can diced tomatoes, 1 (15-ounce) can tomato sauce, 1 tablespoon brown sugar, and ½ teaspoon salt. Simmer for 1 hour and add to white sauce. Divide into 1-cup portions and freeze.

Tuna Bake

This classic dish has stood the test of time. Add variety to the casserole by stirring in a cup of cooked peas, carrots, or broccoli.

YIELDS 6–8 SERVINGS

8 ounces elbow macaroni

4 tablespoons butter

3 tablespoons flour

2 cups heavy cream

½ teaspoon salt

½ teaspoon pepper

2 cups Cheddar cheese, shredded

1½ teaspoons prepared yellow mustard

4 (9-ounce) cans tuna, drained

½–1 cup milk, as needed (used on reheating day)

2 cups crushed cornflakes (used on reheating day)

1 stick butter, melted (used on reheating day)

Freezing Day

1. Cook elbow macaroni al dente (cooked but still firm) and drain.

2. In a large saucepan, melt the butter over medium heat. Add flour and mix well.

3. Slowly add the cream to the butter mixture, stirring as you pour.

4. Bring to just under a boil, stirring constantly for about 5 minutes until the sauce thickens.

5. Add salt, pepper, cheese, and mustard. Continue to stir until all of the cheese is melted.

6. Gently stir in macaroni and tuna and remove from heat to cool. Freeze in a freezer bag.

Reheating Instructions

1. Defrost in the refrigerator overnight.

2. Grease a large baking dish and put tuna mixture in it. Add milk as needed to reach a creamy consistency.

3. Cover the casserole with crushed cornflakes and pour the melted butter over the cornflakes.

4. Bake at 375°F for 30–40 minutes.

Fish Tacos

To serve these tacos without freezing, let the cabbage mixture marinate in the refrigerator for 1–2 hours. Bake spiced fish sticks as directed, then serve with Coleslaw (see recipe in Chapter 6) and salsa in the heated taco shells.

YIELDS 4–6 SERVINGS

1 pound frozen breaded fish sticks

1 teaspoon chili powder

½ teaspoon paprika

⅛ teaspoon cayenne pepper

8 taco shells

1 batch Coleslaw (see recipe in Chapter 6) (used on reheating day)

1 (8-ounce) jar salsa (used on reheating day)

YIELDS 12–18 SERVINGS

3 pounds frozen breaded fish sticks

1 tablespoon chili powder

1½ teaspoons paprika

⅜ teaspoon cayenne pepper

24 taco shells

3 batches Coleslaw (see recipe in Chapter 6) (used on reheating day)

3 (8-ounce) jars salsa (used on reheating day)

Freezing Day

Remove fish sticks from package. Combine chili powder, paprika, and cayenne pepper on a shallow plate and toss fish sticks in this mixture. Place fish sticks and taco shells in separate ziplock bags and freeze. Reserve salsa in the pantry.

Reheating Instructions

Preheat the oven to 400°F. Place frozen fish sticks on a baking sheet and bake for 10–15 minutes, until thoroughly heated. Add frozen taco shells to the baking sheet for the last 4–5 minutes of baking time. Serve Coleslaw and fish sticks in taco shells along with salsa.

Madras Shrimp Tart

To serve this tart without freezing, let it cool for 10 minutes when it comes out of the oven, then slice and serve with more chutney.

YIELDS 6–8 SERVINGS

2 tablespoons oil
¼ cup frozen corn
½ cup finely chopped onion
¼ cup chopped red pepper
1 tablespoon curry powder
2½ cups small cooked shrimp
¼ cup plain yogurt
¼ cup sour cream
2 tablespoons flour
3 tablespoons golden raisins
3 tablespoons chopped almonds
2 eggs
2 Easy Pie Crusts (see recipe in Chapter 12)
2 tablespoons mango chutney

YIELDS 18–24 SERVINGS

6 tablespoons oil
¾ cup frozen corn
1½ cups finely chopped onion
¾ cup chopped red pepper
3 tablespoons curry powder
7½ cups small cooked shrimp
¾ cup plain yogurt
¾ cup sour cream
6 tablespoons flour
9 tablespoons golden raisins
9 tablespoons chopped almonds
6 eggs
6 Easy Pie Crusts (see recipe in Chapter 12)
6 tablespoons mango chutney

Freezing Day

1. In a large skillet, heat oil over medium heat. Add frozen corn, onion, and red pepper; cook and stir for 1 minute. Add curry powder and cook 1 minute more. Stir in shrimp, yogurt, sour cream, flour, and ⅓ each of the raisins and almonds. Remove pan from heat and cool 15 minutes.

2. Preheat the oven to 400°F. Beat eggs in a small bowl and add to filling in the skillet; mix well until combined.

3. Place a pie crust in a 10" tart pan with a removable bottom. Spread chutney over the crust, then spoon shrimp filling over chutney. Sprinkle remaining raisins and almonds over filling. Make a lattice top with another crust and place over the filling, sealing the edges. Bake for 20–35 minutes, until filling is set and crust is golden brown.

4. Cool tart in the refrigerator, uncovered, until completely cold. Wrap in heavy-duty freezer wrap, label, and freeze. Or, slice the tart into wedges and wrap individually to freeze.

Reheating Instructions

Thaw tart overnight in the refrigerator. Bake in a preheated 400°F oven for 15–20 minutes, until thoroughly heated. To reheat individually from frozen, bake in a 400°F oven for 15–25 minutes.

Salmon in Curry Sauce

To serve without freezing, do not cool the sauce; prepare the salmon and add to the sauce. Simmer for 10–15 minutes, until the salmon is thoroughly heated.

YIELDS 6 SERVINGS

2 pounds salmon fillets

1 tablespoon oil

2 tablespoons butter

2 onions, chopped

2 tablespoons flour

2 teaspoons curry powder

¼ teaspoon garlic salt

1 teaspoon sugar

¼ cup evaporated milk

1½ cups fish broth

1 (6-ounce) package couscous (used on reheating day)

1 (8-ounce) jar mango chutney (used on reheating day)

YIELDS 18 SERVINGS

6 pounds salmon fillets

3 tablespoons oil

6 tablespoons butter

6 onions, chopped

6 tablespoons flour

6 teaspoons curry powder

¾ teaspoon garlic salt

1 tablespoon sugar

¾ cup evaporated milk

4½ cups fish broth

3 (6-ounce) packages couscous (used on reheating day)

3 (8-ounce) jars mango chutney (used on reheating day)

Freezing Day

1. Place salmon on a broiler pan and brush with oil. Broil 4–6" from heat source, turning once, for 10–12 minutes, until fish flakes easily when tested with a fork. Remove salmon from the oven and refrigerate.

2. Meanwhile, heat butter over medium heat in a large saucepan until foamy. Add onions; cook and stir until crisp-tender. Sprinkle flour, curry powder, garlic salt, and sugar into the pan; cook and stir for 2–3 minutes, until bubbly. Add evaporated milk and broth; stir well to combine. Cover and simmer for 30 minutes, until sauce is thickened and blended. Cool sauce in an ice-water bath or the refrigerator until cold.

3. Remove skin from cooked salmon fillets and gently break into large chunks. Add to cooled sauce and pack into ziplock bags. Seal bags, label, and freeze. Reserve couscous and chutney in pantry.

Reheating Instructions

Thaw mixture overnight in the refrigerator. Pour into a large saucepan and bring to a simmer, stirring occasionally. Simmer for 8–12 minutes, until salmon is hot and sauce is thoroughly heated. Serve over couscous and top with chutney.

Shrimp Newburg

This dish is perfect for company. To serve without freezing, thaw the shrimp. When the sauce is thickened, add the shrimp and cook until heated, then serve over hot cooked rice or couscous.

YIELDS 4 SERVINGS

1 tablespoon butter

1 tablespoon olive oil

4 cloves garlic, minced

1 shallot, minced

2 tablespoons flour

1 cup evaporated milk

¼ cup cocktail sauce

½ teaspoon salt

⅛ teaspoon white pepper

1 tablespoon Worcestershire sauce

1 pound frozen uncooked shrimp

2 tablespoons sherry (used on reheating day)

YIELDS 12 SERVINGS

3 tablespoons butter

3 tablespoons olive oil

12 cloves garlic, minced

3 shallots, minced

6 tablespoons flour

3 cups evaporated milk

¾ cup cocktail sauce

1½ teaspoons salt

⅜ teaspoon white pepper

3 tablespoons Worcestershire sauce

3 pounds frozen uncooked shrimp

6 tablespoons sherry (used on reheating day)

Freezing Day

1. In a large skillet over medium heat, melt butter with olive oil. Add garlic and shallots; cook and stir for 3–4 minutes, until crisp-tender. Sprinkle flour into skillet; cook and stir until bubbly. Add evaporated milk, cocktail sauce, salt, pepper, and Worcestershire sauce and cook until thickened. Cool sauce in an ice-water bath or in the refrigerator.

2. Pour cooled sauce into a ziplock bag and attach frozen shrimp (do not thaw shrimp). Label package, seal, and freeze. Reserve sherry in pantry.

Reheating Instructions

Thaw sauce overnight in the refrigerator. Thaw shrimp according to package directions. Pour sauce into a medium saucepan and bring to a simmer. Add thawed shrimp and cook, stirring frequently, about 3–7 minutes or until shrimp are pink and cooked. Add sherry just before serving. Serve with hot cooked rice or couscous.

Spinach-Stuffed Fillets

These pretty fillets are good for company and so easy to make. You can serve the cooked fish without freezing.

YIELDS 8 SERVINGS

½ cup minced onion

1 tablespoon olive oil

2 cups frozen spinach, thawed

1 cup soft bread crumbs

1 egg

½ cup ricotta cheese

1 cup grated Havarti cheese

½ teaspoon dried basil leaves

8 (6-ounce) thin red snapper fillets

½ cup grated Parmesan cheese

YIELDS 24 SERVINGS

1½ cups minced onion

3 tablespoons olive oil

6 cups frozen spinach, thawed

3 cups soft bread crumbs

3 eggs

1½ cups ricotta cheese

3 cups grated Havarti cheese

1½ teaspoons dried basil leaves

24 (6-ounce) thin red snapper fillets

1½ cups grated Parmesan cheese

Freezing Day

1. In a heavy skillet over medium heat, cook onion in olive oil until crisp-tender. Drain spinach thoroughly, pressing between paper towels to remove moisture. Add to the skillet and cook for 1–2 minutes longer. Remove the skillet from the heat.

2. Preheat the oven to 350°F. In a medium bowl, combine bread crumbs, egg, cheeses, and basil. Add spinach and onion; mix to combine. Spread spinach mixture on each fillet and roll up to enclose filling; fasten with toothpicks.

3. Roll each fillet in Parmesan cheese to coat. Place rolled fillets on parchment paper–lined baking sheets and bake for 25–30 minutes, until fish flakes when tested with a fork. Cool completely in the refrigerator; then place in rigid containers, wrap, seal, and freeze.

Reheating Instructions

Thaw fish in the refrigerator overnight. Bake at 400°F for 12–18 minutes, until fish is thoroughly heated.

Salmon Quiche

Apple juice adds a sweet note and complements the salmon and Havarti in this special quiche. To serve without freezing, let quiche stand for 5–10 minutes after baking, then slice and serve.

YIELDS 6 SERVINGS

1 onion, chopped
1 clove garlic, minced
2 tablespoons butter
2 tablespoons olive oil
¼ cup flour
½ teaspoon salt
⅛ teaspoon pepper
½ cup apple juice
1 cup evaporated milk
3 eggs, beaten
½ teaspoon dried dill weed
1½ cups shredded Havarti cheese
1 (9") unbaked Easy Pie Crust (see recipe in Chapter 12)
1 (14-ounce) can red salmon
¼ cup grated Parmesan cheese

YIELDS 18 SERVINGS

3 onions, chopped
3 cloves garlic, minced
6 tablespoons butter
6 tablespoons olive oil
¾ cup flour
1½ teaspoons salt
⅜ teaspoon pepper
1½ cups apple juice
3 cups evaporated milk
9 eggs, beaten
1½ teaspoons dried dill weed
4½ cups shredded Havarti cheese
3 (9") unbaked Easy Pie Crusts (see recipe in Chapter 12)
3 (14-ounce) cans red salmon
¾ cup grated Parmesan cheese

Freezing Day

1. Preheat the oven to 400°F. Cook onion and garlic in butter and olive oil in a heavy skillet over medium heat until crisp-tender. Sprinkle flour, salt, and pepper over onions; cook and stir for 3–4 minutes. Stir in apple juice and evaporated milk; cook and stir for 4–5 minutes, until thick. Remove from heat and cool for 10 minutes.

2. Meanwhile, in a medium bowl, beat eggs until foamy; add dill weed. Stir egg mixture into onion mixture and blend well. Sprinkle half of the Havarti cheese into the bottom of the pie crust.

3. Drain salmon and remove and discard skin and bones. Break salmon into chunks and scatter over cheese. Pour onion–egg mixture over salmon and top with remaining Havarti cheese. Sprinkle with Parmesan cheese. Bake for 30–35 minutes, until golden brown and set.

4. Cool in refrigerator, then flash freeze; wrap, label, and freeze. Or, slice quiche into serving pieces before freezing and flash freeze individually.

Reheating Instructions

Thaw quiche overnight in the refrigerator. Bake at 350°F for 20–25 minutes, until heated through. To reheat individually, microwave each frozen slice on medium for 2–4 minutes, then 1 minute on high, until hot.

Sweet-and-Sour Shrimp

To serve this dish without freezing, after the sauce has simmered, add the thawed shrimp and cook as directed in the recipe. Thicken as directed with the cornstarch mixture.

YIELDS 4–6 SERVINGS

1 onion, chopped

3 cloves garlic, minced

2 tablespoons olive oil

1 green pepper, chopped

1 (8-ounce) can pineapple tidbits

1 cup fish broth

¼ cup ketchup

¼ cup apple cider vinegar

¼ cup sugar

1 teaspoon ground ginger

2 tablespoons soy sauce

1 pound frozen uncooked shrimp

2 tablespoons cornstarch (used on reheating day)

¼ cup water (used on reheating day)

YIELDS 12–18 SERVINGS

3 onions, chopped

9 cloves garlic, minced

6 tablespoons olive oil

3 green peppers, chopped

3 (8-ounce) cans pineapple tidbits

3 cups fish broth

¾ cup ketchup

¾ cup apple cider vinegar

¾ cup sugar

1 tablespoon ground ginger

6 tablespoons soy sauce

3 pounds frozen uncooked shrimp

6 tablespoons cornstarch (used on reheating day)

¾ cup water (used on reheating day)

Freezing Day

1. In a large skillet over medium heat, cook onion and garlic in olive oil until crisp-tender. Add green pepper and cook 1–2 minutes longer. Drain pineapple, reserving juice. Set pineapple aside. Add pineapple juice to the skillet, along with broth, ketchup, vinegar, sugar, ginger, and soy sauce. Bring to a boil, reduce heat, and simmer for 5–7 minutes; then add pineapple tidbits. Cool in an ice-water bath or in refrigerator.

2. Place frozen shrimp in a ziplock bag. Pour cooled sauce into a large ziplock bag and attach the shrimp; label, seal, and freeze. Reserve cornstarch in pantry.

Reheating Instructions

Thaw sauce overnight in the refrigerator; keep shrimp frozen. Pour sauce into a large saucepan and bring to a simmer over medium heat. Add shrimp and cook for 4–7 minutes, until shrimp turn pink and are thoroughly cooked. Meanwhile, dissolve cornstarch in water and add to the skillet. Simmer for 1–2 minutes, until sauce thickens. Serve over hot cooked rice.

Thai Fish with Rice

To serve without freezing, thaw fish fillets and combine as directed without chilling the sauce or rice. Bake, covered, at 375°F for 15–25 minutes or until the fish flakes when tested with a fork.

YIELDS 4 SERVINGS

½ cup coconut milk
¼ cup peanut butter
1 teaspoon minced fresh gingerroot
⅛ teaspoon cayenne pepper
⅛ teaspoon white pepper
1 tablespoon olive oil
½ cup minced onion
3 cloves garlic, minced
1 cup rice
2 cups chicken broth
2 tablespoons water
4 frozen fish fillets
¼ cup chopped peanuts

YIELDS 12 SERVINGS

1½ cups coconut milk
¾ cup peanut butter
1 tablespoon minced fresh gingerroot
⅜ teaspoon cayenne pepper
⅜ teaspoon white pepper
3 tablespoons olive oil
1½ cups minced onion
9 cloves garlic, minced
3 cups rice
6 cups chicken broth
6 tablespoons water
12 frozen fish fillets
¾ cup chopped peanuts

Freezing Day

1. In a small bowl, combine coconut milk, peanut butter, gingerroot, cayenne, and white pepper and mix until blended. In a heavy skillet over medium heat, heat olive oil and sauté onion and garlic until crisp-tender. Add coconut milk mixture and cook and stir for 2–3 minutes to blend. Chill sauce in an ice-water bath or the refrigerator.

2. In a heavy saucepan, combine rice and chicken broth. Bring to a boil, then reduce heat, cover, and simmer for 15 minutes, until almost tender. Cool rice in the refrigerator until cold. Place rice in a 9" × 9" baking dish and sprinkle with 2 tablespoons water. Top rice with frozen fish fillets (do not thaw) and pour coconut sauce over fish. Sprinkle with peanuts, wrap casserole, seal, label, and freeze.

Reheating Instructions

Thaw overnight in the refrigerator. Bake in a preheated 375°F oven for 20–35 minutes or until the fish flakes easily when tested with a fork.

Tuna Pot Pie

To serve this pie without freezing, do not cool the sauce or refreeze the pastry. Bake and assemble the pastry as directed.

YIELDS 6–8 SERVINGS

1 sheet puff pastry, thawed
1 onion, chopped
3 cloves garlic, minced
2 tablespoons olive oil
2 tablespoons butter
4 tablespoons flour
½ teaspoon salt
⅛ teaspoon pepper
2 cups half-and-half
1 cup shredded Havarti cheese
1 cup frozen peas
2 cups frozen hash brown potatoes
1 cup frozen broccoli
1 (12-ounce) can chunk tuna, drained
1 egg (optional)
1 tablespoon water (optional)

YIELDS 18–24 SERVINGS

3 sheets puff pastry, thawed
3 onions, chopped
9 cloves garlic, minced
6 tablespoons olive oil
6 tablespoons butter
12 tablespoons flour
1½ teaspoons salt
⅜ teaspoon pepper
6 cups half-and-half
3 cups shredded Havarti cheese
3 cups frozen peas
6 cups frozen hash brown potatoes
3 cups frozen broccoli
3 (12-ounce) cans chunk tuna, drained
3 eggs (optional)
3 tablespoons water (optional)

Freezing Day

1. Place thawed puff pastry on a lightly floured surface and cut a 10" round from the center. Cut out small decorative shapes from the center of the pastry. Wrap pastry in freezer wrap and freeze.

2. In a heavy saucepan over medium heat, sauté onion and garlic in olive oil and butter until crisp-tender. Sprinkle flour, salt, and pepper over onion mixture; cook and stir until bubbly. Stir in half-and-half; cook and stir until slightly thickened. Remove from heat and stir in cheese until melted. Cool sauce in an ice-water bath or the refrigerator.

3. When sauce is cold, stir in frozen vegetables and drained tuna. Place in a 2-quart baking dish, and then wrap dish in freezer wrap, attach puff-pastry top, label, seal, and freeze.

Reheating Instructions

Thaw dish overnight in the refrigerator; keep puff pastry frozen. Bake in a preheated 375°F oven for 20 minutes or until the filling is hot. Top with frozen puff-pastry round. If desired, brush puff pastry with a mixture of 1 beaten egg and 1 tablespoon water. Bake 20–25 minutes longer or until pastry is puffed and golden brown and the filling bubbles.

Shrimp Quiche

To serve without freezing, bake the quiche as directed; let stand for 10 minutes. If you like, substitute bay scallops or chunks of fresh crabmeat for the shrimp.

YIELDS 6 SERVINGS

1 Easy Pie Crust (see recipe in Chapter 12)
2 tablespoons olive oil
1 tablespoon butter
1 pound uncooked medium shrimp
1 onion, chopped
2 tablespoons flour
⅛ teaspoon white pepper
¾ cup evaporated milk
3 eggs
½ cup sour cream
1 cup shredded Havarti cheese
1 cup frozen peas
¼ cup grated Parmesan cheese

YIELDS 18 SERVINGS

3 Easy Pie Crusts (see recipe in Chapter 12)
6 tablespoons olive oil
3 tablespoons butter
3 pounds uncooked medium shrimp
3 onions, chopped
6 tablespoons flour
⅜ teaspoon white pepper
2¼ cups evaporated milk
9 eggs
1½ cups sour cream
3 cups shredded Havarti cheese
3 cups frozen peas
¾ cup grated Parmesan cheese

Freezing Day

1. Preheat the oven to 375°F. Bake empty pie crust for 5 minutes until set. In a heavy skillet over medium heat, heat olive oil and butter and add shrimp; cook and stir for 2–3 minutes until shrimp just turn pink. Remove shrimp from pan and set aside in the refrigerator.

2. Add onion to the pan; cook and stir until crisp-tender. Sprinkle flour and pepper into the pan and cook and stir until bubbly, about 3–4 minutes. Add milk to the pan and bring to a simmer, stirring constantly, until sauce is thickened. Cool sauce in the refrigerator.

3. In a large bowl, beat eggs with sour cream. Add cooled sauce along with Havarti cheese. Place cooled, cooked shrimp and frozen peas in the pie crust and pour egg mixture over. Sprinkle with Parmesan cheese and bake for 20–30 minutes, until pie is puffed, set, and golden brown. Cool in the refrigerator, then flash freeze; wrap, label, and freeze. Or, slice quiche into serving pieces before freezing and flash freeze individually.

Reheating Instructions

Thaw quiche overnight in the refrigerator. Bake at 350°F for 20–25 minutes, until heated through. To reheat individually, microwave each frozen slice on medium for 2–4 minutes, then 1 minute on high, until hot.

Tex-Mex Shrimp

To serve without freezing, thaw shrimp as directed and add to the simmering sauce along with the frozen corn. Simmer for 3–5 minutes or until the shrimp are cooked and tender.

YIELDS 6 SERVINGS

2 pounds frozen uncooked shrimp
2 tablespoons olive oil
1 onion, chopped
5 cloves garlic, minced
1 red bell pepper, chopped
1 jalapeño pepper, minced
2 (14-ounce) cans diced tomatoes
1 (6-ounce) can tomato paste
1 cup fish broth
2 teaspoons sugar
⅛ teaspoon cayenne pepper
¼ teaspoon hot sauce
1 cup frozen corn

YIELDS 18 SERVINGS

6 pounds frozen uncooked shrimp
6 tablespoons olive oil
3 onions, chopped
15 cloves garlic, minced
3 red bell peppers, chopped
3 jalapeño peppers, minced
6 (14-ounce) cans diced tomatoes
3 (6-ounce) cans tomato paste
3 cups fish broth
6 teaspoons sugar
⅜ teaspoon cayenne pepper
¾ teaspoon hot sauce
3 cups frozen corn

Freezing Day

1. Place shrimp in a ziplock bag and freeze. In a heavy skillet over medium heat, heat olive oil; sauté onion and garlic until almost crisp-tender. Add bell pepper and jalapeño pepper; cook and stir 2 minutes longer. Add undrained tomatoes, tomato paste, broth, sugar, cayenne pepper, and hot sauce; simmer 10 minutes to blend flavors.

2. Cool sauce in an ice-water bath or the refrigerator. When sauce is cold, add frozen corn, mix well, and pour into a ziplock bag. Attach the bag of frozen shrimp, seal, label, and freeze.

Reheating Instructions

Place frozen sauce in a heavy saucepan and cook over low heat until thawed. Increase heat to medium and bring the sauce to a simmer. Meanwhile, place frozen shrimp in a colander or strainer and place under cold running water for 3–4 minutes, until thawed. Add thawed and drained shrimp to simmering sauce and cook for 3–4 minutes or until shrimp are curled, pink, and firm, stirring once during cooking.

Fish and Shrimp in Parchment

To serve without freezing, simply bake the assembled packages in a preheated 450°F oven for 15–22 minutes or until the fish is thoroughly cooked.

YIELDS 4 SERVINGS

4 (6-ounce) frozen fish fillets
2 cups medium frozen uncooked shrimp
1 lemon, thinly sliced
2 cloves garlic, minced
2 cups frozen sugar snap peas
2 tablespoons extra-virgin olive oil
½ teaspoon salt
⅛ teaspoon white pepper
½ teaspoon dried marjoram leaves

YIELDS 12 SERVINGS

12 (6-ounce) frozen fish fillets
6 cups medium frozen uncooked shrimp
3 lemons, thinly sliced
6 cloves garlic, minced
6 cups frozen sugar snap peas
6 tablespoons extra-virgin olive oil
1½ teaspoons salt
⅜ teaspoon white pepper
1½ teaspoons dried marjoram leaves

Freezing Day

1. Cut 4 (or 12) 14" × 10" pieces of heavy-duty foil or parchment paper. Place 1 frozen fish fillet in the center of each piece and top with frozen shrimp. Remove seeds from lemon slices and divide slices among packets. Sprinkle with garlic and top with sugar snap peas. Drizzle each with olive oil and sprinkle with salt, pepper, and marjoram.

2. Fold sides of foil or parchment around fish and vegetables and seal with a double fold. Wrap again in freezer paper or heavy-duty foil, label, seal, and freeze.

Reheating Instructions

Preheat the oven to 450°F. Remove the top layer of paper or foil from packages and place packages on a cookie sheet. Bake packages for 18–25 minutes, until shrimp are pink and curled, fish flakes easily when tested with fork, and snap peas are hot. Open carefully at the table.

Shrimp Pesto Linguine

To serve without freezing, thaw the pesto, shrimp, and green beans. Cook shrimp in oil with sautéed vegetables. Bring milk to a boil and add pesto, cooked pasta, and the remaining ingredients; toss and serve with cheese.

YIELDS 6 SERVINGS

4 squares frozen Basil and Pine Nut Pesto (see recipe in Chapter 4)

2 pounds frozen uncooked medium shrimp

2 tablespoons oil

1 onion, chopped

2 cloves garlic, minced

2 cups frozen green beans

½ cup grated Parmesan cheese

1 (15-ounce) can evaporated milk (used on reheating day)

½ pound linguine pasta (used on reheating day)

YIELDS 18 SERVINGS

12 squares frozen Basil and Pine Nut Pesto (see recipe in Chapter 4)

6 pounds frozen uncooked medium shrimp

6 tablespoons oil

3 onions, chopped

6 cloves garlic, minced

6 cups frozen green beans

1½ cups grated Parmesan cheese

3 (15-ounce) cans evaporated milk (used on reheating day)

1½ pounds linguine pasta (used on reheating day)

Freezing Day

1. Place frozen pesto in a ziplock bag and place in the freezer. Place shrimp in another ziplock bag and freeze.

2. In a heavy skillet over medium heat, heat oil and add onion and garlic. Cook and stir until crisp-tender; cool in the refrigerator or an ice-water bath. When cold, mix with frozen green beans and place in another ziplock bag. Place cheese in another bag; place all the bags in a large ziplock bag; label, seal, and freeze. Reserve evaporated milk and pasta in the pantry.

Reheating Instructions

1. Thaw packages overnight in the refrigerator. Place onion mixture in a heavy saucepan and heat over medium heat until sizzling. Add shrimp; cook and stir until shrimp are pink and beans are hot. Cook pasta according to package directions.

2. Meanwhile, in another saucepan, bring milk to a boil. Add pesto to the boiling milk and stir in the shrimp mixture and pasta. Toss together over medium heat for 3–4 minutes; then serve topped with Parmesan cheese.

Crab Quiche

This is wonderful to serve at a brunch. Make a variation of this Crab Quiche for your guests who cannot eat seafood. Fill the second one with browned ground sausage and Cheddar cheese, instead of crab and Swiss cheese.

YIELDS 4–6 SERVINGS

1 (9") unbaked pastry shell
1 tablespoon butter, softened
4 eggs
2 cups heavy cream
½ teaspoon salt
1 teaspoon Old Bay Seasoning
1 cup Swiss cheese, shredded
¼ cup chopped green onion
1 cup crabmeat

Freezing Day

1. Preheat the oven to 375°F. Spread the pastry shell with the softened butter and put in the refrigerator.

2. In a medium bowl, whisk eggs, cream, salt, and Old Bay. Stir in cheese and onion.

3. Remove shell from the refrigerator and line the bottom with crabmeat. Pour egg mixture over the top.

4. Bake the quiche for 20 minutes. It should be a bit under-cooked. Cool and wrap tightly with plastic wrap and freeze.

Reheating Instructions

Bake the frozen quiche at 350°F for 50 minutes, or until it is fully heated.

The Perfect Crust

A perfect quiche crust takes work, but here's how to achieve just that. Ensure the shell is well chilled. Pierce all over with a fork. Line the shell with foil and fill with dried beans or uncooked rice to hold it flat. Bake for 12 minutes at 400°F. Remove from the oven, remove the beans or rice, brush the inside of the shell with beaten egg whites, fill with your quiche mixture, and bake.

Salmon Patties with Dill Sauce

You can vary this recipe by adding 2 table-spoons of capers and a tablespoon of Dijon mustard. Use more or less according to taste. Mix the capers and mustard directly into the salmon patties. Try the salmon with Dill Sauce (see recipe in Chapter 4).

YIELDS 4 SERVINGS

1 (14.75-ounce) can pink salmon, flaked
½ cup bread crumbs
1 egg
1 small onion, chopped
1 teaspoon dill
1 tablespoon olive oil (used on reheating day)
1 batch Dill Sauce (see recipe in Chapter 4)
   (used on reheating day)

Freezing Day

In a medium bowl, mix salmon, bread crumbs, egg, onion, and dill. Form into patties and flash freeze. Transfer to a freezer bag.

Reheating Instructions

Defrost patties in the refrigerator overnight. In a medium skillet over medium heat, heat the oil and cook the patties until they are well browned, about 5 minutes on each side. Top patties with Dill Sauce and serve.

Chapter 10

Vegetarian

Easy Stuffed-Crust Pizza

This is a fast and easy way to make a delicious pizza crust stuffed with mozzarella cheese. These are great to have on hand and allow you to get a pizza into the oven in no time!

YIELDS 1 PIZZA
1 package refrigerator pizza dough
6 or 7 pieces mozzarella string cheese

Freezing Day

1. Preheat the oven to 400°F. Take out your pizza pan. You will be forming the crust in the shape of your pizza pan so on reheating day it will be a perfect fit. Make sure your pan will fit in the freezer because you will be using it to flash freeze the crust. Lightly grease the pan.

2. Open the pizza dough and, with your fingers, press it outward to fit the pan. Continue to press it so it overhangs the pan by 2".

3. Lay the string cheese along the inside edge of the pan.

4. Bring the overhanging dough over the string cheese and use your fingers to seal the edges into the dough. Wet your fingers if needed to create a seal.

5. Partially bake the crust for 6 minutes or until it is very lightly browned. Remove from the oven and cool.

6. Put in the freezer to flash freeze. Once frozen, wrap well with plastic wrap and return to the freezer.

Reheating Instructions

Add desired toppings and cook at 400°F for 15–30 minutes, or until the crust is golden brown. Cooking time depends on the thickness of the dough and the size of the pizza.

Frozen Pizzas

You can also load your pizza crust with toppings before you put it in the freezer. Simply add desired toppings after browning your pizza crust and then put the pizza in the freezer to flash freeze. This pizza can go directly from the freezer to the oven. Cook at 375°F for 15–25 minutes, depending on the thickness of your crust.

Spinach and Cheddar Quiche

Would you like a tailor-made quiche recipe designed just for you? Simply substitute the spinach and cheese for any ingredients you love. Make a feta and tomato quiche; or a mushroom, onion, and provolone quiche.

YIELDS 4 SERVINGS

1 (9") unbaked pastry shell
1 tablespoon butter, softened
4 eggs
2 cups heavy cream
½ teaspoon salt
1 cup Cheddar cheese, shredded
½ cup chopped spinach

Freezing Day

1. Preheat the oven to 375°F. Spread the pastry shell with the softened butter and put it in the refrigerator.
2. In a large bowl, whisk eggs, cream, and salt. Stir in cheese.
3. Remove the shell from the refrigerator and line the bottom with spinach. Pour the egg mixture over the top.
4. Bake the quiche for 20 minutes. It should be a bit under-cooked. Cool, wrap tightly with plastic wrap, and freeze.

Reheating Instructions

Bake frozen quiche at 350°F for 50 minutes, or until it is fully heated.

Portion Control

This recipe calls for the quiche to be slightly undercooked before freezing. To fully cook it and cut into single-serving pieces before freezing, cook for 30 minutes or until a knife inserted into the center comes out clean. Individually wrap each slice of quiche in plastic wrap for the freezer. To cook a frozen piece of quiche, unwrap and heat in the microwave.

Bean Burritos

Set up a burrito-making station in your kitchen and get the whole family to help! The kids will have a great time building and freezing the burritos with you.

2 (16-ounce) cans refried beans
2 (10-ounce) cans enchilada sauce
20 flour tortillas
2 cups shredded Cheddar cheese

Freezing Day

1. In a large bowl, combine 2 cans of refried beans with the 2 cans of enchilada sauce. Mix well.

2. Spread 3 tablespoons of bean mixture down the center of each tortilla, and sprinkle Cheddar cheese on top. Fold the burritos by first folding the bottom of the tortilla about ⅓ of the way up. Next fold the right side of the tortilla over the filling, then fold the left side of the tortilla so it overlaps the right side. Flash freeze on a baking sheet, folded-side down. Once frozen, transfer the burritos to a freezer bag.

Reheating Instructions

Microwave frozen burrito for 1 minute, turn over, and microwave an additional minute.

Easy Baked Ziti

This casserole uses only 4 ingredients on freezer day, so it is quick and easy to put together. If you do not want to use a prepared baking dish, simplify the process even more by freezing the casserole in a throwaway aluminum pan.

YIELDS 6–8 SERVINGS

1 (16-ounce) box ziti
1 (15-ounce) container ricotta cheese
1 egg
1 (24-ounce) jar spaghetti sauce
¼ cup freshly grated Parmesan cheese (used on reheating day)

Freezing Day

1. Cook the ziti according to package directions, but only boil the noodles 8 minutes.
2. In a large mixing bowl, combine ricotta cheese with egg.
3. Prepare a casserole dish for freezing according to the Casserole Method found in Chapter 1.
4. Add the cooked ziti and spaghetti sauce to the ricotta cheese mixture. Mix well.
5. Put the ziti mixture in the baking pan and flash freeze.

Reheating Instructions

1. Defrost the casserole in the refrigerator for 24 hours following the Casserole Method, cover, and bake 30–45 minutes at 350°F.
2. To bake the casserole frozen, add 45 minutes–1 hour to the defrosted cooking time.
3. Uncover the casserole and sprinkle with fresh Parmesan cheese during the last 30 minutes of baking.

Pasta Tips

When you buy ziti, look for ziti with ridges, rather than a smooth pasta. The ridges help hold the sauce to the pasta. When cooking the pasta, use a large pot with lots of water and salt—the water keeps the pasta from sticking together—and never rinse your pasta after draining (unless making pasta salad). The rinsing washes away the delicious pasta flavor.

Lasagna Florentine

Lasagna Florentine is similar to a traditional lasagna, but spinach is substituted for the beef. This vegetarian dish is a nice alternative for your guests who do not enjoy meat.

YIELDS 6–8 SERVINGS

1 (16-ounce) box lasagna noodles
1 onion, diced
1 pound fresh mushrooms, coarsely chopped
1 teaspoon basil
2 tablespoons olive oil
2 cloves garlic, minced
2 (10-ounce) boxes frozen spinach, defrosted and squeezed of excess water
2 (6-ounce) cans tomato paste
2 cups hot water
1 teaspoon Italian seasoning
Salt and pepper to taste
3 cups ricotta cheese
1½ cups Parmesan cheese, freshly grated, divided
2 eggs, beaten
4 cups shredded mozzarella

Freezing Day

1. Cook lasagna noodles according to the directions on the package.

2. In a medium skillet over medium heat, sauté onions, mushrooms, and basil in olive oil for 5–8 minutes until the onions have softened. Add garlic and spinach and sauté 2–3 minutes more. Remove from heat.

3. In a medium saucepan, mix the tomato paste with 2 cups of hot water, Italian seasoning, salt, and pepper. Cook over medium heat for 15 minutes.

4. In a mixing bowl, combine the ricotta cheese, ½ cup Parmesan cheese, and eggs. Add the spinach mixture to the cheese mixture and mix well.

5. In a small mixing bowl combine the remaining Parmesan cheese with the mozzarella cheese.

6. In a casserole dish prepared for the freezer according to the Casserole Method in Chapter 1, put a thin layer of tomato sauce. Add alternating layers of noodles, then spinach mixture, then mozzarella and Parmesan cheese, then tomato sauce. Top with a mozzarella and Parmesan layer.

7. Wrap tightly following the Casserole Method of freezing, and flash freeze the casserole.

Reheating Instructions

Cover frozen lasagna with foil, and bake it at 375°F for 1 hour 30 minutes–1 hour 45 minutes, or until it is fully heated. Remove foil during the last 15 minutes of baking.

Macaroni and Cheese Bake

This baked casserole is one you will make over and over again. Kids love it, and it is a good choice for potluck suppers.

YIELDS 6–8 SERVINGS

8 ounces elbow macaroni
4 tablespoons butter
3 tablespoons flour
2 cups heavy cream
½ teaspoon salt
½ teaspoon pepper
1½ teaspoons yellow or Dijon mustard
2 cups Cheddar cheese, shredded
½–1 cup milk, as needed (used on reheating day)
2 cups crushed cornflakes (used on reheating day)
1 stick butter, melted (used on reheating day)

Freezing Day

1. Undercook elbow macaroni by 5 minutes and drain.
2. In a large saucepan, melt the butter over medium heat. Add flour and mix well.
3. Slowly add the cream to the butter mixture, stirring as you pour.
4. Bring to just under a boil, stirring constantly until the sauce thickens, approximately 5 minutes.
5. Add salt, pepper, mustard, and cheese. Continue to stir until all of the cheese is melted.
6. Gently stir in macaroni and remove from heat to cool. Freeze in a freezer bag.

Reheating Instructions

1. Defrost macaroni and cheese in the refrigerator overnight.
2. Grease a large baking dish and put the macaroni and cheese in it. Stir the milk into the macaroni and cheese to give it a creamy (not soupy) texture.
3. Top the macaroni and cheese with crushed cornflakes and pour the melted butter over the cornflakes.
4. Bake at 375°F for 30–40 minutes.

Freezing Cheese

It is often less expensive to buy a large block of cheese than it is to buy grated cheese. Take advantage of the lower price, and do the grating yourself with a food processor. Divide the grated cheese into 1-cup portions and freeze in a freezer bag.

Cheese Enchilada Casserole

This casserole is a breeze to put together and freeze. Serve it with chips and fresh guacamole or Pico de Gallo (see recipe in Chapter 4).

YIELDS 4–6 SERVINGS

1 cup ricotta cheese
2 cups shredded Cheddar cheese, divided
1 (10-ounce) can Ro-Tel diced tomatoes
¼ teaspoon salt
2 cloves garlic, minced
1 (10-ounce) can enchilada sauce
8 corn tortillas

Freezing Day

1. In a medium mixing bowl, combine ricotta cheese, 1 cup Cheddar cheese, tomatoes (drained), salt, and garlic.

2. Use either a disposable aluminum casserole dish, or prepare a casserole dish for freezing according to the Casserole Method in Chapter 1.

3. Pour a small amount of enchilada sauce on the bottom of the casserole dish.

4. Fill each tortilla with the cheese mixture and put in the casserole dish, seam-side down.

5. Pour remaining enchilada sauce over tortillas, and top with remaining 1 cup cheese.

Reheating Instructions

Bake defrosted casserole, covered, at 375°F for 30 minutes, or frozen casserole, covered, at 375°F for 1 hour 10 minutes–1 hour 20 minutes or until casserole is hot or cheese is melted.

Eggplant Parmigiana

This is a delicious vegetarian casserole that easily goes from the freezer to the oven. You may opt to add the eggplant to the casserole without frying it first.

YIELDS 6–8 SERVINGS

2 medium eggplants

1½ cups Italian bread crumbs

3 eggs

2 tablespoons milk

2 tablespoons olive oil

1 batch Traditional Marinara Sauce (see recipe in Chapter 4)

2 cups mozzarella cheese

½ cup freshly grated Parmesan cheese

Freezing Day

1. Cut the eggplant into ⅓"-thick slices.

2. Put the bread crumbs in a shallow pan.

3. Beat the eggs together in a separate shallow pan. Add the milk to the eggs.

4. Dip each piece of eggplant in the egg mixture and then in the bread crumb mixture, coating all the sides.

5. In a medium skillet over medium heat, add the olive oil and lightly brown both sides of the eggplant in the hot olive oil approximately 2 minutes per side.

6. Prepare a casserole dish for freezing according to the Casserole Method in Chapter 1. Pour a small amount of Traditional Marinara Sauce into the dish, enough to cover the bottom of the casserole. Place alternate layers of eggplant, sauce, and a combination of cheeses, ending with cheese on the top.

7. Wrap tightly according to the Casserole Method and freeze.

Reheating Instructions

Put the frozen casserole into the oven and cook at 350°F, covered, for 1 hour 30 minutes–1 hour 45 minutes, or until casserole is hot.

How to Cook a Frozen Casserole

You can defrost casseroles first, or they can go straight from the freezer to the oven. To go the latter route, add 45 minutes–1 hour to the defrosted cooking time. Cover your casserole with aluminum foil while cooking to keep it from drying out.

Spaghetti and Not-Meatballs

Instead of marinara sauce, try the meatballs with Alfredo Sauce (see recipe in Chapter 4) served over linguine with crusty French bread.

YIELDS 4 SERVINGS

1 batch Traditional Marinara Sauce (see recipe in Chapter 4)

¾ cup pine nuts, finely processed in a food processor

4 eggs

⅔ packet onion soup mix

2 cups grated Asiago cheese

1 cup seasoned bread crumbs

1 teaspoon Italian seasoning

2 cloves garlic, minced

Freezing Day

1. Prepare Traditional Marinara Sauce.

2. Preheat the oven to 375°F. In a medium bowl, mix the pine nuts, eggs, onion soup mix, cheese, bread crumbs, Italian seasoning, and garlic. Form into balls. Place balls on a lightly greased baking sheet and bake for 30 minutes or until balls are browned. Turn balls every 10 minutes.

3. Put balls in the marinara sauce and simmer on low for 45 minutes–1 hour.

4. Cool and freeze in Tupperware or a freezer bag.

Reheating Instructions

Defrost in the refrigerator overnight and heat in a large saucepan over medium-low heat until it reaches the desired temperature. Serve over spaghetti.

Waste Not, Want Not

Make a habit of checking your refrigerator for perishables needing to be cooked. Think of how much money is wasted every year on food that has gone bad while sitting in the refrigerator. You may not be ready to eat a particular food, but surely you can find a freezer recipe that allows you to preserve it for another time.

Zucchini Casserole

Zucchini is a type of summer squash and a popular vegetable to grow at home. You can freeze them in ½" slices, but the vegetable must be blanched in water and quickly cooled first.

YIELDS 6–8 SERVINGS

3 large zucchini
½ cup mushrooms, chopped
¼ cup onions, chopped
½ cup butter, melted
¼ teaspoon garlic powder
1¼ cups saltine crackers, crushed
1 egg, beaten
¼ teaspoon pepper
½ teaspoon salt
1 cup Cheddar cheese, shredded (used on reheating day)

Freezing Day

1. Preheat the oven to 350°F. Grate zucchini and put in a large mixing bowl. Add the remaining ingredients (except cheese) and mix well.
2. Put the mixture in an aluminum casserole dish and partially cook for 20 minutes. Cool and freeze.

Reheating Instructions

Defrost Zucchini Casserole in the refrigerator overnight. Cook at 350°F for 15 minutes. Remove from the oven and sprinkle cheese over the top. Return to the oven for 15 minutes.

Why Blanch Vegetables?

Most raw vegetables need to be blanched before freezing. Vegetables have enzymes that help them mature and ripen, and blanching stops the action of the enzymes. If you do not blanch the vegetables, they will continue to ripen while frozen, causing a change of taste, color, and texture.

Potato Patties

This recipe is a great way to use up your leftover mashed potatoes. These patties can also be made from instant potatoes or Mashed Potatoes (see recipe in Chapter 6).

YIELDS 2–4 SERVINGS

1 cup mashed potatoes
½ teaspoon minced onion
2–4 tablespoons flour
2 teaspoons butter

Freezing Day

1. In a medium mixing bowl, mix mashed potatoes with minced onion. Form mashed potatoes into 4–6 patties. Dip patties in flour.
2. Heat butter in a medium skillet over medium-high heat. Fry potato patties in butter for 3–5 minutes per side, turning once they become browned.
3. Cool patties and flash freeze. Transfer to a freezer bag.

Reheating Instructions

Put a frozen patty in the microwave and heat for 1–2 minutes, or fry a frozen patty in a skillet with butter on medium-high until heated through, about 3–5 minutes.

Spinach-Stuffed Shells

If you prefer to freeze this meal as a casserole, simply prepare a casserole dish for freezing and build the casserole according to the reheating instructions. Cover the casserole tightly and flash freeze.

16 large pasta shells
1 (10-ounce) package frozen spinach, thawed
1 cup ricotta cheese
½ cup Parmesan cheese
1 (28-ounce) jar spaghetti sauce (used on reheating day)
1 cup shredded mozzarella cheese (used on reheating day)

Freezing Day

1. Cook shells for half the recommended cooking time.
2. Squeeze excess water out of the spinach. In a large bowl, mix together the spinach, ricotta cheese, and Parmesan cheese.
3. Stuff the shells with the spinach mixture and flash freeze. Transfer to a freezer bag.

Reheating Instructions

1. Defrost shells completely in the refrigerator for 24 hours. Pour a small amount of spaghetti sauce on the bottom of a casserole dish.
2. Arrange shells in the pan and cover with the remaining spaghetti sauce. Top with mozzarella cheese.
3. Cook for 30 minutes at 350°F.

How to Freeze Fresh Spinach

Only select young and tender spinach to freeze. Wash the spinach and cut off the stems. Blanch the spinach by putting it into boiling water for 2 minutes, then into ice-cold water for 2 minutes. Drain and freeze in a freezer bag. You may flash freeze the leaves before putting them in the freezer bag if desired.

Broccoli Strata

Strata is a casserole made from eggs and bread, and it can also incorporate hash browns and, if desired, meat. Strata is also known as a breakfast casserole and is a great option to serve for brunch.

YIELDS 8-10 SERVINGS

1 loaf Italian bread
1-2 cups grated Cheddar cheese, to taste
2 cups fresh broccoli, cooked
1 stick butter
8 eggs
2 cups milk
2 tablespoons minced onion
½ teaspoon salt
1 teaspoon yellow mustard
Dash red pepper
Dash paprika

Freezing Day

1. Prepare a 9" × 13" casserole dish for freezing according to the Casserole Method in Chapter 1.

2. Slice Italian bread into 1" slices. Line the bottom of the dish with a layer of bread.

3. Layer cheese, then broccoli on top of bread.

4. In a medium saucepan, melt butter. Remove from heat.

5. In a mixing bowl, whisk together the eggs and milk.

6. Add egg mixture and remaining ingredients to the butter and mix well.

7. Slowly pour egg mixture over the top of the casserole. Wrap well according to the Casserole Method in Chapter 1, and freeze.

Reheating Instructions

Following the Casserole Method, defrost casserole in the refrigerator overnight and bake for 45 minutes–1 hour at 350°F, or until the eggs are cooked and a knife inserted into the middle of the dish comes out clean.

Cheese and Rice Enchiladas with Salsa Verde

Bursting with vegetables and topped with fresh Salsa Verde (see recipe in Chapter 4), this flavorful dish is perfect for any night of the week. To serve without freezing, bake as directed.

YIELDS 4–6 SERVINGS

1 red bell pepper, chopped
1 onion, chopped
2 tablespoons olive oil
1 clove garlic, minced
1 (10-ounce) can Ro-Tel diced tomatoes
1 cup enchilada sauce, divided
2 cups rice, cooked
2 cups shredded Cheddar cheese, divided
¼ cup chopped fresh cilantro
8–10 flour tortillas
1 batch Salsa Verde (see recipe in Chapter 4)

Freezing Day

1. In a medium skillet over medium-high heat, sauté the red pepper and onion in olive oil until vegetables are tender-crisp. The vegetables should just begin to get tender but still retain a crisp texture. Add the garlic and sauté 1 minute more.

2. Add Ro-Tel tomatoes, ½ cup enchilada sauce, rice, 1 cup Cheddar cheese, and cilantro. Mix well and heat over medium heat for 5–10 minutes until cheese melts.

3. Prepare a 9" × 13" casserole dish for freezing. See instructions for the Casserole Method in Chapter 1, or use an aluminum pan. Cover the bottom of the casserole dish with the remaining enchilada sauce.

4. Fill each flour tortilla with the rice and cheese mixture. Roll it up, and place it seam-side down in the casserole dish.

5. Sprinkle the remaining cheese over each enchilada, then spoon Salsa Verde over each enchilada.

Reheating Instructions

Following the Casserole Method, defrost the casserole in the refrigerator overnight. Cover the casserole with aluminum foil and bake at 350°F for 30–35 minutes. Remove the cover during the last 10 minutes of cooking time.

Spinach Lasagna

To serve immediately, after layering ingredients in the pan, bake at 375°F for 25–30 minutes or until thoroughly heated and bubbly.

YIELDS 8 SERVINGS

1 (8-ounce) package lasagna noodles
2 tablespoons olive oil
1 tablespoon butter
1 onion, chopped
4 cloves garlic, minced
1 teaspoon dried fennel seed
1 teaspoon salt
⅛ teaspoon white pepper
1 (26-ounce) jar spaghetti sauce
1 (16-ounce) package frozen cut-leaf spinach
2 cups ricotta cheese
1 egg
1 cup shredded mozzarella cheese
1 cup shredded Monterey jack cheese
½ cup grated Parmesan cheese

YIELDS 24 SERVINGS

3 (8-ounce) packages lasagna noodles
6 tablespoons olive oil
3 tablespoons butter
3 onions, chopped
12 cloves garlic, minced
1 tablespoon dried fennel seed
1 tablespoon salt
⅜ teaspoon white pepper
3 (26-ounce) jars spaghetti sauce
3 (16-ounce) packages frozen cut-leaf spinach
6 cups ricotta cheese
3 eggs
3 cups shredded mozzarella cheese
3 cups shredded Monterey jack cheese
1½ cups grated Parmesan cheese

Freezing Day

1. Cook pasta according to package directions until almost tender. Remove from pan, rinse with cold water, and set aside on kitchen towels.

2. In a large saucepan, heat olive oil and butter over medium heat. When foamy, add onion and garlic and cook, stirring, until tender. Add fennel seed, salt, pepper, and spaghetti sauce to the pan. Bring to a boil, then reduce heat, cover the pan, and simmer for 15–20 minutes.

3. Meanwhile, drain spinach thoroughly and combine with ricotta and egg in a medium bowl. Beat well until combined. Add mozzarella and Monterey jack cheeses.

4. Line a 13" × 9" pan with freezer paper and place 1 cup of sauce in pan. Top with 3 lasagna noodles and half of the ricotta mixture. Top with half of the remaining sauce, 3 lasagna noodles, and the rest of the ricotta mixture. Finish layering with 3 remaining lasagna noodles and the remaining sauce. Sprinkle with Parmesan cheese. Cool lasagna in an ice-water bath or the refrigerator, then wrap well, label, and freeze.

Reheating Instructions

Thaw overnight in the refrigerator. Bake in a preheated 375°F oven for 30–45 minutes or until thoroughly heated and bubbly.

Pizza Fondue

To serve without freezing, add cheese to the blended sauce, toast the English muffins, and bake the breadsticks as directed. Place sauce in the fondue pot and serve with dippers.

YIELDS 6 SERVINGS

2 tablespoons olive oil

1 (12-ounce) package frozen meatless crumbles

1 onion, chopped

2 cloves garlic, chopped

1 (24-ounce) can pizza sauce

½ teaspoon dried oregano

½ cup tomato juice

1 (14-ounce) can diced tomatoes, undrained

2 cups shredded Colby-jack cheese

6 English muffins

2 (8-ounce) cans refrigerated breadsticks (used on reheating day)

YIELDS 18 SERVINGS

6 tablespoons olive oil

3 (12-ounce) packages frozen meatless crumbles

3 onions, chopped

6 cloves garlic, chopped

3 (24-ounce) cans pizza sauce

1½ teaspoons dried oregano

1½ cups tomato juice

3 (14-ounce) cans diced tomatoes, undrained

6 cups shredded Colby-jack cheese

18 English muffins

6 (8-ounce) cans refrigerated breadsticks (used on reheating day)

Freezing Day

1. In a heavy skillet, heat olive oil over medium heat and add frozen crumbles, onion, and garlic. Cook, stirring frequently, until vegetables are crisp-tender and crumbles are thawed. Add pizza sauce, oregano, tomato juice, and diced tomatoes. Bring to a boil, then simmer for 15 minutes, stirring occasionally, until blended.

2. Cool sauce in an ice-water bath or in the refrigerator. Pour into a rigid container and attach a freezer bag with the shredded cheese. Attach a freezer bag with the English muffins, label, seal, and freeze. Reserve breadsticks in the refrigerator.

Reheating Instructions

Thaw overnight in the refrigerator. Pour sauce into a medium saucepan and bring to a simmer; simmer 5–10 minutes or until thoroughly heated. Pour into the fondue pot and add shredded cheese; stir to melt cheese. Toast English muffins and cut each into quarters. Prepare breadsticks and bake according to package directions. Serve with fondue.

Chiles Rellenos Casserole

This dish could be considered a shortcut Chiles Rellenos Casserole. For a more authentic flavor, use fresh Anaheim or poblano chilies instead of canned green chilies.

YIELDS 4–6 SERVINGS

Cooking spray

2 (5.75-ounce) cans whole green chilies, drained

½ cup shredded Cheddar cheese

1 (2.25-ounce) can black olives

6 eggs

1 cup milk

2 tablespoons flour

4 tablespoons fresh cilantro, chopped

¼ teaspoon paprika

1 cup shredded Cheddar cheese (used on reheating day)

1 (8-ounce) can enchilada sauce (used on reheating day)

Freezing Day

1. Prepare a 9" × 13" casserole dish for freezing. See instructions for the Casserole Method in Chapter 1, or use an aluminum pan.

2. Spray the pan (or plastic wrap if you are flash freezing) with cooking spray.

3. Place half the chilies on the bottom of the pan. Top with the cheese and olives. Place the other half of the chilies on top.

4. In a separate bowl, whisk together the eggs, milk, flour, cilantro, and paprika. Pour over the top of the chilies.

5. Following the Casserole Method, wrap the casserole well and freeze.

Reheating Instructions

1. Following the Casserole Method, defrost casserole in the refrigerator overnight.

2. Bake at 350°F for 25 minutes. Remove from the oven.

3. Add 1 cup shredded Cheddar cheese to the top of the casserole, and pour the enchilada sauce over the cheese. Return to the oven for 15 minutes.

Roasting Fresh Poblano Peppers for Chiles Rellenos

You may roast them over an open gas flame, in an earthenware pan, or under a broiler. Roast the peppers until the skins are evenly charred. Place freshly roasted peppers in a plastic bag to "sweat" for 15 minutes to make them easier to peel. Peel off charred skin under running water.

Wild Rice Quiche

Wild rice adds a wonderful nutty flavor and a great chewy texture to this classic quiche. To serve immediately, let stand for 10 minutes after baking, then cut into wedges.

YIELDS 6 SERVINGS

1 Easy Pie Crust (see recipe in Chapter 12)

1 cup cooked wild rice

2 tablespoons minced pimientos

1 onion, chopped

3 cloves garlic, minced

1 tablespoon olive oil

3 eggs

1 cup sour cream

1 tablespoon Dijon mustard

⅛ teaspoon white pepper

1 cup shredded Havarti cheese

1 cup shredded Monterey jack cheese

¼ cup grated Parmesan cheese

YIELDS 18 SERVINGS

3 Easy Pie Crusts (see recipe in Chapter 12)

3 cups cooked wild rice

6 tablespoons minced pimientos

3 onions, chopped

9 cloves garlic, minced

3 tablespoons olive oil

9 eggs

3 cups sour cream

3 tablespoons Dijon mustard

⅜ teaspoon white pepper

3 cups shredded Havarti cheese

3 cups shredded Monterey jack cheese

¾ cup grated Parmesan cheese

Freezing Day

1. Preheat the oven to 400°F. Bake unfilled pie shell for 8–10 minutes, until light golden brown. Set aside on a wire rack to cool.

2. Combine wild rice and pimientos in a medium bowl. In a heavy saucepan over medium heat, cook onion and garlic in olive oil until tender, stirring frequently. Add to the wild rice mixture and set aside. In another bowl, combine eggs, sour cream, mustard, and pepper and beat well to blend. Add to the wild rice mixture and stir gently to combine.

3. Combine Havarti and Monterey jack cheeses in a small bowl. Sprinkle 1 cup mixed cheeses in the bottom of the cooled pie shell. Pour wild rice mixture over cheese and sprinkle remaining cheese on top. Sprinkle Parmesan cheese over all. Bake for 30–35 minutes or until the filling is set and golden brown.

4. Cool in the refrigerator, then flash freeze; wrap, label, and freeze. Or, slice quiche into serving pieces before freezing and flash freeze individually.

Reheating Instructions

Thaw quiche overnight in the refrigerator. Bake at 350°F for 20–25 minutes or until heated through. To reheat individually, microwave each slice on medium for 2–4 minutes, then 1 minute on high, or until hot.

Taco Salad

To serve without freezing, add cheese to vegetable mixture and let melt, then serve as directed.

YIELDS 6 SERVINGS

2 tablespoons olive oil

2 onions, chopped

1 green pepper, chopped

1 teaspoon cumin

1 tablespoon chili powder

½ teaspoon Tabasco sauce

1 (14-ounce) can diced tomatoes, undrained

2 (14-ounce) cans kidney beans, rinsed and drained

1 cup diced Cheddar cheese

2 cups corn chips (used on reheating day)

1 (10-ounce) jar salsa (used on reheating day)

1 (10-ounce) bag mixed salad greens (used on reheating day)

YIELDS 18 SERVINGS

6 tablespoons olive oil

6 onions, chopped

3 green peppers, chopped

1 tablespoon cumin

3 tablespoons chili powder

1½ teaspoons Tabasco sauce

3 (14-ounce) cans diced tomatoes, undrained

6 (14-ounce) cans kidney beans, rinsed and drained

3 cups diced Cheddar cheese

6 cups corn chips (used on reheating day)

3 (10-ounce) jars salsa (used on reheating day)

3 (10-ounce) bags mixed salad greens (used on reheating day)

Freezing Day

1. In a heavy skillet over medium heat, heat olive oil and add onions. Cook and stir for 4–5 minutes, until crisp-tender. Add green pepper; cook 2 minutes longer. Add seasonings, tomatoes, and kidney beans; stir. Simmer mixture, stirring occasionally, for 10 minutes. Remove from heat and chill in an ice-water bath or the refrigerator.

2. Pour mixture into a heavy-duty freezer bag and attach a small bag with the Cheddar cheese. Label, seal, and freeze. Reserve chips and salsa in the pantry and greens in the refrigerator (or purchase them the day before serving this salad).

Reheating Instructions

Thaw overnight in the refrigerator. Pour the vegetable mixture into a heavy skillet; heat over medium heat, stirring frequently, until the mixture simmers, about 8–10 minutes. Add cheese, remove from heat, cover, and let stand until cheese is melted. Place corn chips and greens on serving plates and top with the vegetable mixture. Garnish with salsa and serve.

Black Bean Lasagna

To serve without freezing, bake, covered, in a preheated 350°F oven for 50–55 minutes or until noodles are softened. Uncover and bake 10–15 minutes longer.

YIELDS 8 SERVINGS

1 onion, chopped

2 cloves garlic, minced

2 tablespoons olive oil

1 (14-ounce) can diced tomatoes

1 (6-ounce) can tomato paste

1 cup vegetable broth

½ teaspoon dried thyme leaves

½ teaspoon dried oregano leaves

½ teaspoon salt

⅛ teaspoon pepper

2 cups ricotta cheese

2 eggs, beaten

1 cup shredded Muenster cheese

3 cups shredded mozzarella cheese

9 lasagna noodles

2 (14-ounce) cans black beans, drained and rinsed

½ cup grated Parmesan cheese

Freezing Day

1. In a heavy skillet over medium heat, cook onion and garlic in olive oil until crisp-tender. Add undrained tomatoes, tomato paste, broth, thyme, oregano, salt, and pepper. Simmer, covered, for 10–12 minutes, until flavors are blended. In a large bowl, combine ricotta, eggs, Muenster, and the first quantity of mozzarella, and blend well.

2. In a 13" × 9" pan, place 1 cup tomato sauce. Cover with 3 uncooked lasagna noodles. Pour half of tomato sauce over the noodles. Top with 3 more noodles. Spread half of the ricotta mixture over the noodles and top with black beans. Spread remaining ricotta mixture over black beans and top with 3 noodles. Pour remaining tomato sauce over and sprinkle with remaining mozzarella and Parmesan. Cool completely in refrigerator; then wrap, seal, label, and freeze.

Reheating Instructions

Thaw lasagna overnight in the refrigerator. Bake, covered, in a preheated 375°F oven for 55–60 minutes. Uncover and bake 10–15 minutes longer or until cheese is melted and browned.

Spicy Cheese Tortellini

To serve without freezing, add frozen tortellini to the simmering sauce and cook for 3–4 minutes until the tortellini are hot and tender. Serve with Parmesan cheese.

YIELDS 4–6 SERVINGS

2 tablespoons olive oil
1 onion, chopped
2 cloves garlic, minced
1 jalapeño pepper, minced
1 (14-ounce) can diced tomatoes, undrained
1 (8-ounce) can tomato sauce
1 (6-ounce) can tomato paste
2 cups vegetable broth
½ teaspoon salt
⅛ teaspoon white pepper
1 (9-ounce) package frozen cheese tortellini
½ cup grated Parmesan cheese

YIELDS 12–18 SERVINGS

6 tablespoons olive oil
3 onions, chopped
6 cloves garlic, minced
3 jalapeño peppers, minced
3 (14-ounce) cans diced tomatoes, undrained
3 (8-ounce) cans tomato sauce
3 (6-ounce) cans tomato paste
6 cups vegetable broth
1½ teaspoons salt
⅜ teaspoon white pepper
3 (9-ounce) packages frozen cheese tortellini
1½ cups grated Parmesan cheese

Freezing Day

1. Heat olive oil in a large skillet over medium heat and sauté onion and garlic until crisp-tender. Add jalapeño pepper; cook and stir for 1–2 minutes, until fragrant. Add remaining ingredients except for tortellini and Parmesan cheese and stir to blend. Simmer for 5–6 minutes, until flavors are blended.

2. Cool sauce in an ice-water bath or in the refrigerator until cold. Pour into a rigid container and attach a freezer bag of frozen tortellini. Place Parmesan cheese in a small ziplock bag and attach to the sauce. Label, seal, and freeze.

Reheating Instructions

Thaw sauce and cheese overnight in the refrigerator. Do not thaw tortellini. Pour sauce into a saucepan and bring to a simmer. Add frozen tortellini, bring back to a simmer, and cook for 3–4 minutes or until tortellini are hot and tender. Serve with Parmesan cheese.

Spinach Pie

You won't miss the meat in this delicious, cheesy pie. To serve without freezing, when pie is baked, let it stand for 10 minutes before slicing.

YIELDS 6–8 SERVINGS

2 onions, chopped

5 cloves garlic, minced

2 tablespoons olive oil

1 tablespoon flour

2 cups frozen cut-leaf spinach, thawed

1 cup frozen chopped broccoli, thawed

5 eggs

⅛ teaspoon pepper

1 cup ricotta cheese

1 (3-ounce) package cream cheese, softened

2 cups shredded mozzarella cheese

1 cup grated Parmesan cheese

2 Easy Pie Crusts (see recipe in Chapter 12)

1 tablespoon milk

YIELDS 18–24 SERVINGS

6 onions, chopped

15 cloves garlic, minced

6 tablespoons olive oil

3 tablespoons flour

6 cups frozen cut-leaf spinach, thawed

3 cups frozen chopped broccoli, thawed

15 eggs

⅜ teaspoon pepper

3 cups ricotta cheese

3 (3-ounce) packages cream cheese, softened

6 cups shredded mozzarella cheese

3 cups grated Parmesan cheese

6 Easy Pie Crusts (see recipe in Chapter 12)

3 tablespoons milk

Freezing Day

1. Preheat the oven to 375°F. In a heavy skillet over medium heat, cook onion and garlic in olive oil until crisp-tender. Sprinkle flour over vegetables. Cook and stir for 2 minutes; then remove from heat and refrigerate until cold.

2. Drain spinach and broccoli by pressing between paper towels. In a large bowl, beat eggs, pepper, ricotta cheese, and cream cheese until well mixed. Add vegetables, mozzarella cheese, and Parmesan cheese and mix well.

3. Pour spinach mixture into a pie crust–lined pan. Top with a pie crust, seal and flute edges, and cut vent holes in the top of the crust. Brush the crust with milk and bake for 50–65 minutes or until the crust is browned and the pie is set. Cool in the refrigerator, then wrap whole pie and freeze, or cut pie into 8 slices and wrap individually, then freeze.

Reheating Instructions

Thaw overnight in the refrigerator. Bake at 375°F for 25–35 minutes or until thoroughly heated. To thaw and reheat individually, thaw a slice overnight in the refrigerator, then bake at 375°F for 10–15 minutes or until thoroughly heated.

Crisp Phyllo Burritos

These delicious little bundles are a cross between a French pastry and a Mexican burrito. To serve without freezing, bake as directed.

YIELDS 6 SERVINGS

1 tablespoon olive oil
1¼ cups frozen meatless crumbles
½ cup chopped onion
2 cloves garlic, minced
2 tablespoons Taco Seasoning Mix (see recipe in Chapter 4)
¼ cup water
½ cup refried beans
⅓ cup salsa
9 sheets phyllo dough, thawed
¼ cup melted butter
1 cup shredded pepper jack cheese
1 teaspoon smoked paprika (used on reheating day)

YIELDS 18 SERVINGS

3 tablespoons olive oil
3¾ cups frozen meatless crumbles
1½ cups chopped onion
6 cloves garlic, minced
6 tablespoons Taco Seasoning Mix (see recipe in Chapter 4)
¾ cup water
1½ cups refried beans
1 cup salsa
27 sheets phyllo dough, thawed
¾ cup melted butter
3 cups shredded pepper jack cheese
1 tablespoon smoked paprika (used on reheating day)

Freezing Day

1. In a heavy skillet, heat olive oil over medium heat and add crumbles, onion, and garlic. Cook and stir until vegetables are crisp-tender. Stir in taco seasoning, water, and refried beans and mix to blend. Simmer for 5 minutes; then add salsa. Cool this mixture completely in the refrigerator or an ice-water bath.

2. When filling is cold, spread 1 sheet phyllo dough on the work surface and brush with butter. Layer another phyllo sheet on top of the first and brush with butter. Add a third sheet and cut the stack of sheets in half crosswise, making 2 rectangles. Place a spoonful of chilled filling at the short end of the phyllo stack and top with cheese. Roll phyllo dough over filling, folding in ends and sealing edges with butter. Repeat with second phyllo stack.

3. Repeat with remaining phyllo sheets, butter, and filling. Brush bundles with butter. Wrap each bundle in freezer paper and place all in a heavy-duty ziplock bag. Label, seal, and freeze. Reserve paprika in the pantry.

Reheating Instructions

Let thaw overnight in the refrigerator. Preheat the oven to 375°F. Place unwrapped bundles on a cookie sheet, sprinkle each with paprika, and bake at 375°F for 20–25 minutes or until filling is thoroughly heated, cheese is melted, and phyllo dough is browned and crisp. Serve with sour cream and salsa.

Hash Brown Potato Bake

Look for different types of hash brown potatoes; some come packaged with vegetables like onions and peppers. To serve this dish without freezing, bake, covered, at 375°F for 35–40 minutes.

YIELDS 4 SERVINGS

1 tablespoon olive oil
1 shallot, chopped
1 clove garlic, chopped
1 green chili, chopped
½ cup milk
1 (3-ounce) package cream cheese
½ teaspoon salt
⅛ teaspoon white pepper
2 cups frozen hash brown potatoes
1 cup frozen corn
¼ cup grated Parmesan cheese

YIELDS 12 SERVINGS

3 tablespoons olive oil
3 shallots, chopped
3 cloves garlic, chopped
3 green chilies, chopped
1½ cups milk
3 (3-ounce) packages cream cheese
1½ teaspoons salt
⅜ teaspoon white pepper
6 cups frozen hash brown potatoes
3 cups frozen corn
¾ cup grated Parmesan cheese

Freezing Day

1. In a heavy skillet over medium heat, heat olive oil and cook shallot and garlic until crisp-tender, about 3–4 minutes. Add green chili, cook and stir for 1 minute, then add milk, cream cheese, salt, and pepper. Cook and stir over medium heat until cream cheese is melted and sauce is blended. Remove from heat and chill in an ice-water bath or the refrigerator.

2. When sauce is cold, fold in frozen potatoes and frozen corn. Place in an 8" × 8" pan lined with freezer paper and sprinkle with Parmesan cheese. Wrap and freeze casserole until frozen solid, then remove from pan, wrap again, and freeze.

Reheating Instructions

Unwrap casserole and place in an 8" × 8" baking dish; let thaw overnight in the refrigerator. Bake, covered, in a preheated 375°F oven for 20–30 minutes or until casserole is bubbly and hot in the center. Uncover and bake 5–10 minutes longer, until top is browned.

Chapter 11

Sandwiches

Meatball Marinara Sandwiches

To serve these sandwiches immediately, combine hot meatballs and sauce in a saucepan and simmer for 4–5 minutes. Broil and assemble sandwiches as directed.

YIELDS 4 SERVINGS

1 pound lean ground beef
¼ cup dry bread crumbs
3 tablespoons milk
1 egg
½ teaspoon salt
⅛ teaspoon pepper
1 (14-ounce) jar tomato pasta sauce
4 hoagie buns
1 cup shredded Monterey jack cheese

YIELDS 12 SERVINGS

3 pounds lean ground beef
¾ cup dry bread crumbs
9 tablespoons milk
3 eggs
1½ teaspoons salt
⅜ teaspoon pepper
3 (14-ounce) jars tomato pasta sauce
12 hoagie buns
3 cups shredded Monterey jack cheese

Freezing Day

1. Preheat the oven to 350°F. In a large bowl, combine beef, bread crumbs, milk, egg, salt, and pepper and mix gently but thoroughly. Form into 24 meatballs and place on a baking sheet. Bake for 20–30 minutes, until meatballs are thoroughly cooked. Cool in the refrigerator.

2. Combine cooled meatballs with pasta sauce and place in a ziplock bag. Slice hoagie buns and place in a ziplock bag. Place cheese in a ziplock bag. Combine all the bags in one larger bag; label, seal, and freeze.

Reheating Instructions

Thaw hoagie buns at room temperature overnight. Thaw meatballs and sauce and cheese in the refrigerator overnight. Pour meatballs and sauce into a large saucepan and heat over medium heat until sauce bubbles and meatballs are thoroughly heated. Toast sliced hoagie buns under the broiler. Place meatballs and sauce on one half of each toasted bun and top with cheese. Place filled halves of hoagie buns on a broiler pan and broil 4–6" from heat for 4–5 minutes, until cheese melts. Assemble sandwiches and serve.

Mozzarella Basil Burgers

Top this burger with vine-ripened tomato slices or, for a crunchy alternative, add cucumber sliced lengthwise or on the diagonal.

YIELDS 4–6 SERVINGS

2 pounds ground beef

1 batch Ground Beef Seasoning Mix (see recipe in Chapter 4)

1 egg

½ cup bread crumbs

2 tablespoons Worcestershire sauce

1 cup mozzarella cheese, grated

6 ounces cream cheese, softened

¼ cup fresh basil, chopped

Freezing Day

1. In a large bowl, mix ground beef with Ground Beef Seasoning Mix, egg, bread crumbs, and Worcestershire sauce.

2. Divide the ground beef into 8 parts and shape into patties.

3. In a separate bowl, combine the mozzarella cheese, cream cheese, and basil.

4. Spread cheese mixture on 4 patties. Top the 4 patties with the 4 plain patties and seal the edges.

5. Flash freeze and transfer to a freezer bag, or wrap each individually in plastic wrap.

Reheating Instructions

Cook frozen or defrosted burgers in a skillet over medium heat until they reach the desired level of doneness.

Get Out of the Bun!

Part of a great hamburger is the bread you serve it on. For something new, try serving your burger on flatbread, pita bread, yeast rolls, an English muffin, onion rolls, Hawaiian bread, or even your own homemade hamburger buns. Toasting the buns or bread can also give the old burger a new presentation.

Hummus Sandwiches

This recipe for Hummus also makes a delicious appetizer dip for fresh vegetables or a sandwich spread for chicken or roast beef sandwiches. Store it, well covered, in the refrigerator for up to 1 week.

YIELDS 4 SERVINGS

1 (16-ounce) can garbanzo beans, drained
2 tablespoons lemon juice
¼ cup sesame paste
1 tablespoon olive oil
1 teaspoon toasted sesame oil
¼ cup toasted sesame seeds
¼ cup chopped green onions
8 slices whole-wheat bread
2 tablespoons butter, softened

YIELDS 12 SERVINGS

3 (16-ounce) cans garbanzo beans, drained
6 tablespoons lemon juice
¾ cup sesame paste
3 tablespoons olive oil
1 tablespoon toasted sesame oil
¾ cup toasted sesame seeds
¾ cup chopped green onions
24 slices whole-wheat bread
6 tablespoons butter, softened

Freezing Day

1. In a food processor or blender, combine drained garbanzo beans, lemon juice, sesame paste, olive oil, and sesame oil and process until almost smooth. Remove from the processor to a medium bowl and stir in toasted sesame seeds and green onions.

2. Spread 1 side of each slice of bread with butter and divide hummus among bread slices. Make sandwiches and place in ziplock bags. Label bags, seal, and freeze.

Reheating Instructions

Thaw in the refrigerator overnight. Or place, still frozen, in lunchboxes in the morning and let thaw. Make sure the sandwiches are eaten at lunch when thawed.

Black Bean Burgers

Pile on your choice of toppings to make a one-of-a-kind Black Bean Burger. Try tomatoes, avocados, and onions with a dash of sesame oil on a kaiser roll.

YIELDS 4 SERVINGS

2 (16-ounce) cans black beans, fully drained
½ green bell pepper, finely diced
2 tablespoons fresh cilantro, finely diced
3 tablespoons teriyaki sauce
1 tablespoon minced onion
1 egg
1 teaspoon sesame oil
½ cup bread crumbs, or more if needed
3 tablespoons vegetable oil (used on reheating day)

Freezing Day

1. In a large bowl, mash the black beans with a potato masher. Add peppers, cilantro, teriyaki sauce, onion, egg, and sesame oil and mix well.
2. Add bread crumbs a little at a time until the mixture is the right consistency and holds together.
3. Form into patties. Flash freeze on a baking sheet lined with wax paper. Transfer to a freezer bag once frozen.

Reheating Instructions

Cook frozen patties in a medium skillet in oil over medium heat until heated through.

Pimiento Cheese Sandwiches

Using whole pimientos and chopping them yourself makes a better-textured spread. You could use white sandwich bread instead of whole wheat if you'd prefer; make sure it's a firm, thinly sliced white bread.

YIELDS 6 SERVINGS

1 (7-ounce) jar whole pimientos, drained
1 (3-ounce) package cream cheese, softened
½ cup Miracle Whip
2 cups shredded Colby cheese
1 teaspoon Worcestershire sauce
⅛ teaspoon garlic powder
Pinch white pepper
3 tablespoons butter
12 slices whole-wheat bread

YIELDS 18 SERVINGS

3 (7-ounce) jars whole pimientos, drained
3 (3-ounce) packages cream cheese, softened
1½ cups Miracle Whip
6 cups shredded Colby cheese
1 tablespoon Worcestershire sauce
⅜ teaspoon garlic powder
3 pinches white pepper
9 tablespoons butter
36 slices whole-wheat bread

Freezing Day

1. Drain pimientos and chop coarsely. In a medium bowl, combine cream cheese and Miracle Whip and beat until smooth and fluffy. Add pimientos, Colby cheese, Worcestershire sauce, garlic powder, and pepper and stir gently by hand until blended.
2. Spread a thin layer of butter on one side of each slice of bread. Divide pimiento cheese among bread slices and put together to make sandwiches. Wrap each sandwich in freezer wrap, then place all in a large ziplock bag. Label sandwiches, seal bag, and freeze.

Reheating Instructions

Let thaw overnight in the refrigerator, or add to brown-bag lunches in the morning and let thaw until lunchtime. Make sure sandwiches are eaten within 2 hours of being completely thawed.

Turkey Pesto Sandwiches

You can substitute plain cooked turkey for the smoked turkey in these easy sandwiches. They can also be served immediately without freezing, or the spread can be stored in the refrigerator, well covered, and used as desired.

YIELDS 4 SERVINGS

1 (3-ounce) package cream cheese
¼ cup Miracle Whip
3 blocks frozen Basil and Pine Nut Pesto (see recipe in Chapter 4), thawed
¼ cup grated Parmesan cheese
1 cup chopped smoked turkey
8 slices cracked-wheat bread
2 tablespoons butter, softened

YIELDS 12 SERVINGS

3 (3-ounce) packages cream cheese
¾ cup Miracle Whip
9 blocks frozen Basil and Pine Nut Pesto (see recipe in Chapter 4), thawed
¾ cup grated Parmesan cheese
3 cups chopped smoked turkey
24 slices cracked-wheat bread
6 tablespoons butter, softened

Freezing Day

1. In a medium bowl, combine cream cheese and Miracle Whip and beat until well blended. Add pesto and Parmesan cheese and mix well. Stir in turkey and mix well.

2. Spread one side of each slice of bread with softened butter. Divide turkey mixture among bread slices and put together to make sandwiches. Place sandwiches in ziplock bags, seal, label, and freeze.

Reheating Instructions

Thaw in the refrigerator overnight. Or place, still frozen, in lunchboxes in the morning and let thaw. Make sure the sandwiches are eaten at lunch when thawed.

Garlic Roast Beef Sandwiches

Roasting garlic makes it nutty and sweet, adding a perfect touch to tender roast beef. The garlic spread can be stored, well covered, in the refrigerator and used as desired.

YIELDS 4 SERVINGS

6 cloves garlic
2 teaspoons olive oil
3 tablespoons Miracle Whip
2 tablespoons whipped cream cheese
Pinch white pepper
2 tablespoons butter, softened
8 slices sourdough bread
½ pound cooked roast beef, sliced

YIELDS 12 SERVINGS

1 head garlic
2 tablespoons olive oil
9 tablespoons Miracle Whip
6 tablespoons whipped cream cheese
3 pinches white pepper
6 tablespoons butter, softened
24 slices sourdough bread
1½ pounds cooked roast beef, sliced

Freezing Day

1. Preheat the oven to 400°F. Place unpeeled garlic on a square of heavy-duty foil and drizzle with olive oil. Fold foil over garlic, sealing the edges; place on a cookie sheet and roast for 20–25 minutes, until garlic is soft. Let cool until it is easy to handle. Press garlic out of skins with your fingers and place in a small bowl. Add Miracle Whip, whipped cream cheese, and white pepper and mix well until blended.

2. Spread butter on one side of each slice of bread. Spread garlic mixture over butter and lay roast beef on top. Top with another slice of bread, butter-side down. Place each sandwich in a ziplock bag. Seal bags, label, and freeze.

Reheating Instructions

Thaw in the refrigerator overnight. Or place, still frozen, in lunchboxes in the morning and let thaw. Make sure the sandwiches are eaten at lunch when thawed.

Onion Mushroom Burgers

Dijon mustard originated in Dijon, France, and was originally made from brown or black mustard seeds and verjuice, a juice made from unripe grapes. Dijon mustard has a more pungent flavor than yellow mustard, and shouldn't be substituted.

YIELDS 4 SERVINGS

1 pound ground beef

1 batch Ground Beef Seasoning Mix (see recipe in Chapter 4)

1 tablespoon Worcestershire sauce

3–5 tablespoons butter (used on reheating day)

1 onion, sliced into rings (used on reheating day)

½ pound mushrooms, sliced (used on reheating day)

4 tablespoons Dijon mustard (used on reheating day)

¾ cup dry sherry (used on reheating day)

Freezing Day

Mix ground beef with seasoning mix and Worcestershire sauce. Form into 4 patties, flash freeze, and transfer to freezer bag.

Reheating Instructions

1. Defrost hamburger patties in the refrigerator overnight. In a heavy skillet, melt 3 tablespoons butter over medium-high heat. Brown patties 2–3 minutes per side and remove from skillet.

2. Add additional butter to the skillet (if needed) and sauté onions and mushrooms 5–7 minutes. Leave in the skillet, but push to the side to make room for burgers.

3. Spread 1 tablespoon Dijon mustard on each hamburger and return to skillet, Dijon-side down.

4. Pour sherry over the top of the hamburgers. Cook until desired doneness.

5. Serve burgers with sautéed onions and mushrooms on toasted rolls.

Onion Storage

Onions should be stored in a cool, dry place with good airflow. They shouldn't be stored in the refrigerator or in plastic bags, but onions can also be frozen. To freeze the onions, chop them and flash freeze on a baking sheet. Transfer to a freezer bag. When a recipe calls for chopped onion, you can measure right from the freezer bag.

Sweet Ginger Sloppy Joes

Although ground ginger may be substituted for fresh ginger in the correct proportion, it does have a different flavor. Ground ginger is much stronger, so substitute ¼ teaspoon ground ginger for every 4 teaspoons fresh ginger.

YIELDS 4–6 SERVINGS

1 pound ground beef
1 onion, chopped
1½ cups ketchup
¾ cup brown sugar
½ cup soy sauce
4 teaspoons fresh ginger, grated
½ cup water
8 hamburger buns (used on reheating day)

Freezing Day

1. In a medium skillet over medium heat, brown ground beef and onion. Drain.
2. Add remaining ingredients and cook over medium heat for 5 minutes.
3. Freeze mixture in a freezer bag.

Reheating Instructions

Defrost meat. Heat in a saucepan over medium heat for 20 minutes, or until the desired temperature is reached. Make sandwiches using hamburger buns.

Curried Chicken Salad Wraps

These wraps can be served without freezing; in that case, you can place lettuce leaves on the tortillas before adding the chicken salad.

YIELDS 4 SERVINGS

1½ cups cooked, cubed chicken
⅓ cup Miracle Whip
3 tablespoons mango chutney
1 teaspoon curry powder
¼ cup golden raisins
¼ cup chopped green onions
⅓ cup crushed pineapple, well drained
4 (8") flour tortillas

YIELDS 12 SERVINGS

4½ cups cooked, cubed chicken
1 cup Miracle Whip
9 tablespoons mango chutney
1 tablespoon curry powder
¾ cup golden raisins
¾ cup chopped green onions
1 cup crushed pineapple, well drained
12 (8") flour tortillas

Freezing Day

In a medium bowl, combine all the ingredients except the flour tortillas and mix well to blend. Place flour tortillas on a work surface and divide chicken mixture among them. Roll up each tortilla, enclosing filling; then cut in half crosswise. Wrap each filled tortilla half in freezer wrap and place in ziplock bags. Seal bags, label, and freeze.

Reheating Instructions

Let thaw in the refrigerator overnight. Or place, still frozen, in lunchboxes in the morning and let thaw. Make sure the sandwiches are eaten at lunch when thawed.

Apple Turkey Burgers

Make a batch of these burgers to have on hand for lunch or an easy dinner. Serve on a toasted onion roll and top with caramelized onions and thinly sliced Granny Smith apples.

YIELDS 6–8 SERVINGS

2 eggs
½ cup applesauce
2 pounds ground turkey
1 green onion, finely chopped
½–¾ cup bread crumbs
1 teaspoon dried sage
1 clove garlic, minced
1 teaspoon salt
1 teaspoon pepper
1 tablespoon vegetable oil (used on reheating day)

Freezing Day

1. In a medium bowl, beat eggs and stir in applesauce. Mix well.

2. Add ground turkey, onion, ½ cup bread crumbs, sage, garlic, salt, and pepper. Mix well. If mixture is sticky, add additional bread crumbs a tablespoon at a time.

3. Form into patties and flash freeze on a baking sheet lined with wax paper. Once patties are frozen, transfer to a freezer bag.

Reheating Instructions

Cook frozen patties in a medium skillet in oil approximately 4–6 minutes per side until turkey reaches an internal temperature of 165°F.

Salmon Salad Wraps

You can substitute tiny canned shrimp, drained canned crabmeat, or drained canned tuna for the salmon in these delicious wraps. They can be served immediately or wrapped and refrigerated for up to 6 hours.

YIELDS 6 SERVINGS

1 (15-ounce) can red sockeye salmon
1 (3-ounce) package cream cheese, softened
⅓ cup mayonnaise
¼ cup honey mustard salad dressing
½ teaspoon dried thyme leaves
¼ cup minced green onion
2 cups frozen corn
2 tablespoons butter
6 (6") corn tortillas

YIELDS 18 SERVINGS

3 (15-ounce) cans red sockeye salmon
3 (3-ounce) packages cream cheese, softened
1 cup mayonnaise
¾ cup honey mustard salad dressing
1½ teaspoons dried thyme leaves
¾ cup minced green onion
6 cups frozen corn
6 tablespoons butter
18 (6") corn tortillas

Freezing Day

Drain canned salmon and carefully remove skin and bones. Flake salmon into a medium bowl and set aside. In another medium bowl, combine cream cheese and mayonnaise and beat until smooth. Mix with remaining ingredients except butter and tortillas. Spread butter evenly on tortillas. Spread filling over butter and roll up, enclosing filling. Place in ziplock bags, seal, label, and freeze.

Reheating Instructions

Let thaw in the refrigerator overnight. Or place, still frozen, in lunchboxes in the morning and let thaw. Make sure the sandwiches are eaten at lunch when thawed.

Cannellini Bean Spread Wraps

This spread is similar to hummus but is milder; it makes an excellent sandwich spread or an appetizer dip served with vegetables. The sandwiches can be served immediately, or wrapped and stored in the refrigerator for up to 6 hours.

YIELDS 4 SERVINGS

1 (16-ounce) can cannellini beans, drained

2 tablespoons lemon juice

1 (3-ounce) package cream cheese, softened

3 tablespoons olive oil

⅓ cup grated Parmesan cheese

⅛ teaspoon cayenne pepper

½ teaspoon dried marjoram leaves

4 (10") jalapeño-flavored flour tortillas

YIELDS 12 SERVINGS

3 (16-ounce) cans cannellini beans, drained

6 tablespoons lemon juice

3 (3-ounce) packages cream cheese, softened

9 tablespoons olive oil

1 cup grated Parmesan cheese

⅜ teaspoon cayenne pepper

1½ teaspoons dried marjoram leaves

12 (10") jalapeño-flavored flour tortillas

Freezing Day

In a blender container or food processor, combine drained beans with remaining ingredients except tortillas. Blend or process until the mixture is almost smooth. Spread the mixture on tortillas and roll up, enclosing the filling. Cut wraps in half and place in ziplock bags; label, seal, and freeze.

Reheating Instructions

Let thaw in the refrigerator overnight. Or place, still frozen, in lunchboxes in the morning and let thaw. Make sure the wraps are eaten at lunch when thawed.

Spicy Taco Roll-Ups

These roll-ups can be served as an appetizer, a snack, or a main dish. Serve a variety of dips with the roll-ups such as Queso Dip (see recipe in Chapter 4), Pico de Gallo (see recipe in Chapter 4), and ranch dressing.

YIELDS 6–8 SERVINGS

1 pound ground beef

1 cup water

1 batch Taco Seasoning Mix (see recipe in Chapter 4)

1 (16-ounce) can refried beans

¾ cup shredded Cheddar cheese

1 (14.5-ounce) can diced tomatoes with green chilies, drained

3 packages refrigerator crescent rolls

Freezing Day

1. In a heavy skillet over medium heat, brown ground beef. Add water and taco seasoning. Bring to a gentle boil, and cook an additional 15 minutes. Mix in the refried beans, Cheddar cheese, and tomatoes with green chilies. Immediately remove from heat.

2. Open the crescent rolls, and divide package into 4 rectangles. Smooth together the perforation that runs diagonally across each of the rectangles.

3. Roll or press out each rectangle with your fingers so it measures approximately 4" × 4". Cut in half and make 2 (2" × 4") rectangles.

4. In the center of each rectangle, spread 2 tablespoons of the meat mixture. Roll the rectangle the long way (so it looks like a fat pencil) and flash freeze.

Reheating Instructions

1. Defrost rolls in the refrigerator. Bake at 375°F for 11–13 minutes, or until golden brown.

2. Bake frozen rolls at 375°F for 20–25 minutes, or until golden brown.

Hold the Heat

It is easy to make these Spicy Taco Roll-Ups without the hot spices. First, substitute plain diced tomatoes for the diced tomatoes with green chilies. Don't add cayenne pepper when you make the Taco Seasoning Mix. Also, instead of 1 tablespoon chili powder, substitute 1½ teaspoons cumin (in addition to the cumin already listed in the recipe), and 1½ teaspoons oregano.

Blue Cheese Burgers

There are many varieties of blue cheese, and they range in flavor from mild to quite pungent. For these Blue Cheese Burgers, choose either Cabrales or Picón if you enjoy a pungent flavor or Gorgonzola if you prefer a mild flavor.

YIELDS 4 SERVINGS

2 pounds ground beef

1 batch Ground Beef Seasoning Mix (see recipe in Chapter 4)

Salt and pepper to taste

½ cup blue cheese, crumbled

5 ounces cream cheese, softened

¼ cup roasted pine nuts

1 teaspoon Worcestershire sauce

Freezing Day

1. Mix the ground beef with the Ground Beef Seasoning Mix. Divide the ground beef into 8 parts and shape into patties. Salt and pepper each patty.

2. In a separate bowl combine the blue cheese, cream cheese, pine nuts, and Worcestershire sauce.

3. Spread cheese mixture on 4 patties. Top the 4 patties with 4 plain patties and seal the edges.

4. Flash freeze and transfer to a freezer bag, or wrap each individually in plastic wrap.

Reheating Instructions

Cook frozen or defrosted burgers in a skillet over medium heat until they reach the desired level of doneness.

How to Store Seeds and Nuts

The best way to store seeds and nuts is in the freezer, and there is no need to remove the shells! When the nuts are frozen in the shell, they crack much easier. Not only will your nuts and seeds stay fresher longer, but you don't need to defrost them—use them directly from the freezer.

Open-Faced Italian Sandwiches

Hearty and tasty, these sandwiches are perfect after a long day of work or school. Serve them with Roasted Peppers and Tomatoes (see recipe in Chapter 6) for an extra burst of flavor.

YIELDS 2–4 SERVINGS

1 pound ground beef
2 tablespoons onion, chopped
2 cloves garlic, minced
2 teaspoons Italian seasoning
2 tablespoons tomato paste
3–5 tablespoons water
1 loaf Italian bread
8 ounces cream cheese
1–2 cups mozzarella cheese, to taste

Freezing Day

1. In a medium skillet over medium heat, brown ground beef, and onion 7–10 minutes or until meat is thoroughly cooked. Add garlic and cook an additional minute. Drain.
2. Stir in Italian seasoning, tomato paste, and water. Set aside to cool.
3. Cut Italian bread into 1" slices. Spread cream cheese on each slice of bread.
4. On each piece of bread, spread meat mixture over cream cheese, and top with mozzarella cheese.
5. Flash freeze, then transfer to a freezer bag.

Reheating Instructions

Arrange frozen slices of bread on a baking sheet. Bake at 450°F for 8–12 minutes.

Peanut Butter and Jelly Sandwiches

These sandwiches can be packed frozen in a lunchbox, taken on a picnic, or even packed for a trip to the beach! Make them ahead of time and simplify your mornings.

YIELDS 10 SERVINGS

1 loaf sliced sourdough bread
1 jar peanut butter
1 jar of your favorite jam

Freezing Day

1. Spread peanut butter all the way to the edge of 1 slice of bread.
2. Spread jam on another slice of bread, stopping ½" from the edge of the bread.
3. Make into a sandwich, wrap with foil, and freeze.

Reheating Instructions

Defrost in the refrigerator for several hours, or even in a lunchbox, and serve at room temperature.

Black Bean and Corn Wraps

If you prefer corn tortillas to flour tortillas, you have a couple of options. You can bake corn taco shells in the oven and fill with the bean mixture, or heat corn tortillas in a skillet with a bit of oil to soften, then wrap.

YIELDS 4 SERVINGS

1 (15.5-ounce) can black beans, drained
1 (15.5-ounce) can whole-kernel corn, drained
1 (14-ounce) can tomatoes, diced
2 tablespoons tomato paste
3 tablespoons water
2 tablespoons fresh basil, chopped
Salt to taste
1 (8-count) package flour tortillas (used on reheating day)

Freezing Day

Mix all the ingredients, except the tortillas, and freeze in a freezer bag.

Reheating Instructions

1. Defrost bean mixture in the refrigerator overnight. Heat in a saucepan over medium heat for 15–20 minutes or until the desired temperature is reached.

2. Wrap the flour tortillas in moist paper towels and heat in the microwave for 1 minute. Spoon bean mixture down the center of each tortilla. Fold up the bottom and roll in the sides to make a burrito.

Avocado Chicken Burgers

Are you a cheese lover? When you form the burgers, make an indentation in the center of the burger, fill it with your favorite cheese, and close it up again.

YIELDS 4 SERVINGS
1 pound ground chicken
½ teaspoon paprika
1 egg
¼ cup Italian-seasoned bread crumbs
1 tablespoon Worcestershire sauce
Oil
1 ripe avocado (used on reheating day)
1 tablespoon lemon juice (used on reheating day)
2 tablespoons sour cream (used on reheating day)
Salt and pepper to taste (used on reheating day)
4 whole-wheat buns (used on reheating day)
Desired burger toppings such as lettuce, tomato, red onion (used on reheating day)

Freezing Day

1. In a medium bowl, mix chicken, paprika, egg, bread crumbs, and Worcestershire sauce.
2. Form mixture into 4 patties. Flash freeze and transfer to a freezer bag.

Reheating Instructions

1. Cook frozen patties in a medium skillet in a small amount of oil over medium-high heat, 6–8 minutes per side. Cover and cook an additional 2–3 minutes until burgers are fully cooked and no longer pink in the center.
2. To make the sauce, combine avocado, lemon juice, sour cream, salt, and pepper in a small bowl. Spread sauce on buns and top with burgers and desired toppings.

The Perfect Avocado

Use the following tips to select the perfect avocado. If the avocado is bright green or hard, it is not yet ripe. Look for one that is dark green or black. Gently press the avocado with your thumb. It should be soft, but not so soft that you'll pierce the skin. When you slice the avocado open, there should be no dark spots.

Grilled Sirloin Wraps

An alternative to grilling your steak is to stir-fry it. On freezing day, cut steak into ½" strips and put into a freezer bag with the marinade. On cooking day, defrost steak, discard marinade, and stir-fry in a wok or skillet.

YIELDS 6 SERVINGS

2 pounds sirloin steak

½ cup butter

⅓ cup onion, minced

3 teaspoons dried parsley

2 tablespoons Worcestershire sauce

½ teaspoon yellow mustard

¼ teaspoon pepper

½ teaspoon salt

12 flour tortillas (used on reheating day)

½ cup lettuce, shredded (used on reheating day)

2 tomatoes, chopped (used on reheating day)

⅓ cup Vidalia onions, chopped (used on reheating day)

½ cup shredded Cheddar cheese (used on reheating day)

½ cup sour cream (used on reheating day)

Freezing Day

1. Score the top of the steak by cutting slits across the grain.

2. In a medium saucepan over low heat, melt butter. Add onion, parsley, Worcestershire sauce, mustard, pepper, and salt. Cook on low heat 5–10 minutes. Remove marinade from heat and cool.

3. Put the steak in a freezer bag and pour in the marinade. Freeze.

Reheating Instructions

1. Defrost steak and marinade overnight in the refrigerator, then discard marinade. Grill the steak over high heat until desired doneness. Let rest for 5 minutes. Cut steak into ½" strips.

2. To serve, layer each tortilla with steak, lettuce, tomato, onion, cheese, and sour cream. Roll like a burrito.

Let Your Steak Rest

Ever wondered why chefs let steak rest before cutting? During grilling, the juices flow inward and saturate the middle of the steak. When cut immediately after cooking, the juices flooding the middle have nowhere to go but out. By allowing it to rest, the juices have time to be reabsorbed evenly throughout the meat.

Chicken Verde Wraps

Tomatillos are a popular ingredient in many traditional Mexican dishes. They are covered with an inedible husk, but once peeled look like a small green tomato. You can buy them fresh, or you can use jarred tomatillos for this recipe.

YIELDS 2–4 SERVINGS

3 cups cubed chicken, uncooked

3 tablespoons olive oil

1 onion, coarsely diced

1½ cups green tomatillo (jarred)

Salt and pepper to taste

1 package flour tortillas (used on reheating day)

Grated Cheddar cheese (used as a topping on reheating day)

Sour cream (used as a topping on reheating day)

Freezing Day

1. In a large skillet over medium-high heat, sauté the chicken in oil for 4–6 minutes until white in color. Add the onion and sauté until most of the juices have disappeared. Drain any remaining juices.

2. Add the tomatillo and cook over low heat until the mixture thickens. Season the mixture with salt and pepper. Freeze using a freezer bag.

Reheating Instructions

Defrost chicken mixture in the refrigerator overnight, in the microwave, or in cold water. Place in a saucepan and heat over medium heat. Serve burrito style with flour tortillas. Top with Cheddar cheese and sour cream as desired.

Jalapeño Burgers

Top this spicy burger with a slice of Cheddar cheese and spread mayonnaise on the bun. Other options include a slice of tomato and a slice of sweet onion.

YIELDS 4–6 SERVINGS

2 jalapeño peppers

2 pounds ground beef

1 batch Ground Beef Seasoning Mix (see recipe in Chapter 4)

1 egg

½ cup bread crumbs

½ cup jarred picante sauce

Freezing Day

1.   Remove the seeds from the jalapeño peppers, and dice the peppers.

2.   In a large bowl, mix diced peppers, ground beef, Ground Beef Seasoning Mix, egg, bread crumbs, and picante sauce. Mix well. Shape into patties and flash freeze. Transfer to a freezer bag once frozen.

Reheating Instructions

Cook frozen or defrosted burgers in a skillet over medium heat until they are fully cooked.

Delicious Burger Topping

Looking for an easy and flavorful topping for hamburgers cooked in a skillet? After cooking your burgers, turn up the heat and cook the drippings and bits until crisp. Deglaze the pan with red wine or apple cider vinegar and reduce. Stir in 2 tablespoons of half-and-half and mix the reduction into an equal portion of mayonnaise.

Chapter 12

Desserts

Easy Pie Crust

Pair your homemade pie crust with Spinach and Cheddar Quiche (see recipe in Chapter 10), or fill it with the delicious Sweet Berry Filling in this chapter.

> **YIELDS 1 (9") PIE CRUST**
>
> 1 cup flour
> Pinch salt
> ⅓ cup shortening
> 3–8 tablespoons water
> 1 (9") aluminum pie tin

Freezing Day

1. In a food processor, combine the flour and the salt. Add the shortening and pulse until the mixture has a mealy texture.
2. Add 3 tablespoons water to the mixture and pulse about 5 times. Check the consistency by pinching together the mixture with your fingers. If it holds together, you have the right amount of water. If it doesn't hold together, continue to add water until it does.
3. Roll the dough into a ball. On a floured surface, roll the dough into a 12" circle.
4. Place the rolled-out dough into the aluminum pie tin. Crimp the outside edge of the crust by pinching the crust all the way around so it forms a wavy line. As an alternative to crimping, use a fork and press down the outside edge of the pie into the side of the pan leaving tine marks along the edge.
5. Wrap well with plastic wrap and freeze.

Reheating Instructions

Use the frozen pie crust according to your pie recipe.

How to Transfer Dough to a Pie Tin

To check the size, lay your pie tin upside down over the crust. You should have an extra 2" all around. Gently fold your crust in half, then fold in half again. Lay the crust in the pie tin, with the pointed end of the crust in the center. Unfold and use your fingers to push the bottom into place.

Sweet Berry Filling

Pair this fruit filling with the Easy Pie Crust (see recipe in this chapter) for a delicious home-made pie, or use the fruit as a topping on ice cream and other desserts. You can even put it in the blender and make a fruit syrup to pour over Classic French Toast (see recipe in Chapter 2).

YIELDS 1 QUART

1 quart of fruit of your choice
½ cup sugar

Freezing Day

1. Wash and dry fruit and remove any that are bruised or have bad spots.
2. In a large bowl, mix fruit and sugar, coating thoroughly. Freeze in freezer bags.

Reheating Instructions

Defrost in the refrigerator overnight, and use as desired.

Fruity Frozen Pie

This is a great summer treat for your friends and family. Let this dessert defrost 15–20 minutes at room temperature before serving—it makes cutting it easier.

YIELDS 1 PIE

¾ cup sugar
1 (10-ounce) package cream cheese, softened
1 (16-ounce) bag frozen strawberries with juice, thawed
1 (15-ounce) can crushed pineapple, drained
1 (12-ounce) container Cool Whip
2 large bananas, peeled and sliced

Freezing Day

1. In a large mixing bowl, mix sugar and cream cheese.
2. Cut strawberries into pieces and add them and all the extra strawberry juice into the mixing bowl. Add pineapple and Cool Whip. Fold in bananas.
3. Spread mixture into a 9" x 13" pan and freeze.

Reheating Instructions

Remove dessert from the freezer and serve.

Frozen Fruit Combos

Here are some other combinations of fruits that would work well in a Fruity Frozen Pie: orange and pineapple; kiwi and strawberry; apple and any berry; cherry and plum; and cantaloupe and honeydew. For best results, do not mix an acidic fruit with a sweet fruit or melon.

Chocolate Banana Pops

These popsicles are a fun and messy dessert the kids will love making! They are the perfect snack on those hot summer days when the kids want something cool to eat.

YIELDS 6–8 SERVINGS
1 package chocolate chips
6 ripe bananas
12 popsicle sticks
1–2 cups crushed peanuts

Freezing Day

1. Melt chocolate chips in the microwave on 50 percent power for 30 seconds. Stir chips and return to microwave for another 30 seconds at 50 percent. Continue until chips are melted.
2. Cut bananas in half. Push a popsicle stick into the cut side of the banana.
3. Spread peanuts out in a shallow dish.
4. Dip the banana into the chocolate, then into the peanuts.
5. Lay the popsicles on a baking sheet lined with wax paper and flash freeze. Transfer to a freezer bag.

Reheating Instructions

No defrosting necessary. Eat the frozen treats straight from the freezer.

Let Your Imagination Run Wild!

Try dipping half the banana into chocolate and the other half in melted peanut butter chips. Instead of crushed peanuts, try different toppings such as crushed M&M's, crushed Oreo cookies, or even crushed pineapple. Or a mixture of all of them! You are only limited by your imagination.

Hot Fudge Sundae Pie

This dessert takes minutes to make, so with very little preparation you can serve a treat everyone loves. Treat your guests to a hot fudge sundae bar with a variety of topping choices, and let them create their own customized Hot Fudge Sundae Pie!

YIELDS 1 PIE

1 quart vanilla ice cream

1 ready-made graham cracker pie crust

Hot fudge to taste (used on reheating day)

Coconut flakes to taste (used on reheating day)

Chopped nuts to taste (used on reheating day)

Maraschino cherries to taste (used on reheating day)

Whipped cream to taste (used on reheating day)

Freezing Day

Allow the ice cream to soften just a bit. Spread the ice cream into the pie shell to make an ice cream pie. Wrap well with plastic wrap and freeze.

Reheating Instructions

1. Serve the ice cream pie frozen.
2. Set out toppings, cut the pie into wedges, and let people customize their own piece of pie.

Ice Cream Sandwiches

These are a lot of fun for kids to make. Try all kinds of coatings instead of the chocolate morsels listed. Sprinkles, gummy bears, peanut butter chips, or crushed candy bars all are good options.

YIELDS 12 SANDWICHES

24 Chocolate Chip Cookies (see recipe in this chapter)

1 quart vanilla ice cream

1 (12-ounce) package chocolate chip morsels

Freezing Day

1. Line a baking sheet with wax paper. Lay 1 cookie, flat-side up, on the baking sheet. Put a small scoop of ice cream on the cookie and put another cookie on top of the ice cream. Press it down until the ice cream reaches the edge of the cookies.
2. Roll the edge of the ice cream sandwich in the chocolate chip morsels.
3. Flash freeze on the baking sheet, then transfer to a freezer bag.

Reheating Instructions

Eat straight from the freezer.

Light Fruit Cake

Homemade fruit cakes taste far better than store-bought fruit cakes. They are a traditional holiday treat, and make great gifts for your family and friends.

YIELDS 2 LOAVES

1 cup butter
1 cup sugar
4 eggs
3 cups flour
1 teaspoon baking powder
½ cup orange juice
¼ cup light corn syrup
1 teaspoon lemon juice
2 (10-ounce) jars maraschino cherries, drained and chopped
1 cup light raisins
2¼ cups mixed candied fruit
1 cup walnuts, chopped

Freezing Day

1. Preheat the oven to 300°F. In a large mixing bowl, beat butter and sugar until fluffy.
2. Mix in eggs, followed by the rest of the ingredients.
3. Pour into 2 greased and floured loaf pans. Bake for 1 hour 10 minutes. Cool.
4. Wrap well in plastic wrap and freeze.

Reheating Instructions

Defrost fruit cake 2–3 hours at room temperature and serve.

German Spice Cake

This spice cake has a unique flavor that will have your friends talking about it long after they've enjoyed it. It tastes especially good paired with a cup of coffee.

YIELDS 1 CAKE

4 cups flour
2 teaspoons baking powder
2 teaspoons baking soda
3 teaspoons cinnamon
1 teaspoon nutmeg
1 teaspoon allspice
¼ teaspoon ground cloves
1 teaspoon ginger
1½ tablespoons molasses
1 cup hot coffee
1 cup cold water
1 cup brown sugar
1 cup white sugar
1 cup honey

Freezing Day

Preheat the oven to 350°F. In a large bowl, mix the ingredients, starting with the dry ones and then adding the wet ones. Pour into a long loaf pan. Bake for 30 minutes, then lower the temperature to 300°F and bake for 30 minutes. Cool, wrap with plastic wrap, and freeze.

Reheating Instructions

Defrost at room temperature for 2–3 hours, or in the refrigerator overnight, and serve.

Sugar Cookies

These wonderful Sugar Cookies taste delicious plain, or you can decorate them with frosting and sprinkles. Also try the Sugar Cookie Filling (see recipe in this chapter).

YIELDS 30 COOKIES

1 cup butter
2 cups sugar
4 eggs
2 teaspoons vanilla
5 cups flour
4 teaspoons baking powder
¼ teaspoon salt

Freezing Day

1. In a large mixing bowl, cream butter and sugar.
2. Beat in eggs and vanilla.
3. Preheat the oven to 400°F. In a separate bowl, combine the dry ingredients. Add to the butter mixture.
4. Roll out dough ¼" thick and cut out cookie shapes using a biscuit or cookie cutter.
5. Bake for 6 minutes. The cookies should almost be white when done.
6. Flash freeze cookies and transfer to a plastic container or freezer bag.

Reheating Instructions

Defrost cookies at room temperature for 1–2 hours and serve.

Freeze Your Cookie Dough!

There is no need to wait until the cookies have been baked to freeze them. Divide the dough into several balls, wrap in plastic wrap, and put in a freezer bag. The dough will defrost faster when it is divided into the smaller balls, and the double wrapping helps the dough from absorbing freezer odors while it protects from freezer burn.

Sugar Cookie Filling

Use this recipe with Sugar Cookies (see previous recipe). It is a good idea to use a plastic container when you freeze cookies to protect them from breaking. Layer the cookies in the container, and separate each layer with wax paper.

YIELDS 30 SERVINGS

½ cup raisins
½ cup chopped dates
½ cup chopped walnuts
½ cup sugar
Pinch salt
9 tablespoons flour
½ teaspoon vanilla
1 batch Sugar Cookies (see previous recipe)

Freezing Day

1. Preheat the oven to 400°F. Combine all the ingredients, except the vanilla and the Sugar Cookies, in a medium saucepan. Stir and boil over high heat until smooth and thick.
2. Remove from stove and add vanilla.
3. Put 1 tablespoon of filling on one (unbaked) Sugar Cookie.
4. Top with a second cookie and seal the edges.
5. Bake for 6–8 minutes. Cool and flash freeze, then transfer to plastic container or plastic bag.

Reheating Instructions

Defrost cookies at room temperature for 1–2 hours and serve.

Dark Chocolate Cake

Top off this delicious and rich cake with a simple frosting, a glaze, or even a scoop of vanilla ice cream.

YIELDS 1 CAKE

1 cup vegetable oil
2 cups sugar
4 eggs
1 cup sour milk
2½ cups flour
¼ teaspoon salt
3 teaspoons baking soda
¾ cup cocoa
¾ cup boiling water
1 teaspoon vanilla

Freezing Day

1. Preheat the oven to 350°F. In a large mixing bowl, beat together oil, sugar, and eggs.
2. Add remaining ingredients and beat well.
3. Grease a cake pan, pour in the batter, and bake for 45–50 minutes for a 9" × 13" pan, or 1 hour and 10 minutes for a tube pan. Remove from the oven, cool, wrap cake in plastic wrap, and freeze.

Reheating Instructions

Defrost cake at room temperature for 1–2 hours and serve at room temperature.

Sour Milk

There seems to be quite a debate over whether it is safe to use milk for baking that has gone past its expiration date and turned. The safest (and easiest) solution is to make sour milk by mixing 1 tablespoon lemon or vinegar with 1 cup fresh milk.

Freezer Derby Pie

The official Derby Pie is a tradition of the Kentucky Derby. It was first made by the Kern family who decided on the name by pulling it out of a hat. The authentic recipe is closely guarded and only cooked by Kern's Kitchens.

YIELDS 2 PIES

1 cup butter
4 eggs
½ cup brown sugar
1⅛ cups Karo Light Corn Syrup
1 tablespoon flour
1 teaspoon vanilla
⅓ cup bourbon
1½ cups chopped pecans
2 frozen Easy Pie Crusts (see recipe in this chapter)
1½ cups chocolate chips

Freezing Day

1. Preheat the oven to 350°F. In a small saucepan, melt butter.
2. In a mixing bowl, beat eggs slightly. Add melted butter, brown sugar, Karo, flour, vanilla, bourbon, and pecans. Mix well.
3. Line the bottoms of the pie crusts with chocolate chips. Pour the mixture over the chocolate chips.
4. Bake for 45 minutes or until pie sets.
5. Cool pie, wrap well with freezer wrap, and freeze.

Reheating Instructions

Heat frozen pie at 375°F for 20–30 minutes or until pie is the desired temperature.

Tips for Serving Dessert

Dessert is often the favorite part of the meal. To make dessert time extra special, serve this course on an appropriately sized plate, not on the same plate used for dinner. Offer your guests a hot drink, like coffee or tea, to go with dessert, and always have a decaffeinated drink available.

Apple Crisp with Almond Topping

Serve this warm out of the oven with a scoop of vanilla ice cream. If you want to vary it, try adding blueberries or peaches instead of apples!

YIELDS 8–10 SERVINGS

1½ cups flour

2 cups oats

1½ cups brown sugar

1 teaspoon cinnamon

½ teaspoon nutmeg

1½ cups butter, softened

11 or 12 medium Golden Delicious apples, or Granny Smith (if you prefer more tartness) apples, peeled and sliced

1 cup skinless, toasted almonds

Freezing Day

1. Preheat the oven to 350°F. In a mixing bowl, combine flour, oats, brown sugar, cinnamon, and nutmeg.

2. Cut in butter until mixture is crumbly.

3. Press half of the crumb topping mixture on the bottom of a baking dish, and top with cut apples.

4. In a food processor, finely grind almonds. Mix with remaining crumb topping and sprinkle over the apples.

5. Bake for 45 minutes–1 hour or until apples are tender. Cool, wrap tightly with plastic wrap, and freeze.

Reheating Instructions

Defrost apple crisp at room temperature for 2–3 hours and heat approximately 10–15 minutes in a 350°F oven until heated through.

No-Bake Chocolate Cookies

This classic family recipe, also known as boiled cookies, uses only the stovetop to make the cookies! Best of all, they are a cinch to prepare, taste delicious, and freeze wonderfully.

YIELDS 24 COOKIES

2 cups sugar
½ cup butter
¼ cup cocoa
½ cup milk
¼ cup peanut butter
1 teaspoon vanilla
3 cups oatmeal

Freezing Day

1. In a large saucepan, boil the sugar, butter, cocoa, and milk for 1 minute.

2. Remove from the heat and add the peanut butter, vanilla, and oatmeal. Mix well.

3. Drop by the full teaspoon on wax paper and let cool. Flash freeze and transfer to freezer bags.

Reheating Instructions

Defrost cookies 1–2 hours at room temperature and serve at room temperature.

Peanut Butter and Chocolate Bars

Serve on a small plate topped with whipped cream and dusted with cocoa powder or drizzled with chocolate syrup.

YIELDS 6 BARS
½ cup butter
1 cup graham crackers, crushed
1 cup peanut butter chips
1 cup chocolate chips
1 (15-ounce) can sweetened condensed milk

Freezing Day

1. Preheat the oven to 350°F. In a small saucepan, melt butter. Add graham cracker crumbs and mix. Press into the bottom of an 8" × 8" pan.
2. Add peanut butter chips and chocolate chips on top of the crust.
3. Pour the condensed milk over the top.
4. Bake for 30 minutes.
5. Let cool, cut into squares, wrap well with plastic wrap, and freeze.

Reheating Instructions

Defrost at room temperature for 1–2 hours and serve at room temperature.

Belly Up to the Dessert Bar

Almost every dessert can be improved with the right topping. The next time you serve dessert, provide your guests with a fun and innovative dessert bar that offers a number of different toppings that they can add, sprinkle, drizzle, or dollop onto their dessert—and don't forget the coffee!

Chocolate Meringue Pie

Because meringue tends to get tough when it is frozen, this pie is baked in two steps. The first step, the chocolate base of the pie, is completed on freezing day. On the day you plan to serve the pie, you will complete the second step, the meringue topping.

YIELDS 1 PIE

1½ cups sugar
4 tablespoons flour
4 tablespoons cocoa powder
3 egg yolks
1½ cups milk
½ stick butter
1 teaspoon vanilla
1 baked pie crust
3 egg whites, at room temperature (used on reheating day)
1 teaspoon vanilla (used on reheating day)
¼ teaspoon cream of tartar (used on reheating day)
6 tablespoons sugar (used on reheating day)

Freezing Day

1. In a medium saucepan, combine sugar, flour, and cocoa. Add egg yolks, then slowly stir in milk.

2. Place over medium heat, and add butter.

3. Continue to heat and stir 3–5 minutes until the mixture thickens. Remove from heat and add vanilla. Allow to cool.

4. Pour into the pie crust and freeze.

Reheating Instructions

1. Defrost pie in the refrigerator overnight, or at room temperature for 1–2 hours.

2. In a mixing bowl, beat egg whites, vanilla, and cream of tartar to soft peaks. Add sugar 1 tablespoon at a time and beat until stiff.

3. Spread the meringue on top of the pie and bake at 350°F for about 10 minutes until browned.

Chocolate Chip Cookies

Add variety to your Chocolate Chip Cookies by throwing some chopped macadamia nuts or walnuts in the batter the same time you put in the chocolate chips. You can also vary this recipe by using white chocolate chips, or half peanut butter chips and half chocolate chips.

YIELDS 40 COOKIES

2¼ cups flour
1 teaspoon baking soda
½ teaspoon salt
1 teaspoon cinnamon
1 cup butter, softened
¾ cup packed light brown sugar
½ cup sugar
2 eggs
2 teaspoons pure vanilla extract
2 cups chocolate chips

Freezing Day

1. Preheat the oven to 375°F. In a small bowl, mix flour, baking soda, salt, and cinnamon.

2. In a large mixing bowl, cream butter, brown sugar, and sugar until it becomes light and airy.

3. Add eggs and vanilla to the butter mixture, and beat well.

4. Add flour mixture to the butter mixture and beat only until blended.

5. Fold in the chocolate chips.

6. Drop by the heaping teaspoonful onto an ungreased cookie sheet.

7. Bake for 8–10 minutes.

8. Cool completely on a wire rack, wrap well in plastic wrap or put in a plastic container, and freeze.

Reheating Instructions

Defrost cookies at room temperature for 1–2 hours and serve at room temperature.

Chocolate Chip Substitutions

There is a wonderful assortment of other chips available to today's baker that can be substituted for traditional chocolate chips. Besides several varieties of chocolate chips, like white, semisweet, special dark, and milk chocolate, other flavors include butterscotch, peanut butter, carob, and even cherry.

Macadamia Chocolate Squares

Vary this recipe by using pecans or almonds instead of macadamia nuts. You can also stir in ½ cup peanut butter chips or top the squares with toasted coconut.

YIELDS 12 SQUARES

½ cup butter
2 squares unsweetened chocolate
1 cup sugar
2 eggs
½ cup flour
¼ teaspoon salt
½ teaspoon pure vanilla extract
½ cup chopped macadamia nuts

Freezing Day

1. Preheat the oven to 400°F. In a medium saucepan, melt the butter and chocolate over medium-low heat. Stir in sugar and mix well.

2. Add eggs one at a time, mixing well in between each egg.

3. Add flour, salt, vanilla, and nuts. Mix well.

4. Grease and flour a 10" × 15" jellyroll pan and pour in the batter.

5. Bake for 10–15 minutes. Cool completely and cut into squares.

6. Wrap chocolate squares well with plastic wrap and freeze.

Reheating Instructions

Defrost at room temperature 1–2 hours and serve at room temperature.

Marble It!

Before you put the squares in the oven, try marbling them. In a separate bowl, use an electric beater to beat 8 ounces cream cheese with ⅓ cup sugar. Put small spoonfuls of the cream cheese over the top of the chocolate squares batter. Use a knife to pull the cream cheese through the batter, making a marbled effect. Bake as directed.

Peanut Butter Cookies

To make Peanut Butter Chocolate Kiss Cookies, form the dough into a ball but don't flatten. Bake at 350°F for 9–10 minutes. When cookies come out of the oven, press a chocolate kiss into the middle. Let cool.

YIELDS 3 DOZEN COOKIES

1 cup shortening
1½ cups crunchy peanut butter
1 cup white sugar
1 cup brown sugar
2 eggs
1 teaspoon vanilla
3 cups flour
1 teaspoon baking soda
½ teaspoon salt

Freezing Day

1. Preheat the oven to 350°F. In a large bowl, cream together shortening, peanut butter, white sugar, and brown sugar.
2. Add eggs one at a time, followed by vanilla. Mix well.
3. In a separate bowl, sift together flour, baking soda, and salt. Add to peanut butter mixture.
4. Mix dough (it will be very thick). Form into small balls and put on a baking sheet. Press the balls down with a fork.
5. Bake for 9–10 minutes until cookies are lightly browned. Cool and freeze in a plastic container.

Reheating Instructions

Defrost cookies at room temperature for 1–2 hours and serve at room temperature.

Peanut Butter Basics

Peanut butter is nearly 100 percent peanuts; there are very few additional ingredients or additives. The biggest difference between most commercial peanut butters and natural peanut butters is that natural peanut butter does not have hydrogenated oils added to keep the peanut oil from separating from the peanut paste. Natural peanut butter usually needs some mixing prior to use.

Fruit Salad Cupcakes

This makes a cool summertime treat that kids love, and it is also a delicious addition to a breakfast or brunch.

YIELDS 8 CUPCAKES

1 (20-ounce) can crushed pineapples, drained
3 bananas, mashed
1 cup frozen blueberries
8 ounces sour cream
½ cup sugar
½ cup nuts, chopped
1 (16-ounce) container Cool Whip

Freezing Day

1. Combine pineapples, bananas, blueberries, sour cream, sugar, and nuts in a large mixing bowl. Fold in Cool Whip.

2. Fill muffin tins with the mixture and freeze. Once frozen, remove from muffin tins and put in a freezer bag.

Reheating Instructions

Remove from freezer and allow to soften for 15–30 minutes before serving.

Peanut Butter Balls

This is a great recipe to let the kids make since it's a fun, hands-on cooking project that is simple to make and yummy to eat.

YIELDS 30 BALLS

⅔ cup creamy peanut butter
2½ cups Cool Whip
⅓ cup mini chocolate chips
½ cup coconut flakes

Freezing Day

1. Mix together peanut butter, Cool Whip, and chocolate chips in a medium mixing bowl. Put in the freezer for 15 minutes. Remove from the freezer and roll into balls.

2. Put coconut on a plate. Roll the Peanut Butter Balls in the coconut. Flash freeze on a baking sheet lined with wax paper. Transfer to a freezer bag.

Reheating Instructions

No need to defrost—eat straight from the freezer.

Delicious Toppings

For recipes that call for shredded coconut as a topping, consider using one or more of these alternatives: crushed graham crackers; crispy rice cereal; cocoa rice cereal; crushed nuts such as peanuts, cashews, pecans, pistachios, or macadamia nuts; crushed candy bars; crushed Oreo cookies; or crushed chocolate chip cookies.

Applesauce-Raisin Spice Cake

Make muffins out of this recipe by baking in paper-lined muffin or cupcake tins at 350°F for 35 minutes. You can thaw them as you need them if you freeze the muffins individually.

YIELDS 1 CAKE

1¾ cups flour
1 teaspoon baking soda
½ teaspoon salt
1½ teaspoons cinnamon
½ teaspoon nutmeg
½ cup shortening
1 cup sugar
1 egg, beaten
1 cup unsweetened applesauce
1 cup raisins

Freezing Day

1. Preheat the oven to 350°F. In a medium bowl, sift together flour, baking soda, salt, cinnamon, and nutmeg.
2. In a separate bowl, cream the shortening with the sugar. Beat in the egg.
3. Alternate adding the sifted ingredients and the applesauce to the butter and sugar mixture. Stir in raisins.
4. Pour into a greased square pan and bake for 45–50 minutes.
5. Cool, wrap well with plastic wrap, and freeze.

Reheating Instructions

Defrost cake at room temperature for 2–3 hours. Top with a cream cheese icing.

Pecan Cookies

These cookies are perfect for the holidays. Make them ahead of time so you'll have one less thing on your to-do list when the holidays roll around.

YIELDS 4 DOZEN COOKIES

1 cup butter
¼ cup sugar
2 cups flour
2 teaspoons vanilla
2 cups pecans, finely chopped
Powdered sugar, for dipping

Freezing Day

1. Preheat the oven to 325°F. In a large mixing bowl, cream butter and sugar. Add flour and vanilla. Mix well, then stir in pecans.
2. Form the dough into small balls, then press down to make a cookie.
3. Bake for 25 minutes.
4. Once out of the oven, dip the top of the cookie in the powdered sugar.
5. Flash freeze on a baking sheet, then transfer to a freezer bag.

Reheating Instructions

Defrost at room temperature for 1–2 hours and serve at room temperature.

Pumpkin Pie

No need to buy a frozen pie for your next Thanksgiving holiday. You'll see how easy it is to make one from scratch with this delicious recipe.

YIELDS 1 PIE

1 (15-ounce) can pumpkin
¾ cup sugar
1 teaspoon salt
1 teaspoon ginger
1¼ teaspoons cinnamon
½ teaspoon nutmeg
½ teaspoon cloves
3 eggs
1 (12-ounce) can evaporated milk, with enough milk added to make 2 cups
1 unbaked Easy Pie Crust (see recipe in this chapter)

Freezing Day

1. Preheat the oven to 400°F. In a mixing bowl, thoroughly combine pumpkin, sugar, salt, ginger, cinnamon, nutmeg, cloves, and eggs. Blend in milk.
2. Pour mixture into the pie crust.
3. Bake for 50 minutes or until a knife inserted into the center comes out clean.
4. Wrap well with freezer wrap and freeze.

Reheating Instructions

Defrost pie at room temperature for 1–2 hours and serve at room temperature.

Appendix:
U.S./Metric Measurements Conversion Chart

VOLUME CONVERSIONS

U.S. Volume Measure	Metric Equivalent
⅛ teaspoon	0.5 milliliter
¼ teaspoon	1 milliliter
½ teaspoon	2 milliliters
1 teaspoon	5 milliliters
½ tablespoon	7 milliliters
1 tablespoon (3 teaspoons)	15 milliliters
2 tablespoons (1 fluid ounce)	30 milliliters
¼ cup (4 tablespoons)	60 milliliters
⅓ cup	90 milliliters
½ cup (4 fluid ounces)	125 milliliters
⅔ cup	160 milliliters
¾ cup (6 fluid ounces)	180 milliliters
1 cup (16 tablespoons)	250 milliliters
1 pint (2 cups)	500 milliliters
1 quart (4 cups)	1 liter (about)

WEIGHT CONVERSIONS

U.S. Weight Measure	Metric Equivalent
½ ounce	15 grams
1 ounce	30 grams
2 ounces	60 grams
3 ounces	85 grams
¼ pound (4 ounces)	115 grams
½ pound (8 ounces)	225 grams
¾ pound (12 ounces)	340 grams
1 pound (16 ounces)	454 grams

OVEN TEMPERATURE CONVERSIONS

Degrees Fahrenheit	Degrees Celsius
200 degrees F	95 degrees C
250 degrees F	120 degrees C
275 degrees F	135 degrees C
300 degrees F	150 degrees C
325 degrees F	160 degrees C
350 degrees F	180 degrees C
375 degrees F	190 degrees C
400 degrees F	205 degrees C
425 degrees F	220 degrees C
450 degrees F	230 degrees C

BAKING PAN SIZES

U.S.	Metric
8 × 1½ inch round baking pan	20 × 4 cm cake tin
9 × 1½ inch round baking pan	23 × 3.5 cm cake tin
11 × 7 × 1½ inch baking pan	28 × 18 × 4 cm baking tin
13 × 9 × 2 inch baking pan	30 × 20 × 5 cm baking tin
2 quart rectangular baking dish	30 × 20 × 3 cm baking tin
15 × 10 × 2 inch baking pan	30 × 25 × 2 cm baking tin (Swiss roll tin)
9 inch pie plate	22 × 4 or 23 × 4 cm pie plate
7 or 8 inch springform pan	18 or 20 cm springform or loose-bottom cake tin
9 × 5 × 3 inch loaf pan	23 × 13 × 7 cm or 2 lb narrow loaf or pâté tin
1½ quart casserole	1.5 liter casserole
2 quart casserole	2 liter casserole

Index

Note: Page numbers in **bold** indicate recipe category lists.